THE PEOPLE HAVE SPOKEN

THE 2014 ELECTIONS IN FIJI

THE PEOPLE HAVE SPOKEN

THE 2014 ELECTIONS IN FIJI

EDITED BY STEVEN RATUVA
AND STEPHANIE LAWSON

Australian
National
University

PRESS

PACIFIC SERIES

ANU PRESS

Published by ANU Press
The Australian National University
Acton ACT 2601, Australia
Email: anupress@anu.edu.au
This title is also available online at press.anu.edu.au

National Library of Australia Cataloguing-in-Publication entry

Title:	The people have spoken : the 2014 elections in Fiji / editors: Steven Ratuva, Stephanie Lawson.
ISBN:	9781760460013 (paperback) 9781760460020 (ebook)
Subjects:	Elections--Fiji Election law--Fiji. Fiji--Ethnic relations--Political aspects. Fiji--Politics and government.
Other Creators/Contributors:	
	Ratuva, Steven, editor. Lawson, Stephanie, editor.

Dewey Number: 324.99611

Cover design and layout by ANU Press.
Cover photograph: 'The Government Buildings in Suva Fiji' by Stemoc.

Contents

1

'The People Have Spoken …'

Steven Ratuva and Stephanie Lawson

Fiji's general elections of 17 September 2014, held eight years after Fiji's fourth coup, saw some significant firsts, generated largely by new constitutional arrangements. These included a radically deracialised electoral system in which the entire country forms a single electorate and utilises open-list proportional representation. This system, brought in under the regime of coup leader Voreqe (Frank) Bainimarama, was designed first and foremost to encourage a shift away from previous patterns of electoral behaviour which, due in large measure to provisions for communal electorates and voting, were inevitably attuned to communal political identities and the perceived interests attached to them. Elections under such a system certainly allowed 'the people' to speak, but in a way which gave primacy to those particular identities and interests and, arguably, contributed to a political culture that saw democracy itself severely undermined in the process. This was illustrated only too clearly by the recurrence of *coups d'état* between 1987 and 2006 that all revolved, in one way or another, around issues of communal identity expressed through discourses of indigenous Fijian (Taukei) rights versus those of other ethnic or racial communities, especially of those of Indian descent. These discourses remain highly salient politically but, under the Constitution promulgated by the Bainimarama regime in 2013, they are no longer supported institutionally via electoral arrangements. As a result, political parties have generally been forced to at least attempt to appeal to all ethnic communities. These institutional changes have brought Fiji's political system much closer to the standard model of liberal democracy in which 'one person, one vote, one value' is a basic norm.

The elections of September 2014 held under the new system delivered a resounding victory to Bainimarama's newly established political party, FijiFirst, founded on a modernist ideology repudiating the politics of race or ethnicity and emphasising equality and development for all communities in Fiji. However, the notion that election results indicate a clear and unambiguous statement of political intent on the part of the electorate—as reflected in the phrase 'the people have spoken'—is rather simplistic. Although this phrase does emphasise the most basic right of citizens in a democracy, or at least a majority of them, to choose their own government, the people rarely speak with one voice. After all, a key feature of liberal democracy is that it creates space for the expression of contested ideologies, strategies, visions and hopes. There is also the question of the conditions under which the people speak—a particular issue for Fiji's 2014 elections. Freedom of expression and political opposition had been tightly constrained during the period in which Bainimarama's military government had ruled by decree, and remained problematic during the election campaign. These circumstances favoured FijiFirst, which is, when all is said and done, the product of military power. These are among the issues we review below by way of introduction and which are analysed in more detail in the chapters that follow.

Constitutionalism, democracy and elections in Fiji

Politics in Fiji has gone through turbulent and transformational periods since independence in 1970. These have been shaped in part by disagreements over what institutional and normative form democracy should take as well as the particular interests it should serve, for in Fiji it has rarely been simply a matter of serving 'the people' as a whole. This is a reflection of Fiji's 'plural society', in which the claims of the Taukei, who constitute some 57 per cent of the population, have very often been portrayed as trumping those of all other communities, especially citizens of Indian descent, who number around 37 per cent. The remainder of the population is made up of Europeans, part-Europeans, other Pacific Islanders, Chinese, and other small minorities.

In a highly ethnicised political climate, adherence to democratic values for nationalist Taukei leaders was meaningful only if it served the apparent interests of their own ethnic community and, when it failed to do so, democracy as a form of government was considered inappropriate at best and illegitimate at worst. Reactions to the electoral success of those perceived as 'other' ranged from expressions of private displeasure around kava bowls to mass public demonstrations and the overthrow of elected governments. The latter, of course, is the antithesis of democratic constitutionalism, which requires that the rules of the game, once established, be respected by both winners and losers.

Elections in Fiji since independence have been held on an irregular basis, largely as a result of coups. Each coup has had its own peculiar characteristics, impacting on political processes, institutions, practices and discourses, and on people's everyday lives. Coups have unfortunately become the principal chronological and political landmarks from which Fijians take their historical bearing. Prior to the first coup in May 1987, many had seen riots in 1959 as the 'watershed' event in Fiji's history because of the way it united Taukei and Indo-Fijian workers against colonial and foreign corporate hegemony. However, the May 1987 coup, followed by a second intervention in September of the same year, completely eclipsed 1959 as a watershed event, this time appearing as the manifestation of an unbridgeable divide between the two major population groups.

This interpretation did not last long either, as Fiji's political, social and economic fortunes foundered on the rocks created by the system of political apartheid established under the 1990 Constitution. In the ensuing decade, politics took a very different turn with coup leader Rabuka reinventing himself as both a democrat and a multiculturalist and supporting a new, much more liberal constitution, which recognised all Fiji's citizens as 'Fiji Islanders', even though it retained a partly communal electoral system. The vision of a new, liberally oriented, multicultural Fiji seemed to become a reality in 1999 when Fiji's first (and so far only) Indo-Fijian prime minister came to power, thus creating another watershed event. But antagonistic race politics appeared to become re-established as the status quo context for Fiji's politics with the 2000 coup and its aftermath washing away the apparent achievements of the previous decade. Although the civilian 2000 coup leader, George Speight, was prosecuted and subsequently incarcerated for treason, the government established in the wake of the coup, and subsequently legitimated through elections in 2001 and 2006, nonetheless followed an agenda attuned to discourses of race and Taukei privilege promoted by Speight and his supporters.

By the time of the 2006 coup, the term 'watershed' had all but lost its significance in a political environment where coups and elections alternated as defining moments, with new constitutions being promulgated along the way. In some ways, elections have come to play a role as pre-coup and post-coup historical signposts. Memories of an election may now be based on which coup was associated with it. The 1987 elections precipitated the 1987 coup and the 1990 Constitution, although the latter proved so unsatisfactory that it was replaced (without a coup) less than a decade later. This was followed by an election under a new electoral system that produced the unexpected election of an Indo-Fijian prime minister, which in turn precipitated the 2000 coup. The elections of 2001 that followed served partly to legitimate the essential aims of the 2000 coup, even while its prime perpetrators remained behind bars. But it established political stability on a tenuous basis only. The new government's leadership came increasingly into conflict with the military commander Bainimarama, who campaigned vigorously against it in the lead-up to the May 2006 elections. Since, according to Bainimarama, the people 'spoke incorrectly' on this occasion, there followed Fiji's fourth coup in December 2006.

Eight years later, electoral democracy returned to Fiji, albeit with a former military commander and coup leader as prime minister and under yet another new constitution. The 2014 elections were clearly a direct historical offshoot of the 2006 coup—an event claimed by Bainimarama as a 'coup to end all coups'. Certainly, it is unlikely to be the precursor to another in the foreseeable future, at least so long as Bainimarama retains the loyalty of those now in command of Fiji's military forces. It may also require that he retain the confidence of the majority of the electorate. Under the current Constitution, Bainimarama and FijiFirst will face the judgment of the electorate again in 2018, but of course there is no saying how the people will speak then.

In light of these events, democracy in Fiji appears as both a blessing and a curse—a blessing because it created space for multicultural participation in the political process and a curse because multiethnic participation too often revolved around communal interests, thereby sparking inter-communal antagonism. While liberal democracy is predicated on the idea of political plurality, in Fiji this took a different form, labelled elsewhere as 'communal democracy' (Ratuva 2005) or 'ethnic democracy' (Lawson 2012) which, paradoxically, became the nemesis of liberal democracy itself, undermining democratic constitutionalism and the stability it is meant to deliver.

Attempts to craft the 'right' type of democratic architecture through constitutional engineering based on national consensus has faced challenges due to both inter- and intra-communal interests, divided political loyalties and lack of faith in constitutional processes, among other reasons. It is as if exercises in constitutional engineering, which have followed coups, were designed as temporary post-conflict rehabilitation measures addressing immediate concerns rather than having a sustainable long-term trajectory. The latest Constitution, cannibalised from an earlier draft put together by the Constitution Commission under eminent international expert Professor Yash Ghai, but rejected by Bainimarama on the grounds that it pandered to indigenous nationalism, is yet another attempt at resetting the political compass.

Fiji's first three constitutions from the time of independence in 1970 had incorporated electoral systems conceived with communal considerations foremost in mind. The 1970 Constitution attempted to provide for ethnic balance while the 1990 Constitution imposed political hegemony by the Taukei. The 1997 Constitution adopted a halfway position between communalism and individual voting. In 1999 it delivered a multiethnic coalition government led by Fiji's first Indo-Fijian prime minister, Mahendra Chaudhry, subsequently overthrown in the civilian coup of May 2000 led by George Speight. In the 2001 and 2006 elections, however, the same constitution delivered the stridently nationalist government of Laisenia Qarase. This was the government overthrown by Bainimarama in December 2006, ostensibly on the grounds of its highly divisive and retrograde racialist policies.

In contrast with all previous constitutions, the 2013 Constitution removed all traces of communalism in its formal provisions. Although this did not necessarily prevent appeals to communal interests and a certain degree of communal voting behaviour, it clearly represented the most profound institutional change in Fiji's post-independence political history. In opting for proportional representation in a single national constituency without any communally based reserved seats, the new Constitution forces political actors—political parties, individual politicians and voters—to think, behave and act 'nationally'. Although this did work to some extent in September 2014, the new electoral system has created another set of dynamics involving new alliances and contradictions. It requires political parties to become trans-ethnic in appeal if they are to have any chance of forming government. FijiFirst did so with ease because its leadership, which had effectively designed the new Constitution, had repudiated communal politics entirely. On the other hand, other parties that were successors to older communally attuned parties, such as the Social Democratic Liberal Party (SODELPA), effectively the same party that Qarase had led to victory in 2006, and the National Federation Party (NFP), Fiji's oldest political party that had emerged in the colonial period mainly to serve Indo-Fijian political needs and interests, were shackled by their communal history.

Elections in established liberal democracies generally work to legitimise ruling elites and provide the fulcrum for delivering stable governance and social order. In Fiji, as in other post-colonial states, there are additional dimensions that give it a unique character. The prevalence of culture-based chiefly power structures and kinship alliances among indigenous Fijians, which are often intertwined with liberal democratic systems and norms either in a contradictory or complementary way, have produced additional dynamics. These have been at the heart of both intra- and inter-communal politicking, with battle lines drawn and redrawn, and alliances configured and reconfigured in different ways, in different places, at different times. They have interacted with social variables such as religion, kinship ties, tribal loyalty, ethnic consciousness, regional affiliations, professional agendas, socioeconomic interests, political ideologies, gender considerations and personal appeal, all of which play a part in shaping political alliances and voting behaviour. Politics in Fiji has therefore never been a simple contest between the two major population groups.

Indeed, an important but often underemphasised aspect of politics in Fiji has been *intra*-communal contestation. Although always a factor, this became most clearly evident, especially among Taukei, after the first coup of 1987 and continues to this day.

Another key factor in the analysis of Fiji's politics is the coup discourses that also emerged after 1987. Since that time, there has been a latent fear of coups and coup conspiracies before, during and after elections, as reflected in the normalisation of the word coup (or *ku* in Fijian) in everyday vocabulary. There is also the frequent use of coup-related dates and events by scholars, political analysts, journalists and the public at large as historical landmarks around which historical narratives are constructed. Thus coups loom large in people's historical memory and many historical events are understood relative to periods before, during, after or between coups. Bainimarama's coup of 2006, however, was portrayed as the 'coup to end all coups'. While this claim remains to be tested over the longer term, the prospect of another coup following the resounding victory of Bainimarama's FijiFirst party in September 2014 does seem unlikely under FijiFirst rule.

The Bainimarama regime

The results of the September 2014 polls served to confer legitimacy, both nationally and internationally, on a regime that had previously refused to accept the verdict of 'the people' in 2006. Eight years later the newly elected government, headed by former military commander and 2006 coup leader Bainimarama, was more than content to invoke the phrase. But for those on the losing side the rancorous utterance of Dick Turner, a US Democrat unsuccessful in the 1966 California State Senate election, may have had more resonance: 'The people have spoken—the bastards' (Synlick 2006, p. 1).

The 2014 elections followed a period in which Bainimarama's regime deployed coercion and intimidation to implement its own vision of an essential social transformation and to mobilise people's consent to his agenda for change. While these methods were highly undemocratic, the regime did introduce a number of important firsts, which may be seen as enhancing the longer-term prospects for democratic consolidation under FijiFirst rule. For instance, while the first past the post (FPTP) system under the 1970 and 1990 Constitutions and the alternative voting (AV) system under the 1997 Constitution were technically different, they were both largely communally and multi-constituency based. The communal element was a carry-over from the pre-independence period, when electorates were first established on the basis of race. In contrast, the 2013 Constitution, in discarding the communal text, aimed very deliberately to eradicate the politics of race that had characterised all previous elections in Fiji. As any student of electoral engineering knows very well, electoral system design does have an impact on voter attitudes and political culture more generally. If the electoral system is communal, electioneering and voting behaviour will inevitably be oriented to communalism. Under a fully open system with no communal elements the dynamics are likely to change, as indeed they did in 2014, although not entirely.

For these reasons, among others, the 2014 elections may be seen as a turning point in Fiji's politics. The 2013 Constitution, with its radically different electoral system as well as a very significant rebranding of politics—itself very different from previous interventions in terms of its essential justification and subsequent outcomes—has defined a demarcation line between an 'old' Fiji and a 'new' Fiji, created largely by the Bainimarama regime. To many observers, the nation may appear to have reinvented itself, assuming a new identity at least with respect to issues of race or ethnicity. This new Fiji is meant to evince much greater political inclusiveness with the Taukei, Indo-Fijians and other minority groups being treated as equal partners as they move towards a more prosperous future, leaving behind the legacy of a colonial past in which particularistic interests, privileges, agendas and mindsets had become entrenched. Or so the narrative goes.

One point easily overlooked in all this is that the military, which may be seen to still hold ultimate power despite the return to electoral democracy, remains almost 100 per cent Taukei and there are no indications that this is set to change. Also, although the emphasis on equality and inclusiveness in FijiFirst's vision of the country's political future resonates strongly with democratic values, the fact remains that Bainimarama came to power initially through a military coup, ruled by decree, and used repressive measures to enforce his political will on the people of Fiji. This is readily interpreted as the very antithesis of democratic behaviour. So too, of course, are the three coups that occurred in 1987 and 2000 respectively. It is pertinent to note that many of those most vociferously opposed to the Bainimarama coup had supported the previous coups. 'Democracy', at least for some in Fiji, therefore means accepting an electoral result only when one's favoured party wins at the polls. When it loses, 'democracy' may be either rejected because it is not an appropriate form of government for Fiji, redefined to reflect one's own particular interests, values and ideology, or put on hold until such time as the people are 're-educated'.

Bainimarama's regime had put democracy on hold for eight years, during which time it pursued a policy of both radically overhauling the electoral system to eliminate one key form of institutionalised race-based communalism and to re-educate the people to reject the discourses of race that had been so prominent in all previous elections. Even so, the politics of race, played out mainly in the assertion of the superior political rights of the Taukei as the indigenous people of the Fiji islands *vis-à-vis* non-indigenous Fijians (mainly of Indian descent), remained an issue throughout the 2014 elections. SODELPA's policies promoting a 'Christian state' became a proxy for race given that Christianity in Fiji is strongly associated with indigenousness while most Indo-Fijians are Hindu or Muslim. SODELPA also represented an ideology of traditionalism in which Taukei institutions, practices and values, such as those associated with chiefly authority and privileges, were vigorously defended. In contrast, Bainimarama's FijiFirst promoted an ideology of modernism in which real progress and development could be achieved only by the elimination of traditionalism as manifest in the communal electoral system itself, as well as in the political privileges of chiefly authority and all the vested interests associated with these. Having said that, we must be wary of a endorsing a simplistic dichotomy between tradition and modernity, even though these are the general categories adopted, either explicitly or implicitly, by the major contestants themselves.

We now come, very briefly, to the Bainimarama regime's first year as a democratically elected government. With a resounding majority of 60 per cent in favour of FijiFirst, translating into 32 seats in a 50-seat parliament, the balance of power was overwhelmingly in its favour. Theoretically, the AV system is supposed to promote multiparty cooperation, but the strength of FijiFirst's victory means that it does not need to work cooperatively with other parties. The only other parties with seats in the parliament, SODELPA and the NFP, constitute an opposition virtually smothered by FijiFirst's parliamentary hegemony. With parliament so firmly under its control, the Bainimarama government passed numerous items of legislation in its first year; altogether, a total of 413 decrees and statutes were enacted between 2006 and September 2014, one year after the elections.

Much of this legislative activity has supported the continuation of the modernist developmental agenda inaugurated under the previous Bainimarama regime. Interestingly, this approach is characteristic of many South East Asian countries, especially Singapore, where it has succeeded in enhancing the 'performance legitimacy' of semi-authoritarian governments. Here we may note that developmental state theory emphasises the centrality of the state in determining the country's economic direction and in imposing firm control over resources, the bureaucracy and general development policies. In Fiji, post-2006, various reform and development projects relating to the economy, land, infrastructure, social welfare, housing, education, communications and aviation have been implemented following new legislation. The latest measures have been passed with ease in the new parliament. Supporters of FijiFirst may point to Fiji's steady economic growth, which reached 5.3 per cent in 2014. Tourism reached a record high of 692,630 in that year and was expected to easily exceed 700,000 in 2015. Despite this growth, however, there has also been an increase in inequality. This is expected to worsen over time, as it has in other parts of the world where the fruits of development are unevenly distributed.

Parliamentary debates over the economy and development have been vigorous and the opposition has engaged in fierce verbal sparring. The new parliament has become a venue for venting political frustrations, expressing ethnic grievances, articulating ideological interests and publicising religious beliefs. This was to be expected in the new space provided for democratic discourse denied under the previous regime. Not surprisingly, it has caused intense animosity and fractures between and within parties as well as between parliamentarians. It has made the work of the speaker, Jiko Luveni, the first woman speaker in Fiji's political history, very difficult. The speaker herself was allegedly abused in a SODELPA public meeting by party president Ratu Naiqama Lalabalavu, leading to a furious debate in parliament and eventually to Lalabalavu's suspension from the house for two years.

Despite these developments, the committees of the house have worked reasonably well in creating at least some semblance of a bipartisan environment for serious deliberation. However, this has been undermined by the dominance of FijiFirst in the parliamentary votes on committee recommendations, which has killed off much enthusiasm on the part of the minority opposition. Even so, some opposition figures have done some valuable work. The revelations of the parliamentary finance committee, headed by economist Dr Biman Prasad, about previous unaccounted for spending since the 2006 coup has sparked much-needed debate about the financial accountability system of the regime. This illustrates the value of legitimate parliamentary opposition, which was missing throughout the eight years of Bainimarama's post-coup rule by decree.

One year on from the 2014 elections, political parties are already in campaign mode for the 2018 general elections. While FijiFirst is confident of another victory because of the apparent popularity of its intensive nationwide developmentist approach, SODELPA is struggling with internal leadership issues and fractures. The 2018 elections will test whether FijiFirst and its developmental policies can once again be translated into votes and, at the same time, whether the opposition parties have learnt anything from their previous mistakes and can refashion their agendas accordingly.

Analysing the 2014 elections

As the dust from the 2014 elections settles and as Fiji embarks on a fresh journey of democratic rule, questions are being asked from multiple viewpoints about the significance of the 2014 elections. This is what the book is about. It is a collection of chapters by contributors from both academia and outside academia who by no means speak with one voice. The varying positions taken by the authors are in no way an attempt to throw fuel on the fire of Fiji's ideological contestation but rather seek to elucidate some of the deep-felt sentiments on both sides of the political divide, sentiments that are often oversimplified at best, or obscured at worst, in the robust exchanges of politicians and their supporters in the public sphere. The chapters therefore attempt to engage in a serious dialogue about the elections, perhaps the most paradigm shifting of all of Fiji's elections since 1970. The chapters focus primarily on the 2014 elections itself, with some providing relevant historical context to fill out the broader picture. They vary in style, political position and intellectual framings of Fiji politics and the 2014 elections. Unfortunately, despite attempts to solicit chapters from political parties about their experiences during the elections, only SODELPA responded. This is a major gap in the collection.

Chapter 2 by Steven Ratuva provides a broad discussion of electoral engineering, or the process of changing people's voting behaviour and political culture, through electoral system design. Fiji has gone through three different types of electoral systems: the first past the post (FPTP) system under the 1970 and 1990 Constitutions; the alternative vote system (AV) under the 1997 Constitution; and the open list proportional representation (OLPR) system under the 2013 Constitution. Different types of political systems generate different voting patterns and behaviour; the examples presented by the Fiji elections show different patterns of electoral outcomes. The electoral system itself does not determine voters' actual personal choice, but rather influences how people vote and how the results of voting are allocated and counted. There is a complex mix of factors which shape voter psychology and choice, including political and ideological preference, appeal through campaigns and manifestos by political parties, social group (ethnic, religious, cultural and political), individual loyalty, mode of mobilisation and influence of the media, among other things.

Chapter 3 by Stephanie Lawson examines the historical evolution of chiefly politics leading to the 2014 elections. Since independence, the chiefly system in Fiji has been part of the national system, primarily through the Great Council of Chiefs as well as through the role of individual chiefs in state leadership. This has changed over the years as a result of coups and other influences. The 2006 coup was a defining moment in the creation of the political conditions for the demise of chiefly authority in the state system, as exemplified by the abolition of the Great Council of Chiefs, more equal distribution of land lease money and reform of the Fijian administration, among other measures imposed by the pre-election regime. The victory of FijiFirst in the 2014 elections seems to have signalled the death knell for chiefly authority at the national level, although the chiefly system is still strongly embedded within the Fijian community.

Chapter 4 by Brij Lal provides a critical evaluation of some of the forces that shaped Indo-Fijian politics after the 2006 coup and factors that influenced Indo-Fijian votes during the 2014 elections. During the 2001 and 2006 elections, the Fiji Labour Party (FLP) won about 80 per cent of the Indo-Fijian votes, but during the 2003 elections the two predominantly Indo-Fijian parties—the FLP and the NFP—polled very poorly amongst the Indo-Fijian community as more than 70 per cent of them shifted their support to FijiFirst. Included in the numerous factors identified by Lal are issues ranging from an Indo-Fijian sense of insecurity to unrivalled propaganda by the incumbent FijiFirst. A lesson to be learnt from this is that, at least in Fiji where ethnic identification runs deep, group political loyalty can quickly shift when sociopolitical circumstances change.

Chapter 5 by David Robie, both a professional journalist and a scholar, provides an empirical assessment of the media environment and challenges in Fiji, especially after the 2006 coup and immediately before the 2014 elections. The media acts as the information nerve centre in any modern society and plays a vital role in shaping perceptions and values. Because of this, various forms of media often become effective tools for political propaganda, election campaigning and community mobilisation by state forces, political parties and other groups representing particular interests. In Fiji, the media has gone through some challenges posed by the post-2006 coup media decree that is still in force. The struggle to create a freer and better-informed society has been a central dilemma for Fijian journalists and Robie's chapter provides suggestions for positive change in the future.

Chapter 6 discusses the role of the Christian churches after the 2006 coup and during the elections. The author, Lynda Newland, who has carried out considerable fieldwork in Fiji, provides an analysis of the sometimes mutually supportive and sometimes antagonistic relationship between church and state in Fiji. Central to the chapter is the debate relating to the secular state, one of the most contentious issues during the election campaign. Throughout modern history, the relationship between the state and the church has been complex and has assumed different forms, sometimes mutually supportive and sometimes antagonistic. Fiji is no exception. The paper explores the often precarious interface between theology and political ideology, especially how one is used to legitimise and operationalise the other. This interface was manifest in explicit and subtle ways during the 2014 elections and no doubt influenced the way some cast their votes.

Chapter 7 by Sefanaia Sakai focuses on land as a political issue during the 2014 campaign. Land is of the most volatile of all issues in post-colonial Fiji. Sakai's contribution looks at how land has been used by ethno-nationalists to instil fear of an 'Indian takeover' and Taukei marginalisation. He emphasises that land reform, including the equal distribution of lease money amongst all members of the landowning unit (as opposed to a 30 per cent share for chiefs as was the case previously), has empowered ordinary Taukeis. Sakai suggests that fearmongering used by political parties during the elections may have influenced some voters, but was insufficient to draw a significant number of votes away from FijiFirst.

The role of youth in Fijian politics and especially in the elections is discussed by Patrick Vakaoti in Chapter 8. Because of the change in voting age to 18, the number of voters below the age of 35 was in excess of 50 per cent of all voters and so youth naturally became a major target for political parties. But as Vakaoti argues, young voters were not a homogeneous voting bloc but were divided by diverse interests and expectations. The efforts of political parties to target youth voters met with mixed success.

Jone Baledrokadroka's Chapter 9 provides an analysis of the role of the military, as the most powerful coercive institution in Fiji, on political governance and change. His analysis problematises the Fiji military's interventionism, focusing on how it has transformed the political landscape through the use or threat of force since the 2006 coup. Baledrokadroka examines the extent to which support for FijiFirst among the military, and its incumbency, contributed to FijiFirst's victory. He suggests that the post-election period may well see the role of the military becoming more pronounced as an ally of the FijiFirst government and this may give the latter more enthusiasm for unrestrained reform.

The only politician among our contributors, Pio Tabaiwalu, discusses the fortunes and otherwise of SODELPA in Chapter 10. Because of SODELPA's narrow ethnic appeal and campaign to mobilise largely Taukei votes (who constitute about 60 per cent of the electorate), it was virtually impossible for the party to win the elections outright and so it had to seek out coalition partners. But even with the NFP, traditionally an Indo-Fijian party, they could not make up the required 26 seats to control parliament. SODELPA campaigned largely in the shadow of the more resourceful and tactically astute FijiFirst and needs to re-strategise in the next election if it wants to increase its numbers in parliament.

Scott MacWilliam's Chapter 11 looks at SODELPA from the opposite vantage point to Tabaiwalu. While Tabaiwalu places blame on FijiFirst for SODELPA's electoral misfortunes, MacWilliam locates SODELPA's woes squarely within the party itself and its inability to adapt to the demands of a new multiethnic political climate. The chapter also argues a case for demarcating the Fijian political scene along a rural/urban divide, suggesting that this division was also reflected in the party votes.

The coup in 2006, and certainly the 2014 elections, impacted significantly on Fiji's relationship with its neighbours, an issue examined in Chapter 12 by Alexander Stewart. Fiji's suspension from the Commonwealth and the Pacific Islands Forum (PIF) and sanctions by countries like Australia and New Zealand were meant to isolate Fiji as a 'pariah state', and force the Bainimarama regime to hold an election sooner rather than later. Instead, Fiji took advantage of the situation to mobilise support among fellow Melanesian Spearhead Group members as well as countries beyond the region, and to set up the Pacific Islands Development Forum (PIDF). Fiji's new government is now demanding the removal of Australia and New Zealand from the PIF as a precondition for rejoining the organisation.

Chapter 13 by Alisi Daurewa is a personal account of her work as a member of the Fiji Election Commission. The breadth and depth of the work of this organisation has not been fully appreciated, largely because the public's information about them has been based mainly on formal descriptions in the Constitution and electoral decree and media reports. Daurewa's contribution is a story of the more human dimension of the commissioners and electoral officials who expended great energy travelling to the far corners of the country under extremely challenging conditions. Yet, despite these sacrifices, she argues that they were still unfairly vilified by armchair critics.

In Chapter 14 Leonard Chan, who was a member of the international monitoring group (MOG), discusses his personal experience as a member of this group. MOG played a very significant role in ensuring the credibility of the elections in the eyes of the international community. As with the previous chapter, this is a personal story of a kind not usually captured in the media and public discourse.

A note on the use of terms

With ethnic-based contestations over political power and constant shifts in the discourse of race, ethnicity and the definition of cultural boundaries, the use of labels is both complex and sensitive. Until recently, indigenous Fijians were usually known simply as 'Fijians'. The term 'Taukei' (literally 'owners') is now more commonly used, since 'Fijian' officially applies to anyone who is a citizen of Fiji (although this is contentious among more conservative indigenous Fijians). Some readers will be familiar with 'iTaukei'. Here the 'i' stands as the definite article as in *the* Taukei. We use Taukei without the 'i' to avoid the error that often appears when people say 'the iTaukei' (which is the same as saying 'the Taukei'). In the colonial and early post-colonial period, people of Indian descent were usually just called 'Indians'. Then 'Fiji Indians' became more common, but over time the term 'Indo-Fijians' has become standard.

References

Lawson, S 2012, 'Indigenous Nationalism, "Ethnic Democracy" and the Prospects for a Liberal Constitutional Order in Fiji', *Nationalism and Ethnic Politics*, vol. 18, no. 3, pp. 293–315.

Ratuva, S 2005, 'Political and Ethnic Identity in a Post-colonial Communal Democracy: The Case of Fiji', in A Allahar (ed.), *Ethnicity, class and nationalism: Caribbean and extra-Caribbean dimensions*, Lexington Books, Oxford.

Synlick, R 2006, 'Journalist Defends DC Life', *The Observer,* 11 September. Available at ndsmcobserver.com/2006/09/journalist-defends-d-c-life/.

2

Shifting democracy: Electoral changes in Fiji

Steven Ratuva

Electoral systems play a pivotal role in shaping voter political behaviour and choices, the national political culture and institutional political governance processes of a country. Scholars of electoral engineering have often differed on the most appropriate electoral system because different systems have different philosophical assumptions about democracy; and also they tend to create different outcomes based on the type of voting system, how constituency boundaries are designed and how the electoral system is manipulated by political parties and candidates to their advantage. In ethnically divided societies like Fiji, the focus has been increasingly on identifying an electoral system that promotes moderation, provides proportionality and representativeness and enhances inter-group harmony and long-term stability (Fraenkel & Grofman 2006; Horowitz 1997; Lijphart 1994; Reilly 2001). However, some electoral systems are configured specifically to suit the local circumstances or the interests of local elites or particular social groups at a particular point in time. Also, different electoral systems are based on certain assumptions about what democracy means, what it ought to be, how it should work and what the behavioural outcomes should be (Scholdan 2000).

While some theories of constitutional engineering such as the rational choice institutional approach (Norris 2004) have been influential, they tend to be too focused on individual behavioural dispositions and choices and how these interface with institutions; they often ignore the broader ethno-political and cultural dynamics which help shape group choices. In Fiji, constitutional engineering has been influenced by a number of factors. The first past the post (FPTP)–based electoral system under the 1970 Constitution, together with the communal allocation of seats, was inspired by the desire to create ethnic representativeness and balance and inter-ethnic harmony in a potentially volatile ethno-political situation. The shift in the balance of power after the 1987 elections created the conditions for military intervention. Following the coup, the 1970 Constitution was abrogated and a new one was promulgated in 1990 which retained the FPTP system and which was based on the assumption that stability could be achieved only through Taukei (indigenous Fijian) hegemony. This constitution was deemed inoperable in a multiethnic situation and it was amended, leading to the 1997 Constitution, which proposed an alternative voting (AV) system in the hope of creating moderation and stability (Lal 1998). This expectation was shattered by the 2000 coup. Today Fiji's new open list proportional representation (OLPR) electoral system, provided for in the 2013 Constitution, has been justified on the ground that it will steer the country away from an ethnic-based contestation for power and political mobilisation promoted by past FPTP and AV models. While this is true at the institutional level, whether it actually changes people's thinking and political behaviour in a way that negates communal consciousness is a big and challenging question.

This chapter examines some of the broad patterns of electoral change in Fiji, focusing fundamentally on the differences between the FPTP, AV and OLPR – their characteristics and their implications for shaping Fiji's ethno-political landscape.

The first past the post system

The FPTP system is based on a winner takes all approach: it is easy to administer and count and the results from highest to lowest are ordered through a simple process of ranking. The winner is the one who scores a simple majority of one vote above the second highest. Most countries in the Pacific, such as Tonga, Samoa, Solomon Islands and Cook Islands, use the FPTP system. In some cases, the constituencies are so small that the difference between the winner and runner-up is as small as one to three votes. In these cases, recounts often take place and these can be expensive. After the 27 November 2014 elections in Tonga, for example, the former Ha'apai No. 12 people's representative Mo'ale o'ale Finau, who won 532 votes but lost his seat by a margin of three votes, applied for a recount and was required to pay a recount fee of TOP$1,000 (Fonua 2014).

The FPTP voting system was used in Fiji's first election under universal suffrage in 1966 when the Fijian Association, the forerunner to the Alliance Party, won 22 seats. In addition to these, five other independents and Great Council of Chiefs nominees were aligned to the Alliance Party and in total it was able to muster 27 seats in the Legislative Council. The Indo-Fijian National Congress, which later became the National Federation Party (NFP), won nine seats (25 per cent) in the 36-seat legislature (Lal 2008). With three times more votes than the NFP, this was the largest victory the Alliance Party was to ever win. Prior to 1966, Taukei representatives were nominated while Indo-Fijian and European representatives were directly elected by voters. This patronising system was based on the assumption that Taukei interest was best served by chiefs through the Great Council of Chiefs as well as other colonially patronised institutions such as the Native Land Trust Board, Fijian Affairs Board, provincial councils (*Bose ni yasana*), district councils (*Bose ni tikina*) and village councils (*Bose vakoro*).

At the time of independence in 1970, Fiji's dilemma was how to accommodate the distinctive communal interests of competing ethnic groups in an overarching national rubric. It was a classic case of accommodating the often competing and potentially volatile aspirations of ethno-nationalism and civic nationalism (Stavenhagen 1996). The solution, after horse-trading between the leaders of the two major ethnic groups, was a consociationalist arrangement, encapsulated in the 1970 Constitution, whereby the Taukei and Indo-Fijians were to be allocated the same number of seats. To appease the Taukei, who feared political domination by Indo-Fijians and loss of land and political rights, there was agreement that the Senate would provide greater Taukei representation.

The first election under the 1970 Constitution, in 1972, saw shifts in the results compared to the 1966 elections. Based on the FPTP system, the gap between the Alliance Party, which won 33 seats (63 per cent), and the NFP, which won 19 seats (37 per cent), began to close. The allocation of seats under this constitution was largely communal in nature. Of the 52 seats, 22 were reserved for the Taukei, 22 for Indo-Fijians and eight for other minorities, usually categorised as 'General Electors'. The 22 seats for each of the two major ethnic groups were further divided into 12 communal (elected by members of the same community) and 10 national roll seats, to be elected cross-ethnically. For the general electors the division was three communal and five national roll seats (Fiji Government 1970). The ethnic division at this early stage was very clear, with the Alliance Party winning all the Taukei communal seats with the support of 82 per cent of all Taukei votes, and all general communal seats. The NFP won all Indo-Fijian communal seats, securing 73 per cent of all the Indo-Fijian votes. The voter turnout for the communal seats overall was 85.2 per cent.

Based as it was on the FPTP system, elections under the 1970 Constitution should have been relatively straightforward, but they were complicated by the communal allocation of seats in different categories, as mentioned above. Each voter actually had four votes—one in his or her own local communal constituency and one each for the 'national' constituencies for all three communal groups (i.e. Taukei, Indo-Fijian and General). This required four separate ballot papers. For instance, a Taukei voter would vote for a candidate in his or her local communal constituency (in which all the candidates and voters were Taukei), then the same voter would also vote three more times—one for each of the 'national' (cross-communal) seats for Taukei, Indo-Fijians and General Electors.

Because all four votes were counted, the tally of total votes as well as of party votes appeared to be inflated: the total number of votes was 689,673, although the population of Fiji was barely 400,000 in 1972. Another feature of the voting system was the disparity between the proportion of the votes and the number of seats. The Alliance Party polled 57.5 per cent of the votes but won 33 or 63.4 per cent of the seats; the NFP with 33.9 per cent of the votes won 19 or 36.5 per cent of the seats; and the Fijian Independent Party, which won 0.2 per cent of the votes, and independents, who won 6.4 per cent of the votes, both failed to win any seats (Nohlen, Grotz & Hartmann 2001).

The second election under the 1970 Constitution was held in March 1977, when the NFP sent shockwaves through the Taukei political establishment after they won 26 seats to the Alliance's 24 seats, despite the Alliance gaining 46 per cent of the votes as opposed to NFP's 45.2 per cent, an unfortunate disparity created by the FPTP system. Under the current OLPR system, the Alliance could have won the elections with about 24 seats, but the Alliance Party actually lost nine seats and the NFP gained an extra seven seats, while the Fijian Nationalist Party (FNP) and an independent candidate won a seat each. The more than 39,000 votes collected by FNP contributed to the Alliance defeat. There were altogether 47,690 informal votes, a high number indeed (Fiji Elections Office 1977).

The NFP was not able to form a government following the elections due to an internal leadership struggle and other factors and the governor-general, Ratu Sir George Cakobau, invited Ratu Sir Kamisese Mara, the former prime minister and leader of the defeated Alliance, to take over as caretaker prime minister in a 'palace coup' of sorts until the next elections in September of the same year.

 The September 1977 elections saw the Alliance's fortunes shift in their favour. The Alliance won 36 seats, a gain of 12, while the NFP, which by then was divided between the 'flower' and 'dove' factions, lost 11 seats, ending up with 15 (12 for the flower faction and three for the dove faction). The FNP votes declined by more than half as Taukei voters realised that votes for the FNP (which lost almost half of its support) would weaken the Alliance, thus risking the possibility of Taukei losing political power as in the March elections. The number of informal votes increased to 51,713.

Again, as in previous elections, the disparity in the percentage of the votes and number of seats was quite marked. The Alliance Party polled 52.2 per cent of the votes but won a massive 69 per cent of the seats; the NFP (flower) won 23.7 per cent of the votes and won 23.07 per cent of the seats, indeed a rare coincidence of proportionality under the FPTP system; the NFP (dove) won 20.6 per cent of the votes but won only 5.7 per cent of the seats; and perhaps the biggest loser was the FNP, which won 18,854 votes but did not win any seat, while the independent candidate won a seat with only 6,228 votes.

The disparity between votes cast and seats won was not really obvious during the 1982 elections, when the Alliance Party, with 51.8 per cent of the votes, won 53 per cent of the seats, while the NFP won 42 per cent of the seats with 41.2 per cent of the votes. This election saw the entry of the western Viti Levu–based Western United Front (WUF), which won two seats. The number of informal votes reduced to 19,605, a low total compared to the previous elections (Fiji Elections Office 1982).

The last and most significant election under the 1970 Constitution's FPTP system was the April 1987 elections, which led directly to the May and September 1987 coups, following which Fiji's politics was drastically transformed through a serious of coerced regime changes (Ratuva 2011). In 1987, the Alliance Party lost power, winning only 24 seats, although they won 49.5 per cent of the total votes. With only 47.1 per cent of the votes, the NFP–Fiji Labour Party (FLP) coalition won 28 seats, or 54 per cent. One key factor contributing to the coalition victory was the new energy and promise provided by the newly formed FLP. Also the shift of Taukei votes to the WUF and FNP, although the latter once again failed to win a seat, drew votes away from the Alliance Party. The shift in the balance of power away from the Taukei establishment created the conditions for instability in a highly charged ethno-political climate. Again, as in the previous elections, the exaggerated total of over 1 million votes for a population of about half a million was reflective of the type of multiple votes required under Fiji's communal FPTP electoral system.

The FPTP system under the 1970 Constitution had a number of distinguishable factors. The fact that voters had to vote four times complicated the process and inflated the total number of voters by a factor of four. This meant that voters did not necessarily have to vote for the same party on all four ballot papers: one for the voter's communal seat, one for the voter's national seat and two for the national seats of the other two ethnic categories. This system provided a chance for both trans-ethnic and communal voting within the broader rubric of ethnic classification. The complexity of the system led to a large number of informal votes. Another feature was that the seats won were disproportionate to the votes because of the large differences in the size and number of voters in different constituencies.

While the electoral system under the 1970 Constitution was seen as a panacea for Fiji's divergent communal interests because it prescribed a seemingly balanced voting equation (especially the provision for an equal number of seats for Taukei and Indo-Fijians), in some ways that prescription reinforced communalism and entrenched what has been described as 'communal democracy' (Ratuva 2005). These elections did not really serve the purpose of a power-balancing exercise, which the seat allocation formula was assumed to do, but became an arena for both inter- and intra-ethnic contestation of choice and power. When there was a shift in political gravity away from the Alliance Party and, effectively, the Taukei establishment, Fijian democracy, which up until then was underpinned by the notion of paramountcy of Fijian interest, began to unravel in unrestrained ways.

The May 1987 coup, a month after the elections, led to a fundamental transformation of Fiji's political environment, including the declaration of Fiji as a republic and the promulgation of the 1990 Constitution which promoted Taukei political ascendency (Lawson 1991; Norton 1990; Sutherland 1992). There was a dramatic transformation from the discourse of balance to the discourse of communal hegemony, spawned by the waves of Taukei ethno-nationalism that have swept Fiji since 1987. The 1990 Constitution prescribed a FPTP electoral system with 70 parliamentary seats, 37 of which were reserved for Taukei, 27 for Indo-Fijians, one for Rotumans and five for other ethnic minorities (Fiji Government 1990, p. 49). There were no national seats as in the 1970 Constitution. Another significant development was the demise of the Alliance Party and the emergence of the Soqosoqo ni Vakavulewa ni Taukei (SVT) as the dominant Taukei party.

Predictably, the first general elections under the 1990 Constitution, held in 1992, was won by the SVT with 43.6 per cent of the votes and 30 seats, or 43 per cent. This was an unusual coincidence of vote–seat proportionality. Indo-Fijian votes were largely shared between the NFP with 16.1 per cent (14 seats) the FLP with 16.1 per cent (13 seats). This even split in votes can be interpreted as a result of the equal level of appeal of the two political parties amongst Indo-Fijian voters at this time, but that was to change dramatically in the next elections. After a long drought the FNP made a comeback under a new name (Fijian Nationalist United Front), winning three seats. The WUF also made a comeback with two seats and the General Voters' Party (GVP), because it was the only party representing the General Electors, won all five general communal seats (7.14 per cent) but with only 1.4 per cent of the total votes (Fiji Elections Office 1992).

The balance of power in the new parliament was very precarious. With only 30 seats and a slim majority, the SVT struggled to hold on to power and it came as no surprise that a snap election took place two years later in 1994 after the government failed to pass its budget through parliament. The SVT came back strongly in the elections, winning two extra seats with 40.9 per cent of the votes. The NFP also increased its number of seats by six to 20 (17.8 per cent of the votes) at the direct expense of the FLP, which lost six seats and ended up with seven (14.6 per cent of the votes). The newly formed Fijian Association Party (FAP), a direct rival to the SVT, won five seats (9.9 per cent of the votes) while the FNP won 4.1 per cent of the votes and lost its three seats. The number of informal votes was the lowest ever up to that point (Fiji Elections Office 1994). The 1994 elections were the last under the FPTP system before a review of the 1990 Constitution. This review saw major revisions, leading to the 1997 Constitution that introduced the alternative voting (AV) system.

The political dynamics in Fiji had started to swing in a way that the framers of the 1990 Constitution did not envisage. The ethnic distribution of seats to guarantee Taukei hegemony was premised on the assumption that Taukei political interest and aspirations were homogenous and solidarity of the *vanua* (Taukei culture and social structure) was primordially indivisible. This mythical view failed to appreciate and acknowledge the contesting tribal, regional and ideological discourses within the Taukei community, some of which are rooted in pre-European times. The split within the SVT and the formation of the FAP testified to this. The SVT, with only 30 seats, was faced by opposition from both the Taukei and Indo-Fijian political parties.

The voting system under the 1990 Constitution was relatively simple. Every voter voted for only one candidate in the single-member communal constituency. This was a significant contrast to the mixed communal and cross-voting system of the 1970 Constitution, which required four ballot papers for each voter. Because of its simplicity, the informal vote was quite low. Despite this, the undesirability of this electoral system was its ethnically skewed nature, which provided the

Taukei disproportionate political power and simultaneously reduced other ethnic groups into marginalised political subalterns. The system further fragmented Fiji's multicultural society and overseas migration by Indo-Fijians continued unabated as they attempted to escape from the communally restrictive political climate.

The FPTP system under the 1970 and 1990 Constitutions was framed around the reservation of ethnic seats in multiple single-member constituencies. While the 1970 Constitution prescribed a mixture of communal and national rolls to accommodate a mixture of intra- and inter-ethnic votes, the FPTP system under the 1990 Constitution was totally communal, without any trans-ethnic votes. Nevertheless, both variants encouraged ethnic mobilisation and the creation of communally based political cleavages, which contributed to tension and instability. This was because the communally based FPTP system created the conditions for ethnic-based competition for political power on the basis of a winner takes all contest. Ethnic-based political parties became the vehicle for promoting and facilitating the ethnic struggle for political ascendency on the basis of zero-sum gamesmanship. The mixture of the winner takes all principle under FPTP and ethnically exclusive political mobilisation overshadowed the potential for middle-ground compromises. This nurtured the development of a demarcated and antagonistic political culture, which, over time, laced with economic disparity, ethnic competition over state control and deliberate ethnic mobilisation, spawned large-scale ethno-political schism.

A negative feature of the FPTP system was the disparity in the proportionality of votes in relation to the number of seats. We have seen this occur in all the elections under FPTP since universal suffrage was introduced in 1966. The number of seats won by political parties was often disproportionate to the votes they had won. In addition, the figures show that the winners of the elections in 1966, 1970, 1987, 1992 and 1994 did not achieve the 50 per cent threshold to be able to claim majority support. This raises the technical and ethical question of the democratic value of votes and whether attaining victory by winning less than 50 per cent of the votes was sufficient to make a victory legitimate. This was a major dilemma that the AV system attempted to address when it was introduced under the 1997 Constitution.

The alternative voting system

As Fiji moved away from the shadow of the 1987 coup and its associated Constitution of 1990, internal and external pressure for a more ethnically accommodating constitution increased. After a constitutional review process by the constitutional commission, which carried out local and international consultation, parliament unanimously passed the 1997 Constitution. The AV system used in Fiji under the 1997 Constitution was considerably more complex than the FPTP system previously used. A major rationale behind the use of the AV system was a belief in its capacity to ameliorate tension by fostering cooperation and moderation (Horowitz 1997; Reeves, Vakatora & Lal 1996; Reilly 2001). This was because the system allowed for a consociationalist process based on exchange of preferences between political parties. Theoretically the AV system was supposed to provide middle-ground consensus as well as remove extremism and promote opportunities for minority parties to win seats. However, like any other electoral system, the AV system was subject to manipulation by politicians and this, to some extent, had some influence on electoral outcomes.

Of the 71 seats provided for under the 1997 Constitution, 25 were to be open seats in which voters could vote for any candidate from any ethnic group, while 46 seats were reserved for specific communities. In these communal seats, 23 seats were reserved for the Taukei, 19 for Indo-Fijians, one for Rotumans and three for other minorities. The boundaries for 17 of the constituencies were based on the administrative provincial boundaries prescribed under the Fijian Affairs Act; each of the larger provinces of Ba, Tailevu and Cakaudrove were divided into two constituencies, and each of the other provinces became a single constituency. The remaining six constituencies were comprised predominantly of urban and peri-urban areas containing roughly equal numbers (Fiji Government 1997). In terms of the value of votes (determined by seat–voter ratio), the rural provincial constituencies, which were demographically smaller in size, had more advantage than the urban and peri-urban constituencies.

The ballot paper was divided into two parts: the 'above the line' vote required voters to tick the party of their choice and the 'below the line' vote required voters to list the candidates in order of preference from 1 to 5. If no candidate achieved 50 per cent plus one vote of the valid votes cast in a constituency, the votes of the lowest-polling candidate were redistributed among the other candidates according to the preferences listed on the ballot paper. This process was repeated until one candidate had at least 50 per cent plus one vote of the total valid votes cast.

The system of preferential exchange between parties tended to nullify the power of voters to determine the outcome of their votes. In fact it was tantamount to parties 'fixing' the election results, as parties traded preferences to maximise benefits for themselves while conspiring against those they detested. For instance, during the 1999 elections, the first under the AV system, the Veitokani ni Lewenivanua Vakarisito (VLV) and the Party of National Unity (PANU), two moderate Taukei parties, gave high preferences to the Indo-Fijian-dominated FLP as a tactical move to undermine the NFP and Soqosoqo Duavata ni Lewenivanua (SDL), who had formed a close alliance. In the 2001 elections, NFP transferred its votes to SDL, thus enabling it to win, although the NFP failed to win a single seat (Fiji Elections Office 1999).

During the 1999 elections, many voters found the AV system complex and confusing, and the informal vote was as high as 10 per cent. In addition, there was a massive disparity in the proportion of seats in relation to the votes, similar to elections under the FPTP system. For instance, with only 32.2 per cent of the total votes after distribution of preferences, the FLP won 52.1 per cent of the seats. On the other hand, the NFP, with 14.6 per cent of the votes, failed to win a seat, while the Fijian Association Party (FAP), with only 10.1 per cent of the votes, won 10 seats. The UGP, with a mere 1.4 per cent of the votes, won two seats. This disparity in vote value raised fundamental questions about the viability of the AV system as an electoral mechanism for democracy, especially in an ethnically divided society.

The AV system did indeed promote minority parties and interparty cooperation, much more than the FPTP system had. However, the problem was that the inter- and intra-communal formal engagements were still 'floating' on deeply embedded ethnic cleavages and consciousness, whipped up by ethnic entrepreneurs who had personal and political motives. This, together with a host of other factors, including Chaudhry's governance style, built up the momentum towards the 2000 coup.

The attempt by the NFP and SVT, two major ethnic parties, to forge an alliance failed because the leaders, Jai Ram Reddy (NFP) and Sitiveni Rabuka (SVT), could not secure the backing of their respective communities. To the Indo-Fijian voters, Reddy was committing sacrilege by allying himself with the man who staged the 1987 coup against Indo-Fijian political interests. To his Taukei supporters, Rabuka was seen as selling out Taukei interests by crossing the sacred line that kept the Indo-Fijians and Taukei apart. The attempt to move towards a middle ground position was a tectonic shift that reflected the new spirit of the 1997 Constitution and the AV system and the appeal for moderation. However, this came into direct collision with the highly ethnicised political culture nurtured under the communally oriented FPTP. Voters showed their dissatisfaction through the ballot: the SVT lost a total of 24 seats, winning only eight, and there was a mass exodus of Indo-Fijian voters from the NFP to the FLP. The latter won a massive 37 seats while the NFP lost 20. The FLP was now seen as the party representing Indo-Fijian interests, an image propped up by its use of racial fearmongering among Indo-Fijian voters. Its leader, Mahendra Chaudhry, became the first Indo-Fijian prime minister.

The FLP forged a coalition with the FAP and VLV and held power for a year before being overthrown in the coup of May 2000. While the AV system cannot be blamed for the increasing ethnic polarisation, it could not really transform a political culture, which had long thrived on ethno-political polarity in a significant way. The process of party cooperation was not sufficient to heal the ethno-political schism.

The demise of the SVT led to the emergence of the SDL, an even more strongly ethno-nationalist party. During the 2001 elections, the SDL, under the leadership of Laisenia Qarase, who was appointed by the military as interim prime minister after the 2000 coup, won 32 seats with only 26 per cent of the votes, while the FLP, with 34.8 per cent of the votes, won only 27 seats. The Conservative Alliance, a party formed by supporters of George Speight, the ethno-nationalist coup leader, won six seats and subsequently formed a coalition with the SDL (Fiji Elections Office 2002).

The 2006 elections continued to show the dominance of the SDL and FLP as major ethnic political groupings for Taukei and Indo-Fijians respectively. With 44.59 per cent of the votes, the SDL won 36 seats and with 39.18 per cent of the votes, the FLP won 31 seats (Fiji Elections

Office 2006). The results showed an increasingly polarised society, dashing expectations that AV was going to create a middle ground consensus.

The proliferation of political parties under the AV system stemmed from misplaced optimism about its capacity to facilitate minority party interests. The real dynamic behind how the AV system worked was how parties strategically shared their preferences both to benefit themselves and to undermine the chances of parties perceived as arch rivals. By and large, this led to major ethnic parties such as the SDL and the FLP making deals that promoted their interests while undermining intra-ethnic competitors. As we have seen, inter-ethnic deals usually ended up promoting the dominance of a major ethnic party.

Following the military coup in December 2006, which saw the overthrow of the SDL government, a new political order was created after a fundamental political transformation (Ratuva 2011). Among the changes was the creation of a new constitution prescribing an open list proportional representation system (OLPR), which was used for the first time in the 17 September 2014 elections.

The open list proportional representation system and the 2014 elections

The underlying principle of the proportional representation (PR) system is that the proportion of seats won by a party or independent candidate corresponds with the proportion of votes gained. There are basically two types of PR systems: the closed system, in which the political parties provide a list of candidates; and the open system, where the candidates are ranked according to how many votes they win. Fiji uses the 'open' PR system. The ballot paper consists of numbers allocated to the candidates and the voter has to put a tick, a cross or a circle in the box beside the number of the candidate he or she supports. Other variants of the PR system include the mixed member proportional (MMP) system used in New Zealand and the single transferable vote (STV) used in Ireland. About 94 countries in the world use different variants of the PR system. The party list is the most popular, with about 85 countries using it.

The introduction of the open list proportional representation (OLPR) system and the single national constituency system in Fiji is meant to promote trans-ethnic voting, multiethnic political party membership and national unity. As we have seen earlier, communally based constituencies under the FPTP and AV systems promoted ethnic contestation for political power, which contributed to tensions. The single national constituency ensures that politicians are not locked into localised loyalty but rather have a broader national outlook. The open listing is also meant to democratise the elections through the direct choice of the voters rather than allowing the political parties to determine the winning candidates through a closed list system. The number of parliamentary seats has been reduced from 71 to 50 as a way of creating a leaner and less expensive parliament.

The ballot paper is in the form of a grid containing the number allotted to each candidate, picked at random, starting from number 135. This avoided single digit numbers such as 1, which would give some candidates unfair advantage. The design of the ballot paper caused considerable controversy because political parties felt that simply allocating numbers to represent candidates was too simplistic and confusing for voters. An alternative suggestion was a ballot paper with party symbols. The use of the number grid represents an extreme version of design options. The other extreme is to list the names and symbols of all 247 candidates by using a 'tablecloth' ballot paper containing details such as names of candidates and party symbols. This option is not practical but there are other variations in between the two extremes that could show party symbols and even names. These could have been explored.

The vote-counting system uses the D'Hondt method first suggested by Victor D'Hondt, a Belgian mathematician, in 1878. It involves dividing the total number of votes a party receives by a series of denominators from 1 to 50. Thus, the total vote is divided by 1 then the remainder is divided by 2 then the remainder is divided by 3 and then by 4 and so forth, until 50 (because of the 50 seats). The seats are then divided amongst political parties that polled more than the threshold of 5 per cent of the total votes; the allocation of seats is based on the proportion of votes they gain. For instance, a party that polls 50 per cent of the votes gets 50 per cent of the seats and one which polls 10 per cent of the votes receives 10 per cent of the seats. From the party's total seat allocation, the individual seats are then allocated according to their ranking within the party, based on the individual votes they receive. For instance, with 60 per cent of the votes, FijiFirst (FF) was allocated 60 per cent of the seats, which totalled 32 seats. The FijiFirst candidates were then allocated seats on the basis of the 32 highest-polling candidates.

Results of the 2014 elections

As Table 1 shows, the elections delivered a decisive victory for FijiFirst with 59.17 per cent of the votes and 32 seats, followed by the Social Democratic Liberal Party (SODELPA), a renamed version of the SDL. The revived NFP won three seats, while none of the other four parties and two independent candidates reached the 5 per cent threshold and thus they failed to win any seats. In a way, the OLPR system had opened up the space for multiethnic competition, with all the parties claiming to be multiethnic although the degree to which they were in terms of membership or support varied considerably.

Table 1: Election results by political party

Political party	Total no. of votes	Percentage	No. of seats
FijiFirst	293,714	59.17	32
SODELPA	139,857	28.18	15
NFP	27,066	5.15	3
PDP	15,864	3.2	0
FLP	11,670	2.35	0
One Fiji	5,839	1.18	0
FUFP	1,072	0.22	0
Roshika Deo	1,055	0.21	0
Umesh Chand	227	0.05	0
Total	496,364	100	50

Source: Fiji Elections Office (2014).

Note: The figures in this table have been rounded up and do not exactly match the totals supplied.

FijiFirst (FF) turned out to be the biggest beneficiary of the new system by appealing nationally across ethnic groups. The party leader himself, Frank Bainimarama, won a massive 202,459, 41 per cent of all the votes cast, which was 12.6 per cent higher than the total SODELPA votes, 70 per cent of all FF votes and four times more than the votes won by Ro Temumu Kepa, the leader of the SODELPA. Bainimarama's votes created a 'coat-tail effect': his votes enabled members of his party with very low votes to win seats (Fiji Elections Office 2014).

The estimate for the ethnic and party distribution of the votes in Table 2 shows the extent to which FF extended its electoral success across all ethnic groups, winning 50 per cent of Taukei votes, 71 per cent of Indo-Fijian votes and 80 per cent of minority votes. In comparison, SODELPA initially strived to present itself as multiethnic but failed to attract sufficient non-Taukei candidates, winning only 0.4 per cent of Indo-Fijian votes and 1.5 per cent of minority votes. Although its campaign focused on attracting Taukei votes, they managed only 46 per cent of all Taukei votes.

Table 2: Estimates of ethnic votes and percentage

Party	Taukei		Indo-Fijian		Minority		Total
FF	148,909	50%	120,979	71%	23,826	8%	293,714
SODELPA	137,523	46%	751	0.4%	432	1.45%	139,857
Others	11,386	4%	47,034	28%	5,533	18.57%	62,793
Total	297,818	100%	168,764	100%	29,782	100%	496,364

Source: Estimated from Fiji Elections Office figures for 2014.
Note: The figures in this table have been rounded up and do not exactly match the totals supplied.

Because FF had an undisputed dominance over Indo-Fijian and minority votes, the real battle to determine the winner was between FF and SODELPA as they battled over the Taukei votes, which made up 60 per cent of the total voters.

Taukei versus Taukei contest

One of the central trends in the 2014 Fiji general elections was the contestation for political dominance by indigenous Fijian (Taukei) elites representing the two major political parties: the FF and the SODELPA. The differences between FF and SODELPA were deeply rooted in their different conceptualisations of Taukei history, cosmology, culture and the future direction of Taukei social transformation. SODELPA's ideological position supported a protectionist doctrine harking back to the colonial and post-colonial period, while FF was committed to the fundamental transformation of neo-colonial institutions, norms and ideologies.

As already stated, FF scored a decisive victory with almost 59.17 per cent of the total votes and about 50 per cent of the Taukei votes, compared to SODELPA's 28.18 per cent and 46 per cent respectively. The almost 50/50 split in the Taukei votes was indicative of major changes in social dynamics within the Taukei community as well as in the relationship with other communities. This will continue to shape the future trajectory of Fijian politics in significant ways.

The OLPR system opened the way for a three-tier, all-out contest between first, political parties; second, individual candidates of different political parties; and third, candidates of the same party. Taukei votes consisted of 297,818 (60 per cent) of a total of 496,364 votes. As noted above, this was the main battleground for FF and SODELPA. Because SODELPA was a predominantly Taukei party, with an exclusively ethno-nationalist ideology, it was statistically and politically handicapped from the beginning—it had to win 247,188 or 83 per cent of the Taukei votes to be able to reach the 25 (+1) seat threshold to form government in the 50-seat parliament.

The 139,857 votes for SODELPA equated to about 46.9 per cent of Taukei votes. The non-Taukei votes for SODELPA may have come largely from the three Indo-Fijian candidates, whose votes totalled 751, and Mick Beddoes, a member of the minority part-European group, who collected 865 votes. If we assume that about half of Beddoes's votes came from Taukeis then the approximate number of minority groups who voted for SODELPA would be about 432. Thus the total number of non-Taukei votes for SODELPA would be about 1,183 or 0.85 per cent of the total SODELPA votes and 0.2 per cent of the overall national votes. Thus we can conclude that of the total SODELPA votes, about 137,523 or 99.1 per cent, were Taukei. This represented 46 per cent of the total Taukei votes.

Predictably, the last two candidates in the SODELPA list were Indo-Fijians. In the beginning, SODELPA was optimistic about attracting other ethnic groups but abandoned the idea of a multiracial party after failing to attract sufficient non-Taukeis to stand as candidates. If it hopes to have any chance of winning a future election, SODELPA basically has two choices. The first is to increase its share of Taukei votes by 83 per cent and more, a virtually impossible feat. Second, it should reconfigure its ideological and political strategy in a more trans-ethnic direction and compete head on against the FF on the same multiracial platform.

In contrast to SODELPA, FF clearly has a trans-ethnic appeal and therefore had a lower level of difficulty in winning, because all it needed was 50 per cent Taukei votes, 50 per cent Indo-Fijian votes and 50 per cent votes from other minorities to reach the 25 seats threshold. Anything on top of that was a bonus. This meant SODELPA had to work harder by 33 per cent than FF to reach its 83 per cent threshold. With 46 per cent of the Taukei votes going to SODELPA, the share for FF and minority parties was 54 per cent. Assuming that the minority parties' share of Taukei votes was 4 per cent, the other 50 per cent would have voted for FF. This clear division in Taukei votes reflected the shifting nature of Taukei interests, expectations and political choices in a fast-changing social, economic and political environment. This is a significant lesson for electoral strategising in the next elections for political parties who hope to win Taukei votes.

With 148,909 (50 per cent) of Taukei votes (or 29.9 per cent of the total votes) secured, all that FF had to do to ensure total victory was to top up with Indo-Fijian and minority votes. In the end, FF secured 293,714 or 59.17 per cent of the total votes, about twice as many as SODELPA, with 139,857 or 28.18 per cent of the total votes. In addition to the Taukei votes, the Indo-Fijian and minority voters who voted for FF totalled around 144,805 or 29.1 per cent of the total FF votes. Based on the assumption that Indo-Fijians made up 34 per cent of the total votes, the total number of Indo-Fijian votes was 168,764, while the total number of minority votes (again assuming that they made up 6 per cent of the total votes) was 29,782. If we assume that 80 per cent (23,826) of the voters from minorities voted for FF, then about 120,979 (71 per cent) of the Indo-Fijians would have done the same.

The margin of error for these calculations is about 2 to 3 per cent but, by and large, given the absence of any official figures on ethnic categorisation, this estimation, based on the figures available, gives us a good idea of the dynamics of shifting voting patterns. The fact that there was an almost 50/50 split in the Taukei votes between SODELPA and FF means that one cannot talk strictly about a 'Taukei Party'; and in the same way that one can no longer confidently talk about an 'Indo-Fijian Party'.

Election strategies

SODELPA's strategy in carving up the single national constituency into 50 sub-constituencies as the focus of its campaign for the 50 individual candidates was quite innovative and commendable because it won the party most of their seats. Winning SODELPA candidates did well in their allocated local areas by taking advantage of kinship and other sociocultural links within the local community. The only SODELPA candidate who collected substantive votes across the sub-constituency boundaries was party leader Ro Teimumu, with a massive 49,485 votes, light years ahead of Niko Nawaikula, who came second with 7,348 votes. However, while this strategy worked well in rural areas it was less successful in semi-urban and urban areas. These were FF territories.

The FF approach was in direct contrast to that of SODELPA. FF used the 'rock star' phenomenon very strategically by cleverly using the VFR principles (visibility, familiarity and relevance), which underpinned the voter–politician relationship in the OLPR system. The focus was on maximising the VFR of the already well-known party leader Bainimarama to draw votes for the party. This also worked well in the context of the number grid system used in the ballot paper, where one just needed to remember the number 279. Also, FF's presidential campaign style, its use of 'cargo cult' politics (provision of development projects) and a last minute pro-poor manifesto, amongst other strategies, helped to consolidate its dominance. These tactics achieved phenomenal results, especially for the FF leader, who also won votes for another 49 members of the party who collectively won only 30 per cent of the party votes. It is often assumed that one of the advantages of the PR system is to ensure greater parity in the votes between parties, but the lopsidedness of the votes in favour of FF destroyed this assumption.

FF had an advantage over other parties in terms of incumbency and access to state resources as well as through its control over the media and freedom of association during the pre-election period. It also effectively marketed its development projects to voters, sometimes with veiled threats of what might happen if FF did not win the elections. Eight years of unrivalled hegemony entrenched their visibility, familiarity and relevance in voter consciousness.

It is reasonable to assume that if an election had taken place in 2009, FF would have struggled to win because at that time the country was still going through a turbulent period and the Bainimarama regime had very little to market to voters.

Political contestation between FF and SODELPA centred on the very different ideological positions adopted by each. SODELPA's vision of land, the Great Council of Chiefs, identity and the Christian state placed it at the protectionist, ethno-nationalistic and conservative end of the continuum (SODELPA 2014), while FF was more towards the reformist, secularist, modernist and multiethnic end (FijiFirst 2014). What they shared in common were tactics involving psychological coercion in the form of private and public fearmongering. Rumours, conspiracy theories and hate stories were circulated widely through blog sites, social networks and other means, both modern and traditional, of communication. This created much tension and negative energy, which unfortunately did not really wither away after the elections but instead continued unabated into the 2015 parliamentary debates.

The stark ideological distinction between the two parties provided voters with a clear choice. Indo-Fijians and minority groups found the FF position more trans-ethnically embracing and supportive of their long-term security in Fiji compared to the ethnically exclusivist SODELPA position. For the Taukei, the choice was between SODELPA's conservative cultural preservation approach or FF's cultural transformation and socioeconomic modernisation strategy. The patterns of Taukei support for both parties were apparent. SODELPA had massive support in the rural polling stations of Lau, Kadavu and Lomaiviti as well as in Cakaudrove and Bua, while FF performed well in Viti Levu, especially in Nadroga, Nadi, Ba, Serua, Ra, Naitasiri and Tailevu. For instance, Cuvu, Nadroga's 'capital', was overwhelmingly FF, despite the close kinship links between Cuvu and the SODELPA leader. In Tailevu, home of the FF leader, the tussle was quite even but SODELPA dominated in Rewa, home of SODELPA's leader (Fiji Elections Office 2014).

Data from polling stations in urban areas such as Lami, Kinoya, Nausori, Nasinu, Raiwaqa, Nabua, University of the South Pacific, Fiji National University and Suva Civic Centre, amongst others, showed that FF had unsurpassed support (Fiji Elections Office 2014) in these places. Thus it appears that support for SODELPA was strong among the more traditional and conservative members of the rural Taukei community, while support for FF was dominant amongst the more urban and also those who had direct benefit from the government's development projects. But development did not always work as a payoff for party loyalty. For instance, although a large number of development projects in the form of roads and mining had taken place in the Bua province, FF still performed very badly in many Bua polling stations. In a Kadavu polling station, despite the provision of solar electricity to the villages concerned, only two people voted for FF out of a total of 77 voters.

The OLPR system will likely be around for some time yet because provisions for amending the Constitution are very restrictive; for instance, three-quarters of parliamentary votes are required in addition to support by three-quarters of voters in a national referendum. The new system promised hope of representation for minority parties and independents but there were disappointments, as only three parties won seats. While it ensured parity between the number of parliamentary seats a party gained and the number of votes it had received, it still created discrepancies in the actual ranking of individual candidates. For instance, there were winning candidates in FF who collected fewer votes than losing candidates in SODELPA. Bainimarama's coat-tail appeal may have distorted the actual total support for FF, as winning party members actually benefitted from the massive support for Bainimarama. The FF tactic of deliberately and actively promoting their party leader as a political rock star attracted popular votes and worked to their advantage. Perhaps the burning question for FF is what happens when Bainimarama is gone, perhaps in two or three elections' time. This is when competition between political parties will be stiffer and the results more unpredictable.

Conclusion

Fiji has come a long way in its electoral journey from the FPTP used in the first universal suffrage in 1966 and post-independence elections under the 1970 and 1990 Constitutions to the AV system under the 1997 Constitution and eventually the OLPR system under the 2013 Constitution. The FPTP system was used in the context of communally divided constituencies, as reflected in the 1970 and 1990 Constitutions, which helped nurture and reproduce the creation of communal political cleavages and ethnic contestation for political power. Ethnic politics became a significant driver for defining sociocultural identity and social change. One's ethnic identity and political rights became closely linked in an almost symbiotic manner.

Attempts to move away from this communal political culture led to the introduction of the AV system under the 1997 Constitution. Theoretically, the AV system was meant to promote inter-ethnic engagement and moderation but given the simmering ethno-political dynamics in Fiji, the experiences in the 1999, 2001 and 2006 elections showed that sharing of preferences by parties was based not on their desire to move towards moderation but on the desire to leverage the system to maximise self-interest. The results still showed an ethnically polarised pattern of votes.

The introduction of the OLPR system was part of the post-2006 political revolution to transform the sociopolitical landscape by eradicating ethnic mobilisation and consciousness. This has not been fully achieved because of the difficulty in de-ethnicising people's identity and choices. Nevertheless, the rise of FF has shifted political discourse to the centre, where expressions of political choices by different ethnic groups have converged. The results of the 2014 elections appear to show that Fiji's political culture has shifted away from ethnic polarity towards moderation. The next elections in 2018 will indicate whether this shift is substantive or merely temporary.

References

Fiji Elections Office 1977, *Election Results*, Fiji Elections Office, Suva.

Fiji Elections Office 1982, *Election Results*, Fiji Elections Office, Suva.

Fiji Elections Office 1992, *Election Results*, Fiji Elections Office, Suva.

Fiji Elections Office 1994, *Election Results*, Fiji Elections Office, Suva.

Fiji Elections Office 1999, *Election Results*, Fiji Elections Office, Suva.

Fiji Elections Office 2002, *Election Results*, Fiji Elections Office, Suva.

Fiji Elections Office 2006, *Election Results*, Fiji Elections Office, Suva.

Fiji Elections Office 2014, 'Final results for the 2014 general election'. Viewed 5 December 2014 at www.electionsfiji.gov.fj/2014-election-results/.

Fiji Government 1970, *Constitution of the Republic of Fiji Islands*, Government Printing Press, Suva.

Fiji Government 1990, *Constitution of the Republic of Fiji Islands*, Government Printing Press, Suva.

Fiji Government 1997, *Constitution of the Republic of Fiji Islands*, Government Printing Press, Suva.

Fiji Government 2013, *Constitution of the Republic of Fiji*, Government Printing Press, Suva.

FijiFirst 2014, *Manifesto*. Viewed 26 November 2014 at fijifirst.com/our-manifesto/#toggle-id-1.

Fonua, P 2014, 'Ballot recount for Ha'apai 12 candidate', *Matangi Tonga*, 5 December. Viewed 10 December 2014 at matangitonga.to/2014/12/06/ballot-recount-ha-apai-12-candidate.

Fraenkel, J and Grofman, B 2006, 'Does the alternative vote foster moderation in ethnically divided societies? The case of Fiji', *Comparative Political Studies*, vol. 39, no. 5, pp. 623–51.

Horowitz, DL 1997, 'Encouraging electoral accommodation in divided societies', in BV Lal and P Larmour (eds), *Electoral systems in divided societies: The Fiji constitutional review*, The Australian National University, Canberra, pp. 21–37.

Lal, B 1998, *Another way: The politics of constitutional reform in post-coup Fiji*, Asia Pacific Press, Canberra.

Lal, B 2008, *A time bomb lies buried: Fiji's road to independence, 1960–1970*, ANU E Press, Canberra.

Lawson, S 1991, *The failure of democratic politics in Fiji*, Oxford University Press, Oxford.

Lijphart, A 1994, *Electoral systems and party systems*, Oxford University Press, Oxford.

Nohlen, D, Grotz, F and Hartmann, 2001, *Elections in Asia: A data handbook*, Volume II, Oxford University Press, Oxford.

Norris, P 2004, *Electoral engineering: Voting rules and voting behaviour*, University of Cambridge Press, Cambridge.

Norton, B 1990, *Race and politics in Fiji*, University of Queensland Press, St Lucia.

Ratuva, S 2005, 'Political and Ethnic Identity in a Post-colonial Communal Democracy: The Case of Fiji', in A Allahar (ed.), *Ethnicity, class and nationalism: Caribbean and extra-Caribbean dimensions*, Lexington Books, Oxford.

Ratuva, S 2011, 'The Fiji Military Coups: Reactive and Transformative Tendencies', *Journal of Asian Political Science*, vol. 19, no. 1, pp. 96–120.

Ratuva, S 2013, *Politics of preferential development: Trans-global study of affirmative action and ethnic conflict in Fiji, Malaysia and South Africa*, ANU E Press, Canberra.

Reeves, P, Vakatora, TR and Lal, BV 1996, *The Fiji Islands: Towards a united future*, Report of the Fiji Constitutional Review Commission, Parliament of Fiji, Parliamentary Paper No. 34, Fiji Government Printer, Suva.

Reilly, B 2001, *Democracy in divided societies: Electoral engineering for conflict management*, Cambridge University Press, New York.

Scholdan, S 2000, 'Democratisation and electoral engineering in post-ethnic conflict societies,' *Javnost – The Public*, vol.7, no. 1, pp. 25–40.

SODELPA 2014, *Reclaiming Fiji*, SODELPA, Suva.

Stavenhagen, R 1996, *Ethnic conflict and the nation state*, Palgrave Macmillan, London.

Sutherland, W 1992, *Beyond the Politics of Race: An Alternative History of Fiji to 1992*, Research School of Pacific Studies, The Australian National University, Canberra.

3

Chiefly leadership in Fiji after the 2014 elections

Stephanie Lawson

'Chiefdoms are highly variable, but they are all about power.'
(Earle 2011, p. 27)

Introduction

The last quarter century has seen a significant decline of chiefly influence in Fiji's politics, albeit with some periods of enhanced status for the paramount symbol of indigenous Fijian traditionalism, the Great Council of Chiefs (GCC). This body, however, was abolished by decree under the military regime of Commodore Josaia Voreqe (Frank) Bainimarama in March 2012. The September 2014 elections held prospects for the restoration of chiefly authority and the role of traditionalism through the Social Democratic Liberal Party (SODELPA) led by Ro Teimumu Vuikaba Kepa, holder of a prominent chiefly title. A victory by SODELPA would also have seen the restoration of the GCC. With SODELPA's resounding defeat by Bainimarama's FijiFirst Party, such prospects have received a significant blow.

This chapter provides an account of chiefly leadership in national politics, beginning with a survey of Fiji's colonisation, the role of chiefs in the British colonial regime generally, and their domination of national politics up until 1987. The second section reviews the political dynamics surrounding chiefly leadership from 1987 until the Bainimarama-led coup of 2006. The final sections examine chiefly involvement in national politics in the lead-up to the 2014 elections and prospects for the future of traditional chiefly political leadership which, given the results, look somewhat bleak.

British colonialism and chiefly rule

In contrast with many other parts of the world, where colonial rule was imposed by force, the paramount chiefs of Fiji petitioned the British to establish a Crown Colony. This act also ensured that the leading chiefly clans, mainly from the south and east of the island group, were incorporated into the colonial administration and remained entrenched there throughout the colonial period. The Deed of Cession signed on 10 October 1874 was unconditional in terms of ceding authority to the British Crown but it came to be regarded as a charter of native rights, especially those of the chiefs, and a guarantee that these rights would always be paramount over those of settlers in the colony. This 'doctrine of paramountcy' came to underpin traditional chiefly institutions and has constituted the foundational principle from which indigenous nationalist claims proceed (Lawson 2004).

There was no traditional national political authority in pre-cession Fiji but, rather, a range of sociopolitical units that varied across the island group with different structures of authority and landholding practices. But if the sociopolitical groupings throughout the islands and their relationship to the land were complex and varied, it was the task of the colonial administration to simplify and rationalise them. Pre-existing structures therefore underwent something of a transformation, resulting in what is best described as a neo-traditional order (MacNaught 1982). This included the formalisation of the provinces as administrative units and the establishment of provincial councils presided over largely by chiefs.

At the apex of the colonial Fijian Administration was the Great Council of Chiefs or GCC. It had not existed prior to colonisation but arose initially when Fiji's first substantive colonial governor, Sir Arthur Gordon, summoned the high chiefs to a meeting. This event became a more or less annual affair and was in turn transformed into a formal advisory body. When the Legislative Council was established, leading chiefs were appointed to represent indigenous Fijians, with the initial nomination process conducted through the GCC. Reforms in the 1950s allowed a small number of 'commoners' to serve, but indigenous Fijians as a whole were not enfranchised until the early 1960s. The GCC continued to nominate two members of the legislative council until independence, when all seats in the new House of Representatives were filled through elections, albeit on a communal basis. The 1970 Constitution of independent Fiji also provided for a Senate with appointees nominated by the GCC comprising the largest bloc and with the GCC as a whole having a veto over any legislation affecting indigenous Fijian interests. At the same time, GCC membership widened to include all indigenous Fijians elected to the lower house as ex officio members.

The most prominent chiefs of the colonial period had been Ratu Sir Lala Sukuna and his protégé, Ratu Sir Kamisese Mara. Mara became chief minister in the colonial government, then prime minister at independence in 1970 and president from 1993 to 2000. Both Sukuna and Mara enjoyed high chiefly status in the traditional sphere, but both were also highly educated. Sukuna established the Native Land Trust Board, which rationalised the leasing of native land to Indo-Fijian tenant farmers, bringing benefits to both communities at the time (Norton 2005, p. 149). A number of other key chiefly figures who came to occupy high office benefitted from Sukuna's mentorship as well, including Fiji's first two indigenous governors-general, Ratu Sir George Cakobau and Ratu Sir Penaia Ganilau, as well as Ratu Sir Edward Cakobau, a leading politician in the transition to independence and after.

Colonial practices and institutions produced a certain cultural uniformity that provided the basis for an emergent indigenous national identity based squarely on respect for chiefly leadership. This was reinforced through the introduction of a substantial non-indigenous population from India to provide cheap labour for the colony's plantation economy. Gordon's paternalistic policies required commoner Fijians to remain in their own villages and under the control of their chiefs, thus preserving the 'Fijian way of life' in what Gordon, and most of his successors, saw as its 'natural state'. This remained largely the case until the Native Regulations were abolished in 1967, only three years before independence (Madraiwiwi 2005).

Nayacakalou (1975, pp. 7–8) noted that with the emergence of a modern state a different kind of leadership may be required, challenging those who derived their leadership status from traditional sources.

Preservation of the Fijian way of life also meant that Indians were strictly segregated from indigenous Fijians in virtually every sphere of life. When political representation was introduced, Indians, Europeans and Fijians were all catered for separately, giving rise to communal (i.e. race-based) political representation and therefore communal electoral politics that persisted in one form or another right through to the promulgation of Fiji's 2013 Constitution.

The presence of a substantial 'alien' population contributed to an ideology not only of Fijian 'paramountcy of interests' over those of other population groups but also of chiefs as differentiating symbols of racial/ethnic identity and guardians of the *vanua,* a term understood as embodying a sacred connection between chiefs, land and people. This was strengthened rather than undermined by the widespread adoption of Christianity (*lotu*) among indigenous Fijians (Ryle 2012; Tomlinson 2002). Around 98 per cent of indigenous Fijians are Christian and of those about three-quarters are Methodists. Indo-Fijians remain predominantly Hindu while approximately 15 per cent are Muslim and 5 per cent Christian (Fiji Bureau of Statistics 2013).

Chiefly politics and indigenous nationalism in independent Fiji

Under the 1970 Constitution, the establishment of communal seats required that both candidates and electors be classified as indigenous Fijians, Indo-Fijians or General Electors (the latter mainly European and part-European but with small numbers of 'others', such as Chinese or other Pacific Islanders). Additional cross-voting seats modified strict communalism, but electoral politics was inevitably attuned to perceived communal interests. The National Federation Party (NFP) was essentially an Indo-Fijian party. The Alliance initially sought to embrace all communities, and attracted around 25 per cent of the Indo-Fijian vote in the first general elections of 1972, but it could not maintain this backing in a system so oriented to communal politics. Rather, the Alliance came to embody a reified notion of 'Fijian tradition', including the privileged role of chiefs in every sphere of political life from the village to the national level. However, it was challenged in the mid-1970s by an ultra-nationalist Fijian party— the Fijian Nationalist Party (FNP)—led by a disgruntled former Alliance member, Sakeasi Butadroka, who believed the Alliance under Mara was selling out indigenous Fijian interests to 'foreigners', and Indo-Fijians in particular (Lal 2012, p. 76).

The Alliance was never to recapture the popularity it enjoyed in the early 1970s. Butadroka had opened up an aggressive discourse that threatened to outbid the Alliance in catering to indigenous interests, thus forcing the Alliance to shift its own discourse in that direction. The Alliance nonetheless enjoyed the advantage underpinned by its traditional leadership, something that Butadroka as a commoner was unable to challenge effectively at that time. This was despite the fact that the GCC itself had, by the late 1970s, come to include in its membership chiefs of modest rank and non-chiefs from various walks of life (Norton 2009, p. 99).

Developments before the elections of 1987 saw the emergence of the Fiji Labour Party, led by Dr Timoci Bavadra. It grew out of both blue- and white-collar trade union interests and attempted to promote a new discourse attuned to the rights and interests of all middle and lower socioeconomic groups. It became clear, however, that a split in the Indo-Fijian vote would guarantee an Alliance victory, thus prompting a coalition agreement between Labour and the NFP. In the meantime, the Alliance continued to warn of the dangers to indigenous Fijian interests, especially with respect to the land, if the Alliance and its chiefly leadership were to ever lose office. One senior figure argued:

> [T]he chiefs represent the people, the land, the custom. Without a chief there is no Fijian society. When Fijian chiefs are attacked or criticized in whatever capacity – personal or political – it is the Fijian vanua which is also being criticized (quoted in Lawson 1996, p. 62).

Although these were not the only issues of importance during the campaign, the very idea of an overriding threat to indigenous Fijian land, traditional chiefly leadership and their very identity as indigenous Fijians, expressed through the *vanua*, dominated Alliance discourse.

Following victory by the Labour–NFP coalition, nationalist rhetoric focused on the threat to everything that the *vanua* concept stood for. In the following weeks, an emergent Taukei movement (Taukei meaning, literally, 'owners') promoted an extremist nationalist agenda, fomenting civil disorder and violence against Indo-Fijians. Alliance leaders did little or nothing to calm the situation. The fact that indigenous Fijian rights and interests were triply entrenched in the 1970 Constitution, with a GCC veto the final block on any change, was never mentioned by Alliance or Taukei leaders.

When the third-ranking officer of the Royal Fiji Military Forces, Lieutenant-Colonel Sitiveni Rabuka, intervened less than six weeks after the elections by taking the coalition government hostage at gunpoint on the floor of the parliament, Alliance leaders professed shock and amazement. Despite denial all around that anyone but Rabuka and his immediate followers in the military were involved in the plot, there can be little doubt that key Alliance figures had prior knowledge of the plans. Rabuka certainly justified the coup in precisely the same general terms used by Alliance and Taukei figures alike—namely, the threat to the Fijian *vanua* posed by an 'Indian government' accompanied by the aggressive assertion of indigenous nationalist claims (Lawson 1996, p. 64).

There were, however, tensions within the forces aligned with the coup-maker, including some anti-Alliance/anti-Mara antagonism among Taukei members. Norton (2005, p. 153) observes that proponents of the more extreme Taukei/FNP ethno-nationalist vision of exclusivity have typically been commoners while Howard (1991, p. 358) notes that after the first coup, when Mara lost control of the GCC, extremists in the Taukei movement had sought to use it to thwart Mara's quest to regain control. Nonetheless, an interim administration comprising leading Alliance figures was endorsed by the GCC.

A few months later, however, Rabuka led a second intervention, claiming that the 'objectives' of his May coup, namely the permanent entrenchment of indigenous Fijian political and cultural dominance, had been compromised by the interim administration in making too many concessions to Indo-Fijians. On 7 October 1987, Rabuka declared Fiji a republic. But the chiefs were soon back at the helm. Mara became interim prime minister and Ganilau was appointed president. The Taukei movement remained a force, but a diminished one.

It could not 'sustain an aggressive ethnic movement independently of the ideology that affirmed the legitimacy of chiefly leadership.' (Norton 2009, p. 103)

A fresh review of the Constitution led in due course to the promulgation of the 1990 Constitution of the 'Sovereign Democratic Republic of Fiji', approved by the GCC, dictating that all seats in the new parliament were to be communal, with the majority reserved for indigenous Fijians. Reforms to the GCC excluded many lesser chiefs and commoners, thereby boosting the power of higher chiefs. Around two-thirds of the Senate was to be made up of GCC appointees.

Since the Alliance had imploded in the aftermath of the 1987 coups, a new political party sponsored by the GCC was established. Called the Soqosoqo ni Vakavulewa ni Taukei (SVT), its very name embodied indigenous exclusivity. The NFP and Labour went their separate ways, both attempting to maintain a multiethnic character. The SVT, led by Rabuka, now turned civilian politician, won the 1992 elections but serious factionalism in the ranks led to another general election in 1994. The SVT won again but disunity remained a major problem. Although the SVT had initially been sponsored by chiefs, chiefly leadership within the party was rarely in evidence. Indeed, since the departure of Mara before the 1992 elections, no one of chiefly status, low or high, has held the office of prime minister, although high chiefs have continued to be appointed to the symbolic offices of governor-general or president. Mara himself became vice-president and then president of Fiji after Ganilau's death in 1993, a position he retained until the coup of 2000. Mara was succeeded by Ratu Josefa Iloilo and then by Ratu Epeli Nailatikau, who had been the military commander at the time of the 1987 coup (but was absent overseas when it took place). He is a son of the late Ratu Sir Edward Cakobau and is also Mara's son-in-law. He has since become one of Bainimarama's strongest supporters.

Despite, or perhaps because of, guaranteed political predominance, disunity continued to characterise intra-indigenous Fijian politics. This disunity together with continuing international opprobrium surrounding a constitution that discriminated so deeply against a population on grounds of race were no doubt factors that influenced a rethink of political arrangements. Racial discrimination had led to many skilled Indo-Fijians emigrating, taking the edge off the demographic issue of indigenous Fijians being 'swamped' by an immigrant race. After 1994, Rabuka initiated moves to review the Constitution, resulting in the 1997 Constitution of the 'Republic of the Fiji Islands'. Although introducing some open electorates, it retained a significant number of communal seats. Indigenous Fijian primacy of status was reflected in the retention of the GCC's restricted membership and enhanced privileges, which included the right to appoint the president and vice-president, although the number of senators nominated by the GCC was reduced. The GCC had been persuaded to endorse this new constitution by both Mara and Rabuka, an endorsement seen as essential for broader acceptance by indigenous Fijians. But the more extreme nationalists nonetheless saw it as a sell-out.

Opposition was heightened following the result of the 1999 elections, which saw Fiji's first and so far only Indo-Fijian prime minister, Labour's Mahendra Chaudhry, emerge as leader of a coalition which defeated an STV–NFP coalition led by Rabuka and long-standing NFP leader Jai Ram Reddy in a surprise result. The latter coalition, and the compromises it entailed, had inflamed nationalists further and split the indigenous Fijian vote. Chaudhry's cabinet was balanced and included Mara's daughter (and wife of Ratu Epeli Nailatikau), Adi Koila Nailatikau, elected to her father's old seat as a member of a new regionally based party that had joined the Labour-led coalition.

After a difficult year in office, during which issues concerning the renewal of leases on agricultural land further inflamed nationalist sentiment, the Chaudhry government was overthrown on 19 May 2000 in a coup led by failed business entrepreneur George Speight and a handful of disloyal soldiers from the military's Counter-Revolutionary Warfare (CRW) unit, who took government members hostage in the parliamentary compound. Their justification was once again the threat posed to indigenous Fijians by an 'Indian government'. But this was not a military coup, and it was not backed by the Republic of Fiji Military Forces (RFMF) commander Bainimarama. Ratuva (2011, p. 110), reports that some (unnamed) ethno-nationalist politicians had actually approached the military commander some time after the 1999 elections to ask that he lead a coup, but were met with refusal. By the end of the month, however, Bainimarama declared martial law in the absence of an effective government following the Speight intervention, sidelining President Mara. Following a complicated set of events, Mara's position as president became untenable and he eventually tendered a formal resignation.

Bainimarama also sidelined the GCC, which was split between pro- and anti-coup supporters. Norton (2009, p. 105) observes that dissent and rivalries had always been a feature of GCC meetings, but the impasse created by the coup was unprecedented. He further observes that the failure of leading chiefs to unite in support of a constitution they themselves had endorsed was partly due to a long-standing resentment among some Bauan chiefs over the continuing political pre-eminence of the Lauan paramount chief, Mara. Among the Bauans was Adi Litia Cakobau, daughter of the late Ratu Sir George Cakobau and a strong supporter of the Speight coup, who had previously served in the post-1987 government. The GCC later accepted a court ruling that the 1997 Constitution remained the law of the land. In any event, a nationalist government went on to win two general elections held under its auspices, thereby dampening some of the nationalist opposition to the constitution's more liberal provisions. Two weeks after the 2000 coup, Bainimarama declared he was no longer willing to let the chiefs decide who should rule (*Guardian* 2000). This followed Speight's demands that the GCC be granted executive authority (*Guardian* 2000). These were rejected by Bainimarama, and Speight himself was to be sidelined soon enough.

The coup saw Mara's forced resignation as president and the appointment of a caretaker government led by Laisenia Qarase, a former GCC appointee to the Senate. Speight had agreed to this appointment, had relinquished his own claims to office and finally freed the hostages after accepting an amnesty agreement. However, he soon broke the terms of the amnesty, was arrested and subsequently faced trial for treason. He is now serving a life sentence.

The personal tipping point for Bainimarama was an attempted mutiny by a small number of CRW soldiers, which involved a plan to assassinate Bainimarama for his opposition to Speight. It very nearly succeeded, but was thwarted by Bainimarama loyalists. Eight soldiers were killed. Five from the CRW unit were beaten to death by loyalists. No one has ever been charged over the deaths.

In the meantime, Qarase went on to win elections in 2001, espousing nationalist sentiments clearly aligned with those of Speight. Qarase's new government included members of a new party, the Conservative Alliance Matanitu Vanua (CAMV), set up by Speight and his supporters, which had won six seats. Speight won a seat from prison but soon lost it for non-attendance in parliament. Qarase's own party, the Soqosoqo Duavata ni Lewenivanua (SDL), had formed government in coalition with the CAMV (later absorbed into the SDL). Thus the new government rode what seemed to be a high tide of indigenous Fijian nationalism. Qarase also sought to ingratiate himself with the GCC by suggesting that the sovereignty of Fiji be shared between parliament and the GCC. His government also established an independent income stream for the GCC and work on a grand new building next to Government House commenced (Norton 2009, p. 106).

But Qarase failed to ingratiate himself with Bainimarama, and in fact provoked his implacable hostility by attempting to pave the way for the early release of the coup perpetrators and mutineers through the Reconciliation, Tolerance and Unity Bill, which could have provided an amnesty. For Bainimarama, the very idea of an amnesty for the coup perpetrators meant Qarase was contemplating the release of his would-be assassins. Bainimarama's relationship with Qarase had reached the point of no return. For his part, Qarase made several unsuccessful attempts to remove Bainimarama as head of the military (Lal 2012, pp. 29–30), no doubt contributing to Bainimarama's determination to remove *him*. Bainimarama subsequently campaigned strongly against the SDL in the May 2006 elections and although Qarase emerged victorious, Bainimarama refused to accept his government's legitimacy, charging it with corruption, incompetence and racism (Norton 2009, p. 107). These were the principal themes justifying the December 2006 coup.

In the final days before the coup, Qarase attempted to use the GCC to help resolve the confrontation with Bainimarama, but the latter refused to have the GCC involved. As Bainimarama announced his takeover, the GCC chair, the Tui Tavua, Ratu Ovini Bokini, highlighted his betrayal: 'You told the GCC you would protect this country. Now you have turned your back on God, the chiefs, our country and the church …'. (quoted in Norton 2009). Bainimarama certainly promised to bring about not just a change of regime, but a revolution in political thinking and behaviour in Fiji that moved well beyond traditionalism and indigenous nationalism and all that these entailed.

The retreat of traditionalism in post-2006 Fiji

Qarase's SDL government was clearly based on a nationalist/traditionalist ideology with close ties to the GCC, the Methodist church, provincial councils and other smaller groups and organisations (Ratuva 2011, p. 112). But another major institution that had previously been closely aligned with a nationalist ethos was the military itself, around 99 per cent of whose members were indigenous Fijians. Part of Bainimarama's task was to reorient the military away from that ethos, a task not without its difficulties given that a significant proportion of military personnel had probably voted for the SDL (Firth & Fraenkel 2009, p. 117). This task required two key strategies: first, the purging of all elements among senior officers suspected of disloyalty; and second, the re-making of the military's corporate identity separate from, and indeed in opposition to, a nationalist/traditionalist identity (Lawson 2012).

Bainimarama's post-2006 military regime was determined to counter the anti-modernist elements in indigenous Fijian society, again through two key strategies: the political repression of oppositional opinion on the one hand, and the concerted engagement of indigenous Fijians through a major exercise in public relations on the other. The latter was boosted by long-overdue infrastructure works to upgrade roads and bridges, school buildings, water supplies and to extend electrification of villages. Constitutional change would also prove essential to Bainimarama's long-term vision, as we see shortly.

In the meantime, the relationship between the GCC and Bainimarama was deteriorating, even though GCC appointee President Ratu Iloilo had 'meekly accepted being shunted aside' by Bainimarama during the events of 2006, then 'ignominiously [accepted] re-appointment as President, and consequently doing all of Bainimarama's bidding' (Narsey 2012). In April 2007, matters came to a head when the GCC rejected the nomination of Bainimarama supporter Ratu Epeli

Nailatikau for the vice-presidency. Bainimarama responded by suspending the GCC. In February 2008, new regulations for the GCC were introduced, designed to 'depoliticise' it. But this exercise became irrelevant as the GCC was never to meet again.

In April 2009, another major development occurred following a court case in which the coup of 2006 was declared illegal under the Constitution and Bainimarama's interim government invalid. Bainimarama promptly bade Governor-General Iloilo to abrogate the Constitution. Public Emergency Regulations (PERs) were introduced and Bainimarama commenced rule by decree while muzzling the media, trade unions, NGOs and the arch-nationalist Methodist church. The aim was to suppress not just racist/nationalist discourse but any criticism of the regime. The PERs were withdrawn in January 2012, ostensibly to allow public debate on a new constitution, but new amendments to an older public order act simply reinstated them in another form (Welch 2012).

In March 2012, Bainimarama abolished the GCC as an anachronism that could serve no positive function in the new Fiji under construction by his regime. The GCC, he said, 'is a product of our colonial past and Fiji must now focus on a future in which all Fijians are represented on the same basis' (quoted in Ratuva 2013, p. 175). Another product of the colonial past were the privileges chiefs enjoyed as major beneficiaries of rental income generated through native land leases. Part of the logic was that chiefs required this income to meet their traditional obligations *as* chiefs in funding projects for their communities. There had been criticism over the years, however, that many chiefs kept most of the money for themselves. Under the Bainimarama regime, new provisions were made for distributing land rental monies on an equal basis to all members of the landowning units, with chiefs to receive no more and no less than any other member (Fiji iTaukei Land Trust Board 2010; Sakai, this volume).

The abolition of the GCC in 2012 coincided with the announcement of an independent constitutional review committee to draft a new constitution. In the event, Bainimarama rejected many elements of the draft, believing it pandered to the very same groups that had previously brought the country to grief. The draft was therefore amended substantially to reflect the regime's own vision and the new Constitution promulgated in September 2013. A decree relating to the registration of political parties had been issued in January 2013, allowing parties only 28 days to register, severely restricting sources of funding, disqualifying civil servants and trade union officials from candidature as well as undischarged bankrupts, and those who had served a prison sentence for more than six months in the previous five years. Parties were required to use English names, have multiracial membership, and were prohibited from advocating 'racial or religious hatred, incitement or vilification' (Fiji Elections Office 2014a).

The conviction of Qarase in 2012 on corruption charges relating to activities back in the 1990s disqualified him from candidature, while the ruling on party names disallowed the use of Soqosoqo Duavata ni Lewenivanua. The party was renamed 'Social Democratic Liberal Party', an interesting assortment of monikers designed to at least retain 'S', 'D' and 'L' in its acronym, SODELPA. Its new leader was Ro Teimumu, who had succeeded to the paramount chiefly title of Roko Tui Dreketi on the death of her older sister, Ro Lady Lala Mara (wife of Ratu Mara). She had been appointed a senator in 1999 and then served in the Qarase government from 2001 while also a member of the GCC. Chiefly leadership therefore featured once again in Fiji's foremost traditionalist political party.

A statement by Ro Teimumu and the Tui Cakau, Ratu Naiqama Lalabalavu, issued as a critical response to the 2013 Constitution on the 139th anniversary of the signing of the Deed of Cession, referred, among other things, to the regime's undermining of 'group rights' in relation to land and appealing to international instruments underscoring respect for historical treaty obligations, while also claiming that the group rights of indigenous Fijians should be a concern 'of all right thinking Fiji citizens who proudly share in the ownership of its unique identity' (Statement from Rewa and Cakaudrove chiefs 2013).

This last appeal can scarcely have persuaded the great majority of Indo-Fijians to defer to the very institutions of indigenous Fijian tradition that had so often been used to cast them in the role of second-class citizens. Rather, Indo-Fijian political support had swung firmly behind the Bainimarama regime, which promised to make them fully equal citizens in a new Fiji. What is more surprising, however, is the extent to which indigenous Fijians also shifted their support to Bainimarama in the 2014 elections.

The 2014 elections

The 2013 Constitution had abolished communal voting and the elections were conducted on the basis of one voter, one vote, one value under an open list proportional representation system with every citizen over 18 years of age enfranchised on a single national register. The main parties contesting the elections were Bainimarama's FijiFirst, SODELPA, the Fiji Labour Party, the National Federation Party, and the People's Democratic Party (a new party sponsored by the liberal-oriented Citizens' Constitutional Forum). But the main contest was between FijiFirst and SODELPA, the former promising a new, modern, secular Fiji free of the crippling legacies of a racially divided past.

FijiFirst also promised a continuation of development projects that had brought tangible benefits to many towns and villages around the islands and which no doubt played a significant part in attracting indigenous Fijian support. But Bainimarama's efforts to eliminate racist discourse and to curb the power and privileges of chiefs played its part among indigenous Fijians as well as Indo-Fijians. It would be too much to claim that racist discourse has disappeared, as various rather vicious blogs in unregulated cyberspace attest, but public expression of racist/nationalist views and scare tactics were certainly repressed. This was a positive feature of the campaign, although it came at the expense of freedom of expression.

SODELPA, while declaring its sensitivity 'to the traditions of all communities who call Fiji home' (SODELPA 2014a), nonetheless promoted the nationalist cause as far as it could. The manifesto called for the restoration of the GCC and other chiefly privileges lost under the Bainimarama regime, again appealing to the International Labour Organization (ILO) Convention 169 and the UN Declaration on the Rights of Indigenous Peoples, 2007.

> It is important to put to rest the fears of our native Fijians about what they see as the erosion of their rights, interests and place in the islands they first populated. The principles of the UN Declaration and the ILO Convention are not racist ... They are internationally recognized platforms for indigenous populations everywhere ... (SODELPA 2014a).

SODELPA also made much of Bainimarama's support of Fiji as a secular state in which no particular religion was to be elevated over others. In contrast, SODELPA promoted Fiji as a 'Christian state', while denouncing the 2013 Constitution as 'Godless' (SODELPA 2014b).

Neither the NFP nor Labour could match Bainimarama's appeal to both Indo-Fijian and indigenous Fijian voters. Labour, with just 2.4 per cent of the vote, failed to secure a single seat, while the NFP managed just 3 seats with 5.5 per cent. SODELPA gained 28.2 per cent of the votes and 15 seats (Fiji Elections Office 2014b). The victory by Bainimarama's FijiFirst, securing almost 60 per cent of the vote and 32 seats, can only be described as resounding. There were, inevitably, claims of electoral fraud, but international observers declared the elections largely free and fair, at least procedurally. The main limitation on 'free and fair' was not ballot-rigging, of which there was little evidence, but the muzzling of the media, political parties and others with critical opinions to voice.

Even given this, it was remarkable that a country mired so long in racially oriented politics could produce a stunning victory for a leader who had consistently opposed any form of race-based discourse, repudiating virtually everything that indigenous Fijian nationalists had stood for. That he did so largely through the military, an institution that historically has been as much a part of the traditionalist/nationalist superstructure of Fiji as any other, remains a paradox.

Conclusion

Traditional chiefly leadership has been a powerful political force in Fiji's national politics from the moment the Fiji islands became a unified state entity under colonial rule. Initially institutionalised through the colonial administrative structure, supported by a strong traditionalist ideology and allied at times with an uncompromising indigenous nationalism, paramount chiefs held all the higher offices of the Fijian state until 1987. The Great Council of Chiefs maintained an authoritative presence in government until it was suspended and then finally abolished by the Bainimarama regime in 2012. The only remaining high official position still held by a leading chief is the presidency, which the present incumbent holds only by virtue of his support for Bainimarama. The only other official position in the parliamentary system now held by a high chief is Leader of the Opposition.

The future of traditional chiefly leadership in Fiji's national politics therefore looks rather bleak. Bainimarama has not only routed the chiefly establishment, but has also achieved considerable success in quashing nationalist discourses. Although achieved partly through suppression, the apparent strength of electoral support for Bainimarama's vision of a modern, secular Fiji can scarcely be denied. At the same time, it would be foolish to claim that the ideas and beliefs underpinning racism in Fiji—evident among all communities—have been eliminated, as attested by ongoing diatribes in the blogosphere. Nor has the chiefly system as such disappeared. It is likely to continue to hold a valued place among indigenous Fijians in ceremonial life, and may well maintain a strong presence in local and provincial politics. But it seems unlikely that chiefs will ever dominate national politics to the extent that they once did, especially given the persistent tensions within their own ranks. Having said that, Fiji's politics never fail to surprise, and what seems unthinkable at one historical moment may well come to pass at another.

References

Earle, T 2011, 'Chiefs, chieftaincies, chiefdoms, and chiefly confederacies: power in the evolution of political systems', *Social Evolution and History*. vol. 10, no. 1, pp. 27–54.

Fiji Bureau of Statistics 2013, 'Population by religion—2007 census of the population'. Viewed 20 November 2014 at www.statsfiji.gov.fj/index.php/social/9-social-statistics/social-general/147-religion.

Fiji Elections Office 2014a, 'Political Parties Decree'. Viewed 26 November 2014 at www.electionsfiji.gov.fj/political-parties-decree/.

Fiji Elections Office 2014b, 'Final results for the 2014 general election'. Viewed 26 November 2014 at www.electionsfiji.gov.fj/2014-election-results/.

Fiji iTaukei Land Trust Board 2010, 'Land ownership structure'. Viewed 26 November 2014 at www.tltb.com.fj/index.php?option=com_content&task=view&id=67&Itemid=98.

Firth S and Fraenkel J 2009, 'The Fiji Military and Ethno-Nationalism: Analyzing the Paradox', in S Firth, J Fraenkel and BV Lal (eds), *The 2006 military takeover in Fiji*, ANU E Press, Canberra, pp. 117–38.

Guardian 2000, 'Fiji festers as coup talks fail', 4 June. Viewed 24 November 2014 at www.theguardian.com/world/2000/jun/04/fiji.theobserver.

Howard, M 1991, *Fiji: Race and politics in an island state*, UBC Press, Vancouver.

Lal, B 2012, *Fiji before the storm*, ANU E Press, Canberra.

Lawson, S 1996, *Tradition versus democracy in the South Pacific: Fiji, Tonga and Western Samoa*, Cambridge University Press, Cambridge.

Lawson, S 2004, 'Nationalism versus constitutionalism in Fiji', *Nations and Nationalism*, vol. 10, no. 4, pp. 51938.

Lawson, S 2012, 'Indigenous nationalism, "ethnic democracy" and the prospects for a liberal constitutional order in Fiji', *Nationalism and Ethnic Politics*, vol. 18, no. 3, pp. 293–315.

MacNaught, TJ 1982, *The Fijian colonial experience: A study of the neo-traditional order under British colonial rule prior to World War Two*, Australian National University Press, Canberra.

Madraiwiwi, J 2005, 'Governance in Fiji: the interplay between indigenous tradition, culture and politics', Keynote Address, conference on the 'Pacific, globalisation and governance', The Australian National University, Canberra, 26 October. Viewed 19 November 2014 at press.anu.edu.au/ssgm/global_gov/mobile_devices/ch15.html.

Narsey, W 2012, 'Ghai's dilemma: to be more than a tape recorder', 21 May. Viewed 25 November 2014 at narseyonfiji.wordpress.com/2012/05/21/ghais-dilemma-to-be-more-than-a-tape-recorder/.

Nayacakalou, RR 1975, *Leadership in Fiji*, Institute of Pacific Studies, University of the South Pacific, Suva.

Norton, R 2005, 'A paradox of tradition in a modernising society: Chiefs and political development in Fiji', in A Hooper (ed.), *Culture and sustainable development in the Pacific*, ANU E Press, Canberra, pp. 142–158.

Norton, R 2009, ' The changing role of the Great Council of Chiefs', in S Fraenkel and BV Lal (eds), *The 2006 military takeover in Fiji: A coup to end all coups?*, ANU E Press, Canberra, pp. 97–116.

Ratuva, S 2011, 'The military coups in Fiji: Reactive and transformative tendencies', *Asian Journal of Political Science*, vol. 19, no. 1, pp. 96–120.

Ratuva, S 2013, *Politics of preferential development: Transglobal study of affirmative action and ethnic conflict in Fiji, Malaysia and South Africa*, ANU E Press, Canberra.

Ryle, J 2012, *My God, my land: Interwoven paths of Christianity and tradition in Fiji*, Ashgate, Farnham.

SODELPA 2014a, *Manifesto*. Viewed 26 November 2014 at sodelpa.org/SODELPA-Manifesto-LR.pdf.

SODELPA 2014b, 'Secular State'. Viewed 26 November 2014 at www.facebook.com/sodelpa/posts/1397324750488161.

Statement from Rewa and Cakaudrove chiefs (2013). Viewed 5 December 2014 at www.coup5.com/2013/10/the-statement-from-rewa-and-cakaudrove.html.

Tomlinson, M 2002, 'Sacred soil in Kadavu, Fiji,' *Oceania*, vol. 72, no. 4, pp. 237–56.

Welch, D 2012, 'Fijians "double-crossed" over lifting of laws', *Sydney Morning Herald*, 11 January. Viewed 26 November 2014 at www.smh.com.au/world/fijians-doublecrossed-over-lifting-of-laws-20120110-1ptm3.html.

4

Fiji Indians and the Fiji general elections of 2014: Between a rock and a hard place and a few other spots in between

Brij V Lal

In the September 2014 Fiji general elections an estimated 80 per cent of Indo-Fijians voted for Commodore Frank Bainimarama's newly formed FijiFirst Party (Lal 2014; Larson 2014).[1] The extent of the support was startling even though Indo-Fijians have a history of splitting their votes more frequently than indigenous Fijians have. In the 1972 general elections, for instance, 24 per cent of Indo-Fijian votes went to the Alliance Party, with that figure declining significantly over the decades as coups and ensuing convulsions soured race relations and deepened the divide between the two communities (Lal 2006a; Ali 1973). However viewed, the Indo-Fijian shift away from traditionally Indo-Fijian parties to FijiFirst is significant, even perhaps historic. Several factors are responsible. On the one hand was the Bainimarama Government's ruthless use of incumbency to its enormous advantage and to the manifest disadvantage of the opposition parties, inventing and bending rules as it went along, and its generous and unaccounted

---

1   I am grateful to Jon Fraenkel, Padma Lal and Patrick and Vanisha Mishra Vakaoti for their comments and advice for revision. The usual disclaimer applies.

use of the public purse for electioneering (Fraenkel 2015). On the other was a deep sense of fear and foreboding among Indo-Fijian voters: fear of revenge and retribution from Fijian nationalists should the regime lose, and foreboding about their future without the illusion of security provided by the Fijian military. Muzzling of the media through coercive decrees, suppressing dissent and disabling rival centres of power (of the trade unions and non-government organisations, for instance, or the Methodist Church and the Great Council of Chiefs) contributed their share of pressure. Then there were those who made hay while the sun shone or, as the local expression goes, an omelette from eggs broken in the melee.

But just as one swallow does not a summer make, so one election, held under a new and controversial constitution promulgated by a political party intent on remaining in power at all cost, cannot tell us much about the future pattern of political culture in a country with a history of military coups. Contrary to the official narrative, Fiji's future stability is far from assured. Nevertheless, what is clear with the advantage of hindsight is that, wittingly or unwittingly, Indo-Fijian voters have for the time being rejected one model of democracy for another, preferring the rule of a single strongman within an overarching architecture of democracy to the principles of representative democracy of the type enshrined in the conventional Westminster system which Fiji had inherited at independence in 1970. There is change, no doubt, but whether that change is an aberration or permanent, superficial or significant, and whether it will necessarily serve the long-term interests of the Indo-Fijians, and of Fiji more generally, remains an open question.

Any analysis of the 2014 Fijian general elections and of Indo-Fijian political behaviour would have to begin with the political environment in which these took place. To begin with, 2014 was clearly not 1970, 1990 or even 2000 (Firth 2012). All the fundamental and familiar markers of the Fijian political framework had changed. The assumptions and understandings which had governed Fijian political discourse for nearly half a century were gone, gone with the leaders who had engineered them, most notably Ratu Sir Kamisese Mara, the long-reigning prime minister and the pre-eminent Fijian leader of the second half of the 20th century, who died in 2004 (Scarr 2008). The 2013 Constitution, introduced in controversial circumstances without public consultation (Kant & Rakuita 2014), had several features that differentiated it from its predecessors. Communal voting was abolished, although not the practice of voting along ethnic lines. The voting age was reduced from 21 to 18, enfranchising an age cohort that had come of age in an environment corrupted by coups and endless talk of more coups and which yearned for another, steadier, coup-free future. A new electoral system, open list proportional, replaced the former alternative vote system of the 1997 Constitution which itself had replaced the first past the post system adopted at independence. These factors influenced the response of Indo-Fijian voters and the outcome of the elections.

The years since independence had seen Indo-Fijian society change dramatically (Lal 1992; Taylor 1987). In 1970, Indo-Fijians constituted around 50 per cent of the national population. They had overtaken the indigenous Fijians during the Second World War, spawning deep fears among Fijians and Europeans of 'Indian domination'. That fear, whether real or manufactured for political purposes, determined the course of Fiji's political development as it entered the decade of decolonisation in the 1960s (Lal 2006a). Fijian leaders refused to countenance any change towards internal self-government or independence except on their terms. This included the demand for the full retention of the communal system of voting and a tacit acknowledgement of the principle of Fijian political paramountcy in the governance of the country. In other words, Fijian leaders would accept change, including independence, only if they were assured of political control (Norton 2012). A contrived political arrangement, with communal representation and European overrepresentation at its heart, devised by the departing British, delivered that outcome, papering over cracks regarding fundamental issues which divided the country.

Fiji enjoyed fragile political stability during its early post-independence years, but beneath a placid surface and feel-good atmosphere lurked fears and phobias that would wreck its prospects. Fiji was a symbol of hope to the modern world, Pope John Paul II had intoned during his fleeting visit to Fiji in1985, but that was more comforting rhetoric than a reflection of reality.[2] Fijian control of the government depended on unity among Fijians and enough disunity among Indo-Fijians for Fijians to win power. But neither group was homogenous, divided as

---

2   The Fiji Visitors Bureau turned the Pope's words into 'Fiji: The Way the World Should Be' for tourism promotion.

they were (and still are) along regional, religious and cultural lines. Sakeasi Butadroka's Fijian Nationalist Party exposed the fissures among Fijians by polling 25 per cent of the Fijian communal votes in the April 1977 elections, enough to cause the defeat of the ruling Alliance Party. The lesson was quickly relearnt that Fijian political solidarity was the *sine qua non* for Fijian control of government. To that end, the Alliance made strenuous efforts, reclaiming lost ground with a handsome majority in the September elections of that year, helped by a massive split among Indo-Fijians about why they were unable to form government after narrowly winning the elections in April (Lal 2009b). The embers from that distant split glowed for decades afterwards, energising factions and divisions that debilitated Indo-Fijian politics, and still do.

But the Alliance's victory had come at a cost not fully appreciated at the time. It irrevocably fractured the multiracial foundations of the Alliance Party. Its pro-Fijian tilt, evident in the appointments and promotions in the civil service, the allocation of tertiary scholarships and the reservation of Crown land, among other things, saw many founding fathers of the Indian Alliance, including Sir Vijay R Singh and James Shankar Singh, both former cabinet ministers, joining the National Federation Party (NFP). In 1982, when the NFP (24 seats) came close to defeating the Alliance Party (28 seats), the Great Council of Chiefs (GCC), meeting at the historic island of Bau and opened for the first time by a reigning British Monarch, passed resolutions to change the Constitution to entrench permanent political control of government (Lal 2009a). When the Alliance was defeated at the 1987 polls by a nominally multiracial coalition of the Fiji Labour Party and the NFP, the month-old government was overthrown in a military coup carried out by Lieutenant-Colonel Sitiveni Rabuka, the third-ranking officer of the Fiji Military Forces, tacitly supported by the leaders of the defeated Alliance Party and by Fijians more generally. 'Fijian rights in danger' was the catch cry, and it caught on. The depth of Indo-Fijian anger and hurt caused by the coups was not fully apprehended at the time. Two decades later, Commodore Bainimarama would tap into it to his great electoral advantage.

The goals of the coup were entrenched in the decreed 1990 Constitution, allocating a disproportionate number of seats in parliament to indigenous Fijians, abolishing all multiracial voting in favour of communal voting, decreeing a race-based, legally unchallengeable, affirmative action programme, and reserving the offices of prime minister, governor-general, commissioner of police and commander of the military and heads of important government bodies (such as the civil service) to Fijians. The Methodist Church, one of the principal instigators of the coup, added fuel to the fire by demanding a strict observance of the Sabbath, known popularly as Sunday Ban. For that agenda of religious zealotry, it would pay an incalculable price two decades later. And the Taukei Movement, which had morphed into existence from a diverse group of Fijian nationalists soon after the 1987 elections, demanded the complete fulfilment of the 'aims of the coup'. Violence was threatened and begun in some places and leases to Indo-Fijian tenants were not renewed. Race relations in Fiji were strained to breaking point in the post-coup years.

The Indo-Fijian reaction to all this was to try to emigrate. Emigration had been taking place in small numbers since the 1970s, mostly to North America and the United Kingdom, but after the coup that trickle turned into a torrent. In two decades, over 120,000 Indo-Fijians, mostly well-educated professionals, emigrated, depriving the country of much needed skill and talent (Chetty & Prasad 1993). Many departed deeply embittered and their sense of unjust treatment and rejection continued unabated for decades afterwards. Most never forgave Rabuka for the coups, despite his repeated pleas for forgiveness and his convincing claim that he had acted at the behest of others (Sharpham 2000). Revenge and retribution loomed large in their minds, however vocally denied. The shoe, as the saying goes, was finally on the other foot or, to use a colloquialism, Fijians were now tasting their own medicine. So when Commodore Frank Bainimarama deposed the Qarase government in 2006, many in the Fijian diaspora openly supported him, as they still do, deriving perverse satisfaction at the treatment of the Fijian nationalists by the Fijian military, an eventuality they had never contemplated before. No one had: a Fijian military publicly taking on the Fijian establishment and winning. In 2014 the overwhelming majority of Indo-Fijian voters voted for Bainimarama's party.[3] His well-publicised visits to Sydney and Auckland to thank his supporters and benefactors, mostly Indo-Fijians, was proof enough of that. Bainimarama's words at the United Nations General Assembly in

---

3   The 2013 Constitution allowed Fiji nationals living overseas to vote if they were properly registered, whereas before, voters had to be resident in Fiji for two years before the elections, the residency requirement exempted for those on officially authorised absence overseas.

September 2013 were music to their ears: the coup-inspired emigration of Fiji citizens was 'one of the most shameful episodes of our history', he said, 'and I determined that this must never, never happen again. We must never allow a fellow citizen to be a second-class citizen, to be less than the equal of his neighbour'. No Fijian leader had ever spoken such words of remorse and regret in this way before an international audience.

The massive demographic transformation in Fiji was accompanied by profound changes in the life of the Indo-Fijian community post-1987. None was more significant than the changes in the sugar industry, once the lifeblood of the economy but now in visible decline (Lal 2009b). One cause of this was the non-renewal of 30-year-old leases expiring under the Agricultural Landlord and Tenant Act. Leases were not renewed for many reasons. Among them was the genuine desire of some landowners to join the industry as cultivators themselves, attracted by the possibility of making a decent living they saw, or thought they saw, Indo-Fijian tenants making. Closer acquaintance would reveal the appearance of prosperity to be deeply deceptive. Many Indo-Fijians were actually keen to give up farming altogether for a more regular cash income just when Fijians wanted to come in. But political motivation was not far behind. Under Marika Qarikau, the fiercely, almost irrationally, nationalist head of the Native Land Trust Board, an implicit condition for the renewal of leases was Indo-Fijian acceptance of Fijian political supremacy. Land was power, Fijian power, and he wanted to extract the maximum concession from its users in a simple *quid pro quo*.

Non-renewal led to an exodus of displaced tenants from the sugar cane belts of Fiji, especially northern Vanua Levu, on an unprecedented scale. Squatter settlements mushroomed around south-eastern Viti Levu, clogging the Suva–Nausori corridor. Life in these settlements was plainly squalid: there was no running water, electricity, sewerage facilities, employment or educational opportunities. But the evictees had nowhere else to go and no one would have them. In the Cunningham squatter settlement in Suva, the Fijian landlord demanded money for the conduct of religious functions by his Indo-Fijian tenants. Refusal to pay, it was clearly understood, would mean immediate removal. To these people living at the edge of poverty and destitution on the sufferance of others, with little hope or optimism, talk of democracy and good governance and the disclosure of the Auditor General's report, withheld since 2006, was just that: talk, academic talk. They had heard of such things before, to no avail. What they wanted was relief and respite from misery.

Here the Bainimarama regime had the upper hand, freely dispensing goods and services from the public purse. Most importantly, the regime promised squatters on state land 99-year leases, a dream come true for hundreds who had never imagined a place of their own, and their gratitude to Bainimarama was unbounded. The government also addressed, through active military patrols, the perennial problem of violent burglary in urban and peri-urban areas. On this frontier of lawlessness and violence, the voters knew that only Commodore Bainimarama could deliver. Often, the protocols of natural justice were blatantly breached. But the savage beatings of escaped prisoners beamed around the world to great consternation over the abuse of human rights in Fiji meant little to the squatters, who were often themselves targets of violent crime. They saw Bainimarama as the upholder of law and order, a leader who was finally on their side. The impression created was of a government at last caring for a group that had long lived literally and metaphorically on the unlovely fringes of society. They therefore rallied behind FijiFirst, as indeed did those who, following the decline of the rural sector, were making a meagre living in urban and peri-urban areas as casual labourers, domestic helpers, mechanics, drivers, or carpenters. Rural decline increased over some time, and will continue to swell the numbers of the desperate urban poor.

Bainimarama's rhetoric justifying the coup also attracted many Indo-Fijians to his side. His was not a coup, he said repeatedly, if unconvincingly, in the face of undeniable evidence, it was a 'clean-up campaign'. He wanted to cleanse the country of corruption. His call resonated with ordinary citizens, who knew in their bones that greasing the palm had become an endemic feature of life in the country, and that things were getting worse by the day, not better. Many Indo-Fijians therefore gave him the benefit of the doubt, and their early support bought the military regime valuable time to consolidate itself. By the time people saw that there was more to the coup than what the Commodore had claimed—that corruption and mismanagement in various guises were alive and well, that what was alleged was never actually proven in a court of law (no big fish were ever caught)—it was too late.

Over time, Bainimarama, with the help of adroit image makers, including the American public relations company Qorvis, specialists in refurbishing the image of dictators and tyrants around the world, was portrayed as a selfless soldier embarking on a path to remake Fiji into a modern, vibrant, non-racial society, with Singapore as a model in mind. He was steadily transformed in the public eye from a tongue-tied, temperamentally volatile, short-fused military strongman into a man of the people, an appealing leader, modest and engaging, photographed sitting cross-legged on a mat with cheering uniformed school children, sharing a cup of tea with rural Indo-Fijian housewives, inspecting government projects in shorts and floral bula shirt. No leader had done that before. His 'visit diplomacy' to previously neglected areas in remote regions was good theatre: on horseback, riding through stony rivers and rough terrain, with admirers in tow. Would a 'dictator' ever do that, people asked? He was anti-politics, he said, and blamed 'old' politicians for all the ills of Fiji's past, overlooking the inconvenient fact that several 'old' politicians who had played key roles in previous coups (such as foreign minister Inoke Kubuabola) were serving in his own cabinet. And not altogether subtly, Bainimarama made it clear that it was he, and he alone, who stood between chaos and stability. There would be no coup as long as he was in charge, he told voters. People believed him. They had no reason not to. He was, after all, a former military commander still in touch with his former troops, his eyes and ears still firmly watching and listening to them.

Of all the leaders standing in the elections, Bainimarama was the only one who had the unquestioned loyalty of the military, whose leaders had said often enough that they would prefer him to continue. It was understood, though it did not need to be said, that the military would move in 'to protect the Constitution' if Bainimarama was dislodged. Some political parties had questioned the immunity provisions of the 2013 Constitution, which spawned fear and anger among the rank and file of the military. Bainimarama was on their side. The military needed him as much as he needed them. Mutual self-interest was set in concrete. No one wanted another coup. The attraction of stability and security to a people long at the receiving end of previous coups counted for a lot. People reposed their faith in the coup leader. He was a strong man of action. As he often said, time for talk was over, time for action was now. He had stood up to the GCC and the Methodist Church and hobbled them unceremoniously. He had stood up for Fiji against international opposition to his regime. Finer points about democratic principles and implications of the government's policies in the long term, and the inherent dangers of relying on the whims of one man to govern, did not register with the voters. It was often said that nothing good had happened in Fiji until Bainimarama had come on the scene, and that Fiji would revert to its failed past without him at the helm. It was a familiar tactic of military dictators and authoritarian leaders around the world, who portray themselves as the very embodiment of the national spirit, indispensable to the destiny of the nation. Rabuka had done that in 1987 and Bainimarama was doing it now.

This narrative was given unfettered play in the local media, operating under severe restrictions imposed by the Media Industry Development Decree (29/2010). The *Fiji Sun* newspaper became an unabashed cheerleader for the regime, with screaming front-page headlines praising the government for everything it did or purported to do, while belittling the motivations and modus operandi of its opponents. Fiji had not seen such grovelling journalism before nor such blatantly biased reporting. Unsurprisingly, Commodore Bainimarama was the newspaper's choice for the 'Person of the Year'. Radio stations, both commercial and state-owned, and the FBC television station, were similarly pro-regime. The national broadcaster was run by the younger brother of the regime's attorney general. A prominent Indo-Fijian radio announcer, a household name among Indo-Fijians, pretended neutrality in her questioning of candidates who appeared on her show, but then on the eve of the elections suddenly resigned to stand for Bainimarama's party. The chief executive officer of the Media Industry Development Authority similarly professed impartiality but (unsuccessfully) stood for FijiFirst.[4] It was disturbing to see such boundaries crossed with such impunity and in full public view. Decency demanded some distance, but none was forthcoming. Now anything was possible, any transgression forgiven, if you were with FijiFirst.[5]

---

4   In early 2016, Matai Akauola, chief executive officer of the Media Industry Development Authority, entered parliament under the d'Hondt system of voting when a seat became vacant on the government benches.

5   By contrast, students who campaigned for rival political parties were threatened with the cancellation of their scholarships, even as the regime encouraged the participation in politics of young people.

In the upshot, the people heard only what the military regime wanted them to hear while neutral or contrary voices were noticeably absent from the public domain. The Media Authority, for its part, mouthed platitudes about fairness and responsibility and accuracy and balance in reporting, but it was in truth itself nothing more than a coercive and compliant instrument of and for the regime.[6] Critics took to social media, but ordinary folk in the countryside without access to the Internet were innocent of the contrary views and voices floating in the cyber traffic.[7] In the end, the regime's manipulation of the media was as unprecedented as it was complete; it had learned well from the example of authoritarian regimes around the world that consolidation and unhindered and unaccountable exercise of power required a pliant media. And it had all the power in its hands to bend the media to its knees (by giving Fiji TV a six-month license, for example, or imposing huge fines for breaches of the Media Decree, and by restricting foreign ownership of the local media).

Several aspects of the 2013 Constitution helped to attract Indo-Fijian voters to Bainimarama's FijiFirst Party. One was the abolition of communal voting that had been a defining feature of all Fiji constitutions from the early 20th century (Ali 2007). 'One person, one vote, one value' was the new mantra. In truth, all votes were not equal under the open list proportional system, as the results showed, but what the regime said went. A common roll had been the catch cry of the Indo-Fijian community since 1929, when they first got the franchise, and it had been the signature platform of the NFP in the decolonising decade of the 1960s (Lal 1997). FijiFirst told Indo-Fijian voters it was doing nothing more than meeting a demand the leaders of the Indo-Fijians had been making for generations and therefore deserved its votes, not its condemnation. To see former staunch NFP members such as Praveen Bala (now the minister for housing and local government) in the FijiFirst line-up muddied the waters. Atul Patel, the eldest son of the founding father of the NFP, AD Patel, endorsed this common roll platform of FijiFirst and Faiyaz Koya, the elder son

---

6   Petitions asking for the investigation of biased reporting from pro-regime sources and their refusal to publish views critical of the regime were routinely ignored. For instances, see blog site 'Wadan Narsey on Fiji – for fairness and freedom'.

7   The most trenchant critiques of the practices and policies of the Bainimarama Government appeared on Coupfourpointfive and on Wadan Narsey's 'Fiji – for fairness and freedom'. 'Fijileaks' made important revelations. On the pro-regime side were 'Grubsheet' and to a lesser extent Cros Walsh's blog site 'Fiji: The Way it Was, Is and Can Be'.

of another NFP founder and opposition leader, Siddiq Koya, stood as a candidate for FijiFirst and is now the minister for trade and tourism (after a few short days as attorney general).[8] Their actual and virtual presence behind Bainimarama swayed many voters, who were asking why the NFP was opposing a man who was giving them what the party had been asking for all along: political equality, equal citizenship and a common roll.

On the surface, the question was compelling: why, indeed? The truth was that Bainimarama's brand of strongman, military-backed democracy was not what the NFP had been fighting for. Their quest all along had been for genuine representative democracy, with, right at the heart of it, a robust parliament of men and women elected in their own right rather than riding the coat-tails of their leader. Their platform was for a parliament that would be the ultimate guardian of the country's freely adopted, rather than unilaterally imposed, Constitution; not for an unelected, ethnically lopsided military as the protector of multiracialism and as the arbiter of the national interest. NFP had stood all along for a democracy where power flowed from the ballot box, not from the barrel of a gun. That FijiFirst invoked the name of the NFP in support of its campaign platform was as incomprehensible as it was ironic.

Another feature of the 2013 Constitution that had a bearing on the outcome of the 2014 elections was the lowering of the voting age from 21 to 18. This was recommended by the Reeves Commission in 1996 (Reeves, Vakatora & Lal 1996) but was rejected by a subcommittee of the Parliamentary Select Committee, chaired by none other than Inoke Kubuabola, on the grounds that in Fijian culture 18-year-olds were considered children, not adults, to be seen rather than heard.[9] In 2014, a third of voters were below the age of 30. They had come of age during an era of coups in Fiji. They had very little knowledge or understanding of the country's past and, more to the point, no interest in it. History was rarely taught in schools, and what little was taught was sanitised, brushed clean of the mud and muck of the past, ignoring the unarguable fact that Fiji had a fractured past with little common, unifying narrative. The new generation was obsessively focused

---

8   Though his younger brother, Faizal Koya, stood for the NFP, saying 'I was born in NFP and I will die in NFP'.

9   This I base on conversation with a member of the committee.

on the Internet-dependent present. Not the book, but Facebook, was their source of information and knowledge and enlightenment. They believed Bainimarama when he blamed Fiji's ill-fated past on corrupt politicians; they believed him rather than the obvious truth that it was the military, aided and abetted by some 'old' politicians, which was the real cause of Fiji's problems. They liked his empowering rhetoric of non-racialism and common citizenship, his standing up for Fiji against Australia and New Zealand (though they all secretly hope to migrate there one day and not to Fiji's new-found friends in Iran and North Korea). And reflecting an international trend, a rich vein of anti-political sentiment ran among the youth of Fiji, to Bainimarama's clear benefit. This is not to say that all young people voted for FijiFirst, but a substantial number did, out of a curious combination of apathy, indifference, naiveté, and misguided enthusiasm.

The new open list proportional system worked to Bainimarama's great benefit. In the new system, the 50 seats in the House of Representatives had to be contested from a single national constituency, dispensing with the constituency boundaries of the past. Voters had to vote for a single candidate (with no indication of their name or party affiliation), with the vote for the individual candidate being automatically counted for his or her party. Seats in parliament would be allocated in proportion to the votes a party won. All parties and independent candidates would have to meet the 5 per cent threshold for victory. Theoretically, the open list system gives the voters, not the party, the power to choose whom they vote for, but FijiFirst encouraged voters to cast their vote for one person, party leader Frank Bainimarama. And that is precisely what happened. Bainimarama got 202,459 votes, nearly 70 per cent of the votes cast for FijiFirst and 40.8 per cent of all the votes cast. The system delivered handsomely for FijiFirst, but whether it augurs well for representative parliamentary democracy is another matter. What happens when Bainimarama is no longer around? Is Fiji fated to be governed from now on by strong men (and perhaps women too) backed by the military within an overarching illusion of democratic governance? In 2009, I wrote: 'A militarized democracy seems in the offing in Fiji' (Lal 2009a, p. 444). Sadly, that prospect is looking more and more likely.

Support for Bainimarama and his party seems to have been fairly widespread across the Indo-Fijian community. Major Indo-Fijian businessmen were in his camp, with financial donations and public expressions of support. Among the most prominent of them were CJ Patel, the Tappoos, the Damodars and Gokals, the Dewan Maharajs and owners of big transport and construction companies. Their commitment to Fiji is questionable, as many have substantial assets outside the country and often their families too, with permanent residency papers in order. It is a truism that businessmen everywhere have a cosy relationship with those in power, but the Fiji business community seems to be a particularly myopic lot. There is no sense of loyalty or allegiance to any cause or ideology beyond turning a profit for themselves. They will readily embrace the next person in power, whatever their political ideology, as long as their coffers are full.

Less easy to explain is the support given by Fiji's educational and moral leaders. The vice chancellor of the University of the South Pacific (USP), Rajesh Chandra, an academic bureaucrat par excellence, was a strong supporter of the coup and its leader from the beginning. His staff took his cue, fearful of reprisals. USP's most vocal anti-regime academic, Wadan Narsey, was forced to resign from the university, with the vice chancellor acceding to the military regime's demand. Chandra knew which side of the bread was buttered, as the expression goes in Fiji, but he was also embittered by the denial, unfair as he saw it, of the top job at the regional university some years back because of Fiji's refusal to support his nomination. This was his way of exacting revenge. The vice chancellor of the Fiji National University (FNU), Ganesh Chand, a former Labour politician, was also in the Bainimarama corner, both by choice as well as by necessity. The FNU is a government-funded institution, and not all members of staff were always supportive of him for a variety of reasons, both personal as well as political. Despite his services to the regime, Chand was removed from his position in December 2014. For the historical record, not all Indo-Fijian academics in Fiji or in the Fijian expatriate community were with the regime. There were many, myself included, who opposed the coup through their writings and interventions in the media, but media censorship in Fiji and other forms of overt and covert harassment ensured that contrary narratives did not reach the mainstream public. We mostly talked in the cyberspace through emails and blog sites and Facebook accounts.

From abroad, retired academics in the twilight of their careers and other former Fiji professionals returned to lend support and write in praise of the regime and its leader, ostensibly convinced by the regime's rhetoric of creating a new Fiji. Most had left Fiji disillusioned after previous coups, and were returning now to settle old scores and to set things right, often for lucrative fees or appointments and the small, transient privileges of a fading limelight. Some were no doubt diligent, hoping to use the 'opportunity' of the coup to restructure Fiji's political culture towards greater non-racialism and accountable and effective governance. The National Council for Building a Better Fiji became the vehicle for their effort on the clear premise that all changes made would be within the overarching framework of the 1997 Constitution. Bainimarama gave that undertaking, but then proceeded to abrogate the Constitution in April 2009 after the council had completed its work and given the coup leader his much-heralded roadmap back to parliamentary democracy. He also discarded the process of political dialogue he had been urged to undertake by the Commonwealth, among others. He reneged on his promise to the Pacific Islands Forum to hold elections in 2009. Promises were made only to be broken at will. The Commodore tactically outmanoeuvred everyone; in the end, he had the last laugh.

It was often said before and during the campaign that the 2006 coup was a Muslim coup. This was supposedly due to the support for it, vocal or tacit, by many prominent Muslims, such as Aiyaz Sayed-Khaiyum, Shaista Shameem, former head of the Fiji Human Rights Commission, and her younger sister and former high court judge Nazhat Shameem, now in Geneva as Fiji's ambassador to the United Nations after a short stint as a private legal practitioner in Fiji and destined, many believe, to even higher offices in Fiji.[10] The visible presence of Muslims in statutory organisations and government bodies reinforced that perception. But Muslims did not instigate the coup;[11] they were as divided over the event as other communities, and there are opportunists among Muslims as there are in other groups. What is beyond doubt, though, is that over time, as the picture of the political landscape became clearer, and realisation dawned that Bainimarama would be around for a long time, Muslim support firmed up for

---

10   Michael Green (2013, p. 186) writes about Nazhat Shameem's deep disappointment with the Qarase government for not nominating her for an international judicial post, urging the New Zealand government to sponsor her instead. Only Shameem will ever know if her sense of disappointment with the Qarase government was sufficient for her to adopt a 'softer' approach to the coup and all that followed.

11   Among the strongest opponents of the coup were Shamima Ali of the Women's Crisis Centre, and Imrana Jalal, a human rights lawyer, both Muslims.

FijiFirst. They voted in very large numbers for the party. Without that, Aiyaz Sayed-Khaiyum, widely distrusted among Indo-Fijians and among most Fijians for his controlling ways, confrontational approach and palpable love of power, and whose large hand was seen in the dismantling of many Fijian institutions, would not have got the votes he did (13,753 or 2.8 per cent of the votes cast), more than the total votes cast for the Fiji Labour Party.

But Muslims were not the only ones who supported the military regime. It was the same in other communities as the reality of Bainimarama's determination to remain at the helm sank in. The leaders of Arya Samaj were among its early supporters, with one of them, former high school teacher Kamlesh Arya, appointed high commissioner to Australia without any discernible qualification for that important position. The leaders of the largest Fijian Hindu organisation, the Sanatan Dharma, were not far behind; its then national president Dewan Maharaj, the owner of Quality Print, was among the early prominent backers of the regime. One of the schools in Nausori run by that organisation invited Bainimarama for a function and the welcoming ceremony included washing his feet while he sat on a chair smiling enigmatically, whether in bemused amazement or in genuine puzzlement at this gesture it is difficult to say. The abasing symbolism was arresting as an indicator of desperation. The ceremony is normally performed at serious religious or ritually significant occasions (washing the feet of deities, for instance, or formally welcoming a bridegroom at a wedding by the bride's side), not for ordinary mortals, let alone politicians. Self-interest obviously played a part as organisations vied for government handouts. There were many Hindus who made a show of supporting Bainimarama to prevent him from falling completely into 'the Muslim camp'. But there were other factors as well. Bainimarama's firm rejection of the Methodist Church demand (and the Social Democratic Liberal Party's (SODELPA) also) that Fiji become a Christian state was widely welcomed by Hindus and Muslims. Many had witnessed at first hand the ugly religious bigotry of the late 1980s—the Sunday Ban and the ransacking, looting and burning of Hindu and Muslim places of worship—and they did not want those episodes ever to be repeated. Bainimarama's confrontational attitude towards the Methodist Church, preventing it from holding its annual conferences and insisting that the church dissociate itself from party politics, was welcome among most Indo-Fijians.

Alternative political parties could not match what FijiFirst had to offer the Indo-Fijian voters. Let us take SODELPA. This was the old Soqosoqo Duavata ni Lewenivanua (SDL) under a new name, fulfilling the requirement that all political parties have English names.[12] SDL held bad memories for most Indo-Fijians. Its pro-Fijian policies under the Qarase government (the 'Fijian Blueprint', scholarship programs for indigenous Fijians, subsidies to Fijian-only schools, among others) had deeply disenchanted many. Racist utterances by some of its parliamentarians (Asenaca Caucau, for instance, who likened Indo-Fijians to noxious weeds and went un-reprimanded) were not forgotten or forgiven. Insult and humiliation are hardly ever forgotten among Indo-Fijians; hurtful memories last a long time. The renamed party began with a progressive agenda, but soon started espousing what can broadly be described as a pro-Fijian platform. Many Fijians were understandably angry with the Bainimarama regime for its dismissive policies towards Fijian institutions and protocols, such as abolishing the GCC, using 'Fijian' as the name for all Fijian citizens irrespective of ethnicity, appointing the chairmen of provincial councils, altering the formula of land rent distribution, and dismantling many race-based affirmative action programs.

Hoping to tap into what appeared to be a swelling pool of indigenous Fijian resentment and anger about the regime's policies, SODELPA soon jettisoned any pretence of being a multiracial party, becoming, instead, the vehicle for indigenous Fijian views and concerns. The GCC would be brought back, the party said, Christianity could become the state religion, and the name Fijian would be reserved for indigenous Fijians only. In short, SODELPA once again became the champion for the cause of Fijian paramountcy, though of a more subdued variety than that demanded by the supporters of the 1987 coup. It had little to say to the non-indigenous citizens of Fiji. It fielded only three Indo-Fijian candidates out of 50, among them a former SDL minister, George Shiu Raj, and one of the founders of the People's Democratic Party, Nirmal Singh. They all polled miserably. SODELPA's Fijian reach was strong but its urban base was fractured. The party must adopt a broader, more non-ethnic platform if it is become a serious contender for power in Fiji.

---

12   Under the Political Parties (Registration, Conduct, Funding and Disclosures) Decree 4/2013. The Decree also required all parties to register or re-register with 5,000 signatures from registered voters, with specified numbers from each of the country's four administrative divisions.

Indo-Fijian voters had three other parties to choose from: the Fiji Labour Party (FLP), People's Democratic Party (PDP) and the National Federation Party (NFP). None of them got the traction they hoped for. FLP's fate was particularly tragic, winning only 11,670 (2.4 per cent) of the votes cast and for the first time in its history without a seat in parliament. Formed in 1985, the party had won government in 1987 in coalition with the NFP, only to be overthrown in a military coup after a month in office. Its founding leader, Dr Timoci Bavadra, died in 1989, and was succeeded by the long-time trade unionist Mahendra Chaudhry, secretary of the Fiji Public Service Association, after a short stint at the helm by Bavadra's widow, Adi Kuini Bavadra. Adept and politically astute, Chaudhry was also in a hurry to wrest the leadership of the Indo-Fijian community from the NFP, determined, in his own words, to 'finish NFP off' (Lal 2009a). To that end, throughout the 1990s he deployed his considerable political capital, emerging victorious in the 1999 general elections and becoming the country's first Indo-Fijian prime minister. But his government, too, was overthrown in a quasi-coup after a year in office. The policies of his successor, Laisenia Qarase, kept Chaudhry out of government despite the power-sharing provisions of the 1997 Constitution by offering Labour miniscule ministries of no significance.[13] By the time Qarase honoured the power-sharing formula after the 2006 elections, Chaudhry's cup of disillusionment was full. He concentrated all his efforts on derailing the Qarase government, in which several of his own senior party members were ministers, though he himself had opted to stay out of the Cabinet (Green 2013). In that endeavour, he found an unlikely ally in the commander of the Fiji military forces, Commodore Frank Bainimarama, who had his own private grievance against the government besides genuine anger at proposed bills, in particular the Promotion of Reconciliation, Truth and Unity Bill, which could have granted amnesty to rebel soldiers involved in the mutiny in the military in November 2007, in which several loyalist soldiers had died.

Chaudhry did not use his considerable political weight to oppose the impending coup. As the late Michael Green, New Zealand's high commissioner to Fiji, put it, 'Chaudhry would not stand in the way

---

13   The 1997 Constitution provided that any political party with more than 5 per cent of seats in the House of Representatives was entitled to be invited into cabinet in proportion to its numbers.

of a coup, let alone use his considerable influence to prevent one' (Green 2013, p. 168). Instead, he joined the military cabinet in early 2007. This was significant. Widely recognised as the leader of the Indo-Fijian community, his joining the regime cabinet brought considerable Indo-Fijian support to Bainimarama, bought him valuable time and helped him consolidate his position. A year and a half later, in August 2008, Chaudhry was forced out of the Bainimarama cabinet—left voluntarily, according to Chaudhry—and became a relentlessly vocal critic of the regime. But the regime had the last laugh. On the eve of the elections, Chaudhry was convicted of breaching the country's Foreign Exchange Act for failure to declare ownership of foreign currency without the express permission of the Reserve Bank. As a result of the conviction, he was barred from contesting the elections. Without him, the Labour Party was nothing. Its makeshift leader, former academic Rohit Kishore, was an unimpressive novice. The party, which had once won the hearts and minds of the Indo-Fijian community and formed the government of the country, had lost its peoples' affection and support. The reputation of its leader was now tarnished beyond repair. Indo-Fijians understandably saw no reason to vote for it.

The People's Democratic Party was formed by a group that had broken away from Chaudhry's Labour Party over disagreement about his leadership style. It included leading trade unionists. The PDP was genuinely multiracial and had members with fine talent but with little political experience beyond trade union circles. It lacked rural reach and political credibility too, in the eyes of many. The Fiji Trade Union Congress (FTUC) maintained a low profile in the early days of the coup, and general secretary Felix Anthony accepted his appointment to statutory boards by the military regime. For him to turn around now and condemn the regime sounded incongruous. Nonetheless, the party had socially progressive policies on law and justice and on protecting rights and freedoms, and about protecting workers' rights and media freedom, among many other policies. Such policies were in truth unexceptionable but they failed to impress the Indo-Fijian electorate attuned to other offers and other voices. PDP's policies on indigenous issues were sensitive and sensible, but they directly contradicted those of FijiFirst. The PDP declared in its manifesto that it 'respects the central place of iTaukei within Fiji's wider multicultural society and will pursue policies and programs consistent with the UN Indigenous Tribal and Peoples Convention'. FijiFirst's policy, which many Indo-Fijians found more appealing, placed everyone on an *equal* footing, not giving any group prior rights and privileges. On the GCC, the PDP recognised 'the important role of the GCC as an institution and the role of chiefs in modern Fiji'. Therefore, it would 'reinstate the GCC and will assist it to promote indigenous customs and traditions and to improve the economic well-being of indigenous people', while being guided by its advice 'on all matters relating to the protection of indigenous rights and interests'.

More Indo-Fijians were listening to FijiFirst on indigenous rights, which emphasised 'mainstreaming' indigenous practices. Aiyaz Sayed-Khaiyum had written about a 'sunset clause' on separate traditional institutions in his master's thesis at the University of Hong Kong, under the supervision of Professor Yash Ghai (who would later chair the ill-fated Fiji Constitution Commission, whose report was unceremoniously discarded by the Bainimarama regime). And most Indo-Fijians saw the GCC as a part of the problem, not part of the solution, remembering its support for previous coups and its being out of touch with the realities of a modern Fiji in a rapidly globalising world. The fact that the PDP was new on the scene with no track record did not help its cause. It won 15,864 (3.2 per cent) of the votes cast. Soon after the elections, its leader Felix Anthony rejoined FTUC, which under the present dispensation would prevent him from participating in electoral politics. Without his active participation at the helm, the party's future looks uncertain. It is likely to wither on the vine of public apathy and indifference.

Finally, there was the National Federation Party, which won 27,066 (5.5 per cent) of the votes and three seats in parliament, ending an absence of over a decade. The NFP is Fiji's oldest political party, founded in 1964, based in the Indo-Fijian community but with a non-racial platform, and in the vanguard of the movement for independence on the basis of a common roll. But it was communal representation which won the day and which was entrenched in the 1970 Constitution. Communal politics took root and racial divisions hardened to the point that a government elected with Indo-Fijian support was deposed in a military coup. The decreed 1990 Constitution entrenched racial apartheid. Nonetheless, the NFP leaders, principally Jai Ram Reddy, worked tirelessly with the Fijian leaders, principally the coup maker

Sitiveni Rabuka, to produce a moderate, multiracial 1997 Constitution. It was a massive achievement in the most unlikely of circumstances, but its significance was not appreciated by Indo-Fijians.

The politics of moderation always loses in an atmosphere of polarised racial politics, and Fijian politics in the 1990s was deeply polarised. Both Rabuka and Reddy fell in the 1999 general elections. The NFP did not win a single seat then, or in the 2001 and 2006 elections. There was talk of closing shop, but the party persisted. It gained moderate momentum on the eve of the 2014 elections. It mattered that the party was led by a team untainted by a political past. Its leader was the academic economist Biman Prasad from USP, and its president was a young Fijian lawyer, Tupou Draunidalo. Her elevation to the presidency fulfilled the party's founding non-racial vision. In the party's line-up were several Fijian women and men with successful professional careers of their own. A decade or so ago, this would have been unthinkable, and likened to treachery. But it was to the party's credit that it had broadened its multiracial base to this extent. Its policies were principled, moderate and progressive, appealing more to the electorate's intellect than to its heart. Its credentials as a party of principle were credible. Like all other parties, the NFP had been in the wilderness for the previous eight years, and the military regime had done all it could to hobble its prospects. The constraints were considerable. So too were its achievements: three parliamentary seats, won in the most difficult of circumstances. The NFP has a future if it maintains its multiethnic character and outlook and continues to infuse fresh blood into the party.

Indo-Fijian support for FijiFirst was due not only to the weaknesses and constraints of other parties; it was also due to its own strengths and appeal. From 2007 onwards, despite the downturn in the economy, Bainimarama spared little effort to win popular support, including among Indo-Fijian voters, and the voting figures show he managed to do so to a large degree. He exploited the military regime's power of incumbency to the maximum, pointing to its record of achievements and making specific promises to the electorate, especially in the lower socioeconomic strata. Such promises had considerable attraction: an electricity subsidy for low-income families, water free of charge to those earning less than FJD$30,000 a year, price control and removal of value-added tax on basic food items and pharmaceutical items, free milk to all first-year primary school children, streamlining the

Tertiary Education Loan Scheme, providing free education to primary, secondary and pre-school students, and giving 99-year residential leases to squatters on state land were only some of the many promises the regime made, promises it was emphasised were backed by a record of achievements.

No other party could give such concrete promises and no other party would have been likely to be believed even if it did. While other parties struggled to get their messages through to the electorate, FijiFirst used the full extent of government machinery and the services of a compliant media to campaign. It helped the party's fortunes that all the district commissioners were former military men, along with many heads of government departments, some of who declared their intention to contest the elections within weeks of resigning their public service positions. This made a mockery of Commodore Bainimarama's promise at the time of the coup that no one in his administration would benefit politically or stand for elections. But no one seemed to be overly concerned about broken promises. It was all a part of the 'game' of politics. And in any case, it was said with no sense of irony at all that Bainimarama was standing not because he wanted to but because the people of Fiji would not have it any other way—and the will of the people had to reign supreme, over and above personal preferences. That, after all, was the essence of democracy.

After the elections, Indo-Fijians were commonly blamed for their short-sighted and self-centred choice and their unwillingness to consider the long-term implications of their actions. But it is understandable that Indo-Fijians, by choice as well as by necessity, voted the way they did. Taking a long-term view of democracy and governance is not a strong suit for a people struggling to make ends meet and keen to leave for other lands at the first opportunity. The best and the brightest of the Indo-Fijian community have left, are leaving, or will leave, leaving behind those who cannot migrate because they lack the skills or resources to do so. To them, the immediate fulfilment of their pressing daily needs was what mattered. By this criterion, FijiFirst had a clear advantage over its rivals. Democracy based on the will and whims of one strongman is dangerous, and Fiji may yet pay a heavy price for this; but for many this one strongman also stood for stability against chaos. Indo-Fijians knew well that if Bainimarama failed, they would be done for. More than anything else, ordinary people wanted peace and security, and insurance against future coups. Bainimarama offered to be the buffer, and he was believed. But what happens when the well runs dry, or when some other saviour appears on the horizon, who has a different agenda, a different vision, perhaps even a nationalistic one? Does the military, for all practical purposes an indigenous institution itself, really have a multiracial vision? Do the Commodore's own supporters, many of whom were in previous coup camps, have such a vision? In 2014, Indo-Fijians made the pragmatic assessment that, for the moment, Bainimarama, with the military solidly behind him, was their man. Tomorrow, as they say, is another day.

Democracy has had an ill-fated history in Fiji, having to contend with military coups as the vehicle for effecting political change in the country. Democracy was alive all these years more in its symbolism than in its substance, dependent on the goodwill of powerful men rather than implanted in the hearts of ordinary citizens or embedded in the sinews of its public institutions. It had few true defenders but many fair weather friends, who habitually deserted it in its moments of greatest need. Democratic values have been steadily eroding in Fiji since the 1987 coups and disillusionment with politics and politicians. All this made the Indo-Fijian reaction in 2014 understandable, but it is also true that Indo-Fijians have planted in the process the seeds of a new political order, a new kind of democracy, which is fundamentally at odds with the principles of representative democracy. Putting it colloquially, placing all your eggs in one basket in an uncertain environment is never prudent; nor is it prudent to pin all your hopes on one man to be your saviour, however good or great that saviour might turn out to be. The rule of law, freely arrived at, is infinitely superior to the rule of a group of men, however well intentioned they might be. Fiji is going through a massive process of transition from one order to another. Inevitably, there will be uncertainty, confusion, error, disenchantment and disappointment. The larger question is whether, to borrow words from *Rosencrantz and Guildenstern are Dead*, the exit from one place will lead to an entrance somewhere else. For the sake of Fiji, one hopes it will be entrance to a better place. That remains to be seen, but is something very much to be hoped for.

References

Ali, Ahmed 1973, 'The Fiji General elections of 1972', *The Journal of Pacific History,* vol. 8, pp. 171–80.

Ali, Ahmed 2007, *Fiji and the franchise: A history of political representation, 1900–1937,* iUniverse, Indiana.

Chetty, Kishor Nand and Prasad, Satendra 1993, *Fiji's Emigration: An examination of contemporary trends and issues,* University of the South Pacific, Suva.

Firth, Stewart 2012, 'Reflections on Fiji since Independence', *Round Table: The Commonwealth Journal of International Affairs*, vol. 101, no. 6, pp. 575–83.

Fraenkel, Jon 2015, 'The remorseless power of incumbency in Fiji's September 2014 election', *The Round Table*: *The Commonwealth Journal of International Affairs,* vol. 104, no. 2, pp. 151–64.

Fraenkel, Jon, Firth, Stewart, and Lal, Brij V (eds) 2009, *The 2006 Military Takeover in Fiji: A coup to end all coups*, ANU E Press, Canberra.

Green, Michael 2013, *Persona non grata: Breaking the bond: Fiji and New Zealand, 2004–2007*, Dunmore Publishing, Auckland.

Kant, Romitesh and Rakuita, Eroni 2014, 'Public participation & constitution-making in Fiji: A critique of the 2012 constitution-making process', *State, Society and Governance in Melanesia Program Discussion Paper 6*, The Australian National University.

Lal, Brij V 1992, *Broken Waves: A history of Fiji in the 20th century*, University of Hawaii Press, Honolulu.

Lal, Brij V 1997. *A vision for change: AD Patel and the politics of Fiji*, Asia Pacific Press, Canberra.

Lal, Brij V 2006a, *Islands of turmoil: Elections and politics in Fiji*, Asia Pacific Press, Canberra.

Lal, Brij V 2006b (ed.), *Fiji: British documents on the end of empire*, The Stationery Office, London.

Lal, Brij V 2009a, 'One hand clapping: Reflections on the first anniversary of Fiji's 2006 coup', in John Fraenkel, Stewart Firth and Brij Lal (eds), *The 2006 Military takeover in Fiji: A coup to end all coups?* ANU E Press, Canberra, pp. 425–48.

Lal, Brij V 2009b. *In the eye of the storm: Jai Ram Reddy and the politics of Fiji*, Asia Pacific Press, Canberra.

Lal, Brij V 2013, 'The strange career of Commodore Frank Bainimarama's 2006 Fiji coup', *State, Society and Governance in Melanesia Program Discussion Paper 8*, The Australian National University.

Lal, Brij V 2014, 'In Frank Bainimarama's shadow: Fiji, elections and the future', *Journal of Pacific History*, vol. 49, no. 4, pp. 457–68.

Lal, Padma Narsey 2008, *Ganna: Portrait of the Fiji sugar industry*, Fiji Sugar Commission, Lautoka.

Larson, Eric 2014, 'Fiji's 2014 parliamentary election', *Journal of Electoral Studies*, December 2014, pp. 235–39.

Norton, Robert 2000, 'Reconciling ethnicity and nation: Contending discourses in Fiji constitutional reform', *The Contemporary Pacific*, vol. 12, no. 1, pp. 83–122.

Norton, Robert 2012, 'A pre-eminent right to political rule: Indigenous Fijian power and the multi-ethnic nation building', *Round Table: The Commonwealth Journal of International Affairs*, vol. 101, no. 6, pp. 537–55.

Reeves, Sir Paul, Vakatora, Tomasi Rayal and Lal, Brij V 1996. *Towards a united future: Report of the Fiji Constitution Review Commission*, Parliament of Fiji, Suva.

Scarr, Deryck 2008, *Tuimacilai: A life of Ratu Sir Kamisese Mara*, Crawford House, Adelaide.

Sharpham, John 2000, *Rabuka of Fiji: The authorized biography of Major General Sitiveni Rabuka,* Central Queensland University Press, Rockhampton.

Taylor, Michael (ed.) 1987, *Fiji: Future imperfect*, Allen & Unwin, Sydney.

5

'Unfree and unfair'?: Media intimidation in Fiji's 2014 elections

David Robie

Introduction

Fiji was a media pariah among Pacific nations, as well as a political outcast, for much of the eight years after Voreqe Bainimarama's military coup in December 2006. But while some media credibility was restored in the months leading up to the 2014 general elections and during the ballot itself, the elephant is still in the room: the 2010 Media Industry Development Decree (Fijian Government 2010). While this Decree remains in force, Fiji can hardly claim to have a truly free and fair media.

Just seven months out from the September 17 elections, Fiji was ranked 107th out of 179 countries listed in the 2014 World Press Freedom Index prepared by the Paris-based global media freedom organisation Reporters Without Borders (RSF). That ranking was an improvement on the previous year (RSF 2014a), rising 10 places from the 2013 ranking. The major reason for this improvement was the adoption of the new Constitution on 6 September 2013, criticised as it was in many quarters during that year, and the promise of 'free and fair' elections by 30 September 2014. The elections gave Fiji's ranking a further boost, rising 14 places to 93rd (RSF 2015).

There was considerable hope among news media and civil society groups that the general elections would open the door to a free media climate, which had been lacking since the coup. Over the past few months there has been a marked improvement in public debate and news media have been relatively more robust in terms of published political comment and debate, particularly in news columns and in letters to the editor.

A major problem previously had been a 'divided media' and a void in professional leadership by the now-defunct Fiji Media Council, which had been 'accused of failing to handle ethical lapses and controversies satisfactorily or fast enough' (Morris 2014, p. 3). According to Ricardo Morris, editor of *Repúblika* and president of the recently revived Fijian Media Association, who spoke at the 20th Anniversary of *Pacific Journalism Review* conference in Auckland about the problems facing the media industry some seven weeks after the elections:

> [I]t can be argued that such division was one reason [why] it was easy for the military government to force the Media Decree in 2010. The government justified its actions with reference to some of the unscrupulous journalist practices that should rightly be condemned. And I should point out here that the Fiji Media Council's legacy does live here in the form of the code of ethics for media workers embedded in the Media Decree.
>
> We realised a bit too late that we were all in this together despite our personal political views or those of the companies that we worked for. United we stand, divided we fall. (Morris 2014, p. 3)

Barriers to freedom of information

In a joint submission (RSF 2014b) to the United Nations Human Rights Council Second Universal Periodic Review, the Auckland-based Pacific Media Centre (PMC) and Paris-based RSF argued that the Constitution, described by the Fiji government as 'coup proof', still restricted freedom of the press in four particular areas (CCF 2013). The first criticism is that too much executive power is placed with the offices of the Prime Minister and the Attorney-General, as they control nearly all appointments to the judiciary and independent commissions. The Attorney-General has far wider powers than are given to holders of the equivalent office in other Commonwealth constitutions. The Constitution does not provide the necessary structural protections for the judiciary to be seen to be independent. Secondly, the Chief Justice and President of the Court of Appeal will effectively be political appointments and there is a risk of abuse of power. Journalists are worried that the judiciary could be used by government officials to their own advantage. Fearing judicial reprisals if they criticise the government when covering its activities, many journalists have continued to censor themselves.

Thirdly, the Bill of Rights is weakened by 'severe limitations on many rights'. For example, future governments will no longer need to justify before an independent court that laws which limit rights are 'necessary in a free and democratic society' (as in the abrogated 1997 Constitution). In what is known as the 'claw-back clause', they will simply need to show that a limitation is 'reasonable' (s.6.5.c). Previously there had been a state clampdown on independent journalists, bloggers and netizens (Robie 2009; Walsh 2010). This so-called claw-back clause makes them vulnerable to selective government pressure in the future.

Fourthly, there are also few avenues under the Constitution for citizens to participate in and ensure 'good and transparent government'. While there has been more vibrant debate in online commentaries and letters to the editors in the Fiji national press in recent months in the lead-up to the elections, there has nevertheless been a climate of self-censorship that has prevailed for the past eight years. The Constitution does not give clear enough guarantees of freedom of expression that cannot later be curbed by an unscrupulous government.

The 2013 Constitution makes provision for the new national Parliament of Fiji to pass a law after the elections to allow members of the public to exercise their right to access information (s.150). This Freedom of Information provision is the same as in the 1997 Constitution, except there is now no longer any requirement for such a law to be passed 'as soon as practicable'. As well as Freedom of Information, the new Constitution provides some safeguards for a free press in Fiji while 'simultaneously allow[ing]' the curtailment of such rights if the government wishes. Chapter 1 proclaims the values of 'human rights, freedom and the rule of law', but does not specifically declare freedom of the press. However, section 17 under the Bill of Rights provides for the 'right to freedom of speech, expression, thought, opinion and publication', including 'freedom of imagination and creativity'. It further specifically states 'freedom of the press, including print, electronic and other media' as a right. Even so, section 17(3) says the law 'may limit, or authorise the limitation' of these freedoms in the interests of national security, public safety, public order, public morality, public health and other circumstances, including the curbing of 'ill will between ethnic or religious groups'. Under section 17(4), the right of citizens to be free of 'hate speech', whether directed against individuals or groups, is endorsed. While a preliminary reading of these media freedom rights may suggest conflict with some of the draconian provisions of the 2010 Fiji Media Industry Development Decree, section 17(3) may in fact be providing a legal cloak justifying these elements of the Decree (Fijian Government 2010).

Mixed responses by government on issues of media freedom

In October 2012 the High Court in Suva ruled that the major daily newspaper, *The Fiji Times*, was in contempt of court over an article republished in November 2011 from a New Zealand national weekly newspaper, the *Sunday Star-Times*, that questioned judicial independence in Fiji. Chief editor Fred Wesley and former publisher Brian O'Flaherty had been found guilty but were not actually sentenced until February 2013. A High Court judge fined the newspaper FJD$300,000 (US$160,000) and ordered it to publish an apology within 28 days, fined publisher O'Flaherty FJD$10,000 (US$5,300) and also sentenced editor Wesley to six months' imprisonment suspended for two years. The penalties were widely criticised as being unreasonably harsh and condemned as politically inspired, *The Fiji Times* being unpopular with the Fiji government (Loanakadavu 2013).

In June 2013 a prominent Fiji Television sports editor, Satish Narayan, was forced to resign after he had complained on camera that the daughter of the country's leader, Prime Minister Voreqe Bainimarama, was playing music too loud at an outdoor event. The high school athletics event was organised by the Fiji Sports Council, whose chief executive was Bainimarama's eldest daughter, Litiana Loabuka. The broadcaster was threatened with the loss of its licence if the editor did not leave (Field 2013).

In August 2013, the executive director of the Citizens' Constitutional Forum (CCF) was sentenced to three months imprisonment suspended for one year for contempt of court after publishing an article about the Fiji judiciary in the organisation's newsletter. The article outlined research by the United Kingdom's Law Society, which had reported that the judiciary in Fiji was not independent. Executive director Reverend Akuila Yabaki, who is also the newsletter's chief editor, and the CFF were ordered to pay FJD$20,000 (US$10,700) in fines and court costs (PMW8385 2013).

This climate of intimidation over the months leading up to the elections hardly encouraged a vigorous and independent media. Even though the prosecutions had not come under the umbrella of the Media Decree, but rather through the Public Order Decree, the 'chilling' impact was effectively the same. The medley of decrees and regulations stifle the practice of 'truly robust and critical journalism', as Morris has argued: 'Sometimes you get the impression that everybody with a little power to exercise will unreasonably limit journalists in their work. And it's not only locals doing it' (Morris 2014, p. 4).

The media blackout: 'Draconian and unenforceable'

A total of 450 journalists and media staff were accredited to cover the elections—33 of them working for foreign news groups, arguably the largest team ever assembled to cover a Fijian general elections (MIDA 2014). Certainly, surprisingly, given limited media commitment to international and Pacific news coverage, New Zealand had the largest contingent, numbering 15, more than double the number of journalists from Australia. The largest group was from the pro-FijiFirst Auckland station Radio Tarana (6) and, apart from the *New Zealand Herald*, Radio New Zealand, Television New Zealand, and MediaWorks representatives, controversial right-wing *Whale Oil* blogger Cameron Slater was there as a freelance correspondent. The largest of the local media election teams was the state-run Fiji Broadcasting Corporation (97 accredited staff), followed by *The Fiji Times* (80)—double that of their rival, the *Fiji Sun* (40). The University of the South Pacific's journalism school also had 40 student journalists accredited, including one on assignment from New Zealand's Auckland University of Technology (AUT). Another AUT student journalist was also a member of the *República* team's eight accredited staff. Small international teams represented Agence France-Presse, Al Jazeera, *Asahi Shimbun*, Kyodo News, Nikkei, Nippon Hoso Kyokai and others.

The Electoral Decree imposed a two-day media blackout in Fiji just ahead of the general elections (Fijian Government 2014). News media and journalists faced jail time or fines if they provided any election coverage from 7.30am on Monday 15 September until close of polls at 6pm on Wednesday 17 September. The blackout banned all political advertising on radio and television and required all campaign posters to be removed. News media were allowed to publish information provided by the National Electoral Office only if they submitted their reports to the Media Industry Development Authority (MIDA) for 'vetting' before publication. The International Federation of Journalists (IFJ) and RSF strongly condemned this ban, with IFJ's acting Asia-Pacific director Jane Worthington describing it as a 'gross violation of the freedom of the media ahead of one of the most pivotal elections in Fiji's history' (IFJ 2014) and RSF's Asia-Pacific head Benjamin Ismaïl saying the ban was 'draconian and unenforceable' (RSF 2014c). The Decree also applied to international journalists if their media was accessible to the Fijian public. As I wrote at the time on my media transparency weblog *Café Pacific*:

> BLACKOUT DAY—day one of the 'silence window' in Fiji leading up to the close of polling in the general election at 6pm on Wednesday. And this is under the draconian threat of a $10,000 fine or five years in jail for breaches.
>
> These are the penalties cited in a media briefing distributed to journalists covering the elections last week. But a closer reading of Part 4 'Electoral campaigns and the media' in the Electoral Decree 2014 reveals that there are even harsher penalties of up to $50,000 and 10 years in jail for offenders.
>
> And this could include social media offenders.
>
> (Robie 2014a).

In an interview with Radio New Zealand *Mediawatch* presenter Colin Peacock, who has a keen interest in digital media developments, the Pacific Media Centre's Thomas Carnegie was told the penalties were 'unduly harsh' and would restrict political debate just when it was needed the most (PMC 2014). Confusion and frustration was evident in Suva as the global media contingent tried to get a handle on the full implications of the decree for their news operations. Some media tested the apparent boundaries.

Pacific Scoop and Radio New Zealand broadcast stories about a massive hoarding with an imposing image of FijiFirst leader Voreqe Bainimarama, which appeared to be violating the blackout. But when journalists challenged this apparent breach, MIDA defended the 'buckle up' billboard as a road safety advertisement and part of ongoing ordinary government business (Anneberg 2014).

According to the Section 118 media guidelines:

> Media must not allow any political activity, including advertisements, interview and political actors, and conduct debates or commentaries that would be deemed to be advocacy or has the potential to influence voters—e.g. no candidate can be interviewed on a radio talkback show [after] 7.30am.

> Publication of all material pertaining to political activity in the mainstream media, including magazines, must cease at 7.30am on Monday. Anything published in magazines prior to the blackout period may remain as is.

> (Fijian Government 2014)

But during this 'silent' period, the media were still expected to report on electoral 'administration' activity. RSF criticised the Fiji authorities for not explaining how the Decree would be enforced and ultimately nobody was reported to have been prosecuted under the provisions. RSF's Benjamin Ismaïl commented:

> The scale of the censorship imposed by this decree is out of all proportion. While restrictions on publishing opinion polls, projections, partial results and even political advertising are completely understandable, banning all political commenting for several days and introducing prior censorship is both draconian and unenforceable.

> (RSF 2014c)

During the blackout, Bainimarama was also able to gain some political mileage on freedom for 45 Fijian peacekeeping soldiers at a thanksgiving ceremony at a venue next door to the election National Media Centre less than 24 hours before polling stations were due to open on 17 September. The UN peacekeepers, who had been serving in the Quneitra Crossing demilitarised zone between the Israel-occupied Golan Heights and Syria, had been held captive for the two weeks since 28 August by Jabhat al-Nusra, a Syrian rebel group linked to al-Qaeda but a rival to the Islamic State of Iraq and the Levant (ISIL), which had seized large swathes of Iraq and Syria (Vuru 2014; Weaver 2014). According to media reports in Israel, United Nations negotiators secured the release of the Fiji hostages through payment of a US$25 million ransom by the Qatar government. This deal 'made a mockery of UN and Western leaders' rhetoric against doing deals with terrorists and paying ransoms for the release of hostages' (Ben Zion 2014). UN and Fiji government sources have never admitted the truth of this claim.

The elections provided an important opportunity to change the way Fiji addressed human rights, stated Human Rights Watch (HRW) in an analysis barely a week before the elections (HRW 2014). Among key rights challenges raised by HRW were freedom of expression, allowing human rights' defenders to carry out their peaceful work, judicial independence, labour rights, and constitutional reform. In letters addressed to the five major parties fielding candidates, HRW appealed to them to 'seriously address' and give priority to these issues after the elections. None of these concerns bothered *Whale Oil* blogger Cameron Slater, who was on the ground in Fiji covering the elections just days before the New Zealand ballot. He reported:

> Fiji has voted, and rejected racism.
>
> SODELPA has been spanked; they stood on a platform of racism and lies and the electorate has resounding [sic] rejected those policies.
>
> The early votes that came in were from traditional iTaukei areas in the North and even there Bainimarama was winning. That was the point at which I saw the smiles erupt …
>
> Today is the start of a promising future for Fiji. The people have voted to reject racism and voted for progress and the vision of Frank Bainimarama and Fiji First for Fiji.

(Slater 2014)

A week after the elections were over, a senior HRW research associate, Shaivalini Parmar, followed up by acknowledging the credibility of the ballot, saying the fact that it had proceeded 'without significant disruptions' was a positive outcome (Parmar 2014). She pointed to the strong endorsement by international electoral monitors overseeing the elections as an important indicator. So too was the relatively quick praise from previously critical countries such as Australia, New Zealand and the United States, although Parmar noted they were overlooking Bainimarama's 'troubling human rights record'.

> Elections are a mandate to act and Bainimarama needs to make a commitment to concrete human rights reform. Real reform would involve bold steps to reverse a culture of impunity that has been a significant marker of Bainimarama's rule.

> If Bainimarama is committed to democratic change, he should create a 100-day plan to restore human rights and media freedom, and to reform laws that restrict rights. He needs to make explicit policies to improve the country's human rights record after eight long years of military rule.

> The Fiji First party should break with abusive policies that the military rulers long carried out, by revoking draconian laws and policies that restrict the media and passing other laws to ensure judicial independence. (Parmar 2014)

At the time of writing this chapter, the 100-day honeymoon had lapsed with little indication of a shift around the media laws. Shaivalini Parmar also referred to 'significant barriers' preventing the realisation of fundamental rights, saying that media freedom was of key concern:

> Newsrooms no longer host censors as they did at certain times in the post-coup period, but continuing allegations of government intimidation and interference with the media indicate much more progress is needed. (Parmar 2014)

An example of the ongoing intimidation was a statement by MIDA's Ashwin Raj to the UN Human Rights Council Universal Periodic Review (UPR) in Geneva in October in which he accused Al Jazeera and Radio New Zealand of 'racist, unbalanced and inaccurate' reporting during the elections and claimed they had 'apologised and retracted' (PMW9034 2014b). Typically, Raj was long on obscure wordage but short on facts and Radio New Zealand (RNZ) responded with a denial. In a subsequent RNZ report claiming Raj had 'changed his tune', chief executive Paul Thompson stated he had written to the UN saying there had been no apology over the racism, imbalance or inaccuracy claim. Raj then withdrew the racism allegation and redirected it against Al Jazeera without substantiation (PMW9062 2014c). Accusing Raj of 'amnesia' over the previous eight years of military-backed rule, economist and media commentator Professor Wadan Narsey (2014) said his ready condemnation of Al Jazeera, Radio New Zealand International and local journalists for 'running alleged "hate speeches"' and his reluctance to subject the Bainimarama Government to the same scrutiny 'might suggest that MIDA is being used more to regulate the media in the interests of the Bainimarama Government'.

Ashwin Raj's abrasive and biased style of tenure at MIDA has contrasted sharply with that of his low-key predecessors, professors Subramani and Satendra Nandan, who constantly sought a collegial approach to integrity and ethics, and a 'fresh air of freedom and responsibility of the highest kind' (Nandan 2014, p. 18). The founding chair of MIDA, Dr Nandan, an emeritus professor at the University of Canberra, presented a thoughtful view of freedom of expression in *República* some months prior to the elections (Nandan 2014). He argued that the greater the power, the greater the responsibility, referring to the news media faced with a recent history of coups.

> In Fiji, too much damage has been done by tendentious propaganda by a few that has frayed the fabric of the Fijian society at so many levels of social harmony and political growth of a young democratic nation. And once a nation (and a person) suffers heart attacks, it must take care of its daily diet and exercise both restraint and responsibility. This is never more important than during an election. (Nandan 2014, p. 20)

In Nandan's view, the 2014 general elections has made a major contribution to ending corrupt political and disinformation practices of the past. He argues that the Electoral Commission ought to be able to strip a party which, or a member of Parliament who, wins a seat on the basis of falsification of facts as a 'deterrent to unscrupulous demagogues' (p. 21). Nandan condemned an opposition political leader for claiming during the election campaign that native land tenure in Fiji was in jeopardy.

The [native land tenure] issue has been so falsely and fallaciously used in Fiji for so long that it's no longer funny: the Electoral Commission has the power, I think, to put an end to this kind of lurid and ludicrous propaganda. (Nandan 2014)

Four days before the elections, *The Interpreter* columnist Alex Stewart (2014) concluded that 'by world standards of elections after prolonged military rule, Fiji is doing well'. But he added a cautionary observation about allegations of unbalanced media coverage, participation of non-government organisations in the electoral process, and issues surrounding candidate nominations. All three points were made in response to a 'string of controversies and criticisms' of how the Bainimarama Government was approaching the transition to independence:

[A] truly free and fair election requires more than the absence of extra ballots stuffed into the box. Yes, voters need to be free to make their choice on the day, but the process by which they reach their decision also needs to be fair. In a free and fair election, political parties compete on as level a playing field as the system can enforce. This is where the election process in Fiji stands on shakier ground. (Stewart 2014)

As Stewart acknowledged, there had been repeated accusations by rival parties that Bainimarama's FijiFirst party had 'received unfair media advantages' (Fox 2014). ABC Radio's Liam Fox reported as part of a series of news stories and commentaries prior to the elections that 'while opposition parties and independents battle to be heard, Frank Bainimarama has no such worries, with every move of his FijiFirst Party relayed by the media' (Fox 2014). Stewart noted the 'strenuous denials' by both news outlets and by MIDA, adding: 'It is always difficult to distinguish between legitimate editorialising and bias. But the fact that these claims have persisted is concerning.'

Even two experienced postgraduate student journalists from AUT's Pacific Media Centre, on internship with *República* and *Wansolwara* as the first New Zealand-based students to cover a Pacific election, observed evidence of bias. Alistar Kata, an award-winning broadcast journalist with Ngapuhi and Cook Islands heritage, noted: 'From my unbiased vantage point as a student journalist from New Zealand, the local Fijian media coverage of the elections could sometimes be biased. I was surprised, shocked, at some examples of reporting that were allowed to air or be published' (*Spasifik* 2014, p. 18). But her colleague, Mads Anneberg, an experienced Danish political journalist, was also impressed with an ability to make an impact with quality journalism: 'When you take strict media rules and recent censorship out of the equation, Fiji is a dream for the nostalgic journalist; in some ways it reminds you of the old days, like a Pacific Hunter S. Thompson novel' (*Spasifik* 2014, p. 17).

At least one Fiji-based researcher carried out a systematic analysis of local news coverage of the elections and concluded in a paper prepared for the 20th anniversary of the *Pacific Journalism Review* 'Political journalism in the Asia-Pacific' conference in Auckland in November 2014 that the elections were flawed with 'recently activated political parties struggling to have their voices heard' by the media. (Bhim 2015, p. 108). Mosmi Bhim, an academic at Fiji National University and a former researcher with the CCF, cited a litany of examples of where news media coverage had been unbalanced in favour of Bainimarama's party.

> In an atmosphere of lavish campaign advertisements on billboards, public transport vehicles and the print and television news media by the post-coup Prime Minister Voreqe Bainimarama's political party FijiFirst, recently activated political parties struggled to have their voices heard. Two daily media companies—the Fiji Broadcasting Corporation and the Fiji Sun—displayed bias towards the FijiFirst party by providing them with excessive and preferential coverage and portraying other parties in a negative light; other media organisations attempted to give fairer coverage. (Bhim 2015, p. 109).

Referring to the Declaration on Criteria for Free and Fair Elections adopted by the Inter-Parliamentary Union Council in 1994 and using Fiji's new electoral and media legislation as a yardstick, Bhim produced considerable evidence to support her analysis. As a result of the media and other flaws, she argued that elections only satisfied some of the international criteria for 'free and fair elections' as 'all citizens were unable to participate freely and fully in the 2014 elections' (Bhim 2015, p. 108).

Bhim cited a report on ABC News explaining how MIDA planned to establish an independent unit to monitor media coverage of the election campaign in an attempt to identify political bias (ABC News 2014). The announcement was made by Raj at a media conference called to justify a complaint made against the ABC and veteran Pacific correspondent Sean Dorney, who had been expelled by the Bainimarama Government in 2009. The ABC quoted Suva reporter Samisoni Pareti as saying:

> they [MIDA] took offence to an interview that Sean Dorney did some weeks back [about a Melanesian Spearhead Group summit in Noumea, New Caledonia]. Apparently Mr Dorney made some remarks concerning the freeness of the media, or otherwise, in Fiji. So they took that up.

Little has been reported about this 'monitoring' of Fiji media since.

During the election campaign, in the wake of reported death threats against two Fiji women journalists on 9 September, Ashwin Raj appealed to Fijians to refrain from using the media, including social media, to incite violence through use of inflammatory language to intimidate voters (*Fiji Sun* 2014; RSF 2014d). Two women journalists—Vosita Kotowasawasa of the Fiji Broadcasting Corporation and Jyoti Pratibha of the *Fiji Sun*—reportedly received death threats over their previous day's coverage of the cancellation of a live TV debate between the leading contenders for the post of prime minister. Raj stated in a media conference: 'The media must also remain independent, give equal space to all political actors, must not be seen as aiding and abetting the agenda of one political party over others' (PMW8955 2014a). But as Bhim pointed out in her research paper, Raj made no mention of any inflammatory reporting by the Fiji Broadcasting Corporation or the *Fiji Sun* or against 'their biased reporting towards the FijiFirst party' (Bhim 2015, p. 117). This, argued Bhim, had led to questions being raised about the 'effectiveness and impartiality' of MIDA and whether such a body was actually needed.

Also speaking at the *Pacific Journalism Review* conference, Fijian Media Association president Ricardo Morris raised the issue of the 'fear that hangs over journalists and their media companies—fear of breaching the [Media] Decree and perhaps catching a fine, which could very well cripple any media company' (Morris 2015, p. 37). This threat, argued Morris, was even more serious for small, independent media operators and was omnipresent in the background during coverage of the election campaign. One overall outcome was that many times journalism 'presented to the people of Fiji is bland and unexciting'. Thus 'infotainment and puff pieces' could be much safer and more profitable.

But Morris added that not all news media in Fiji faced the fear of the Decree: 'It is well-known that the *Fiji Sun* newspaper is unconditionally supportive of Bainimarama's vision for a "new Fiji" and will consistently praise any policies of the government and denounce anybody with a differing view.' To be branded with an 'anti-Fiji' or 'anti-government' label by the *Fiji Sun* could make 'life and business very difficult' for any media group. For example, almost all government advertisements have been booked with the *Sun* to punish *The Fiji Times*, the nation's oldest and possibly still most influential newspaper, for its past opposition to the government. Nevertheless, Morris was not entirely pessimistic about the future of media in Fiji. In spite of a 'huge brain drain' (Morris 2015, p. 36) within the media industry through migration of some of the country's senior media workers ever since the first two coups in 1987, there were signs after the elections that the political and media environment could be improving.

> We have recently begun Parliamentary sessions and for the majority of those involved—from the Speaker, to MPs, the Secretary-General and journalists covering Parliament—it is a new experience. Learning parliamentary procedure and understanding the Standing Orders will take some time to master but we are getting there. In the meantime, the effects of dictatorship still hang over much of the process. (Morris 2014, p. 4)

The Media Industry Development Decree

The Media Industry Development Decree has clearly had an impact on the news industry by promoting a climate of self-censorship following the military censorship under the previous 2009 Public Emergency Regulation (PER). According to a national survey of the Fiji media conducted by the Pacific Media Assistance Scheme State of the Media and Communication Report in 2013, power had been delegated under the Media Decree 'to the Fiji Media Industry Development Authority (MIDA), which has an ongoing responsibility to censor material that is considered threatening to the public interest or order' (PACMAS 2013).

The report added that MIDA 'has the power to penalize journalists and media companies that publish content considered unsuitable'. However, in September 2013, then director of MIDA Matai Akauola, formerly general manager of the regional Pacific Islands News

Association, condemned Australian and New Zealand opposition to Fiji's 'homegrown solutions'. He told Pacific Media Watch in an interview that Australian and New Zealand media 'try to dictate to us how we live our lives' (Drageset 2013). But this is balanced by an acceptance that more vigorous debate has been allowed by the news media. In January 2014, Akauola told Radio New Zealand International:

> There is freedom of expression so anyone and everyone can come on board into a nationally televised discussion on issues; we're talking issues and how to progress this nation rather than going back to the old political rivalries. (*Dateline Pacific* 2014)

For Bob Pratt, executive secretary of the defunct self-regulatory Fiji Media Council, the rulings that this body had adjudicated for a decade through its published code of ethics and practice, prepared by the Thomson Foundation, had been 'unanimously accepted' by all main media organisations. He has argued for a return to a self-regulatory regime (Pratt n.d.). However, because the council did not have the power to punish transgressors it had been labelled a 'toothless tiger'— and most of the complaints came from politicians. The council's codes were adopted as part of the Media Decree.

> Prior to the implementation of the Media Decree, government called a meeting of media stakeholders and explained what was proposed. The decree used almost word for word the Council's code of ethics and practice. The main difference was the replacing of the word 'should' with the word 'must'. In addition, it made provision for offenders to be fined. The fines were excessive, but they were the answer to critics of the Media Council. Many of those who had loudly criticised the failure of the Council to punish now complained just as loudly at the ability to punish under the decree. (Pratt n.d.)

In a discussion paper about the Decree, Pratt conceded that the main offender during this period had been 'without doubt *The Fiji Times*— while they played lip service to the media codes they offended regularly and only issued limited retractions after a lot of pressure' (Pratt n.d.). However, he qualified this view:

> It should be borne in mind that Fiji was not alone in facing problems with the Murdoch press. It was felt in some quarters that the lack of media freedom in Fiji stemmed from the intransigence of the old *Fiji Times* and it was believed that once the ownership changed, the pressure on the media would be relaxed; this, however, has proved not to be the case. (Pratt n.d.)

During the UN Human Rights Council's Second Universal Periodic review in October 2014, the Fiji government was presented with 39 recommendations, which included a review of the 2013 Constitution, and was invited to review, amend or repeal restrictive decrees—including the Media Decree. The Fiji government was also called on to 'end intimidation and harassment of those [who] express criticism of the State, to change the climate of fear and self-censorship and to ensure that no-one is arbitrarily arrested and detained for exercising their rights' (PIR 2014). Justice Minister Aiyaz Sayed-Khaiyum told the Council that the recommendations would be examined by Fiji and that relevant independent institutions and government agencies would be consulted.

Among recommendations over Freedom of Information legislation and the Media Decree were those by Germany (including a repeal of the Media Decree so that it would end intimidation and harassment of critics of the State) and Canada (a call for a review of the Decree and introduction of a Freedom of Information law that complies with international human rights standards to ensure respect for freedom of expression and protection of journalists). Also recommending a repeal of the Decree was the joint submission from the PMC and RSF, which called on the government of Fiji to:

- modify its Constitution in order to ensure independence of the judiciary and prevent any dissuasive effect or use of the judiciary to intimidate the media
- stop issuing indirect threats and refrain from any editorial interference
- take measures to ensure more transparency and access to information
- enact a Freedom of Information law with some urgency
- significantly encourage participation in public debate without hindrance
- revoke the Media Industry Development Decree and its draconian punitive measures against journalists, editors and media organisations and adopt a self-regulatory media framework encouraging a free press
- encourage international media reporting and scrutiny, and lift bans on individual journalists.

In July 2015, there was a modest improvement in the Decree with the stripping of the of the Media Industry Development Tribunal's power to fine individual journalists but, as critics said, this 'did not resolve the issue of media censorship in the country' (*ABC Pacific Beat* 2015). While Parliament was reported as having voted unanimously to remove the power of the tribunal to impose fines on journalists for breaching the Decree, the CCF's programme director Ken Cokanasiga was quoted by the ABC's *Pacific Beat* as saying 'this doesn't bring about any significant change to the restrictive media environment'.

Conclusion: Restoring public-good journalism

Two months after the Fiji post-coup general elections, the First Vice-President of the European Union, Frans Timmermans, told a delegation of journalists in Brussels that sustaining quality journalism and putting media freedom back on track was high on his agenda. Among his commissioner responsibilities is a Charter of Fundamental Rights and he acknowledges that the crisis in the European media industry is affecting journalists' rights, jobs and journalism as a public good (EFJ 2014). The comments by Timmermans reflect a worldwide crisis affecting journalism in democratic societies, which has also seriously eroded the quality of journalism and media pluralism in Fiji's southern neighbours, Australia and New Zealand. 'Support for professional and good quality journalism must go hand in hand with transparent media ownership to regain trust in the media', remarked Timmermans (EFJ 2014*)*.

My most recent book, *Don't Spoil My Beautiful Face: Media, Mayhem and Human Rights in the Pacific* (Robie 2014b), explored issues of media freedom and credibility in the Asia Pacific region and argued for a critical development journalism approach. The book included Fiji in the lead-up to the elections and offered several models on how a more vigorous brand of journalism, tempered by responsibility as a public good, could be achieved. This is not an isolated plea for better political journalism. Other authors, such as journalism educator Dr Angela Romano (2010) with her edited work on case studies on international journalism and democracy with 'civil engagement models', and Kunda Dixit (2010) have canvased parallel concepts. Both argue for the empowerment of citizens. Even in a specifically

Fijian context, the head of journalism at the University of the South Pacific, Dr Shailendra Singh, and current opposition parliamentary finance and media spokesman Professor Biman Prasad, have argued along similar lines (Singh & Prasad 2008).

Removing the elephant in the room—the Media Decree—is not enough. While arguing in my book that Pacific journalists now have a greater task than ever in encouraging 'democratisation' of the region, including Fiji, and seeking solutions (p. 339), I identified the poor education of many journalists working in Fijian newsrooms and the constant creaming off of university journalism graduates to more highly paid regional and international non-government organisation jobs: 'This continual loss of staff makes it very difficult to achieve stable and consistent editorial standards and policies' (Robie 2014b, p. 345).

Ricardo Morris also identifies the 'brain drain' of journalists since the coups as damaging for the media industry. 'The majority of young journalists in Fiji today have never worked in a completely free media environment', he laments (Morris 2015, p. 38). 'Many have grown up in a dictatorship and the repressive environment that it entails for the media and have known nothing else.' Now, more than ever, Fiji needs journalists who not only know their craft, but have the critical and analytical skills provided at the university-based journalism schools, such as the University of the South Pacific and Fiji National University, to have the self-confidence to be truly committed public-good journalists in a partially revived democracy.

In January 2015, barely four months after the elections, opposition National Federation Party leader Professor Biman Prasad called for an end to the eight-year-long 'siege' of the nation's news media and for the contentious Media Decree to be repealed. He declared that Fiji's social, economic and political future could not be guaranteed unless there was free expression through a 'free, fair and credible media'. He also made a plea for enacting the Freedom of Information Bill.

> Where is the balance and fairness government is preaching about? Where is the accountability? ... [s. 22 which prohibits publishing material against the public interest or order] is like a noose around the media's neck. This provision is unnecessary because offences are already adequately covered under [the] Crimes Decree [and] under the Public Order Act on racial and religious vilification, hate speech and economic sabotage. (PMW9104 2015)

Three months later, Dr Prasad steered an opposition motion in Parliament seeking a repeal or review of the Media Decree (Narayan 2015). Although it was defeated 17-24, with nine abstentions, the motion succeeded in opening a wider national debate and challenging the validity of the military-backed law, which has had such a shackling impact on the media. Dr Prasad described the Fiji media in his motion speech as having been 'under siege' since the 2006 coup, and the mediascape had been 'turbulent and devastating' since the imposition of the Media Decree. Except for a brief period after the 1987 coups, the work of the media had been 'remarkable, balanced, informative and impartial'. 'The Decree is regressive and suppresses media freedom because it imposes restrictions and prescribes heavy penalties', he said (Prasad 2015, p. 2). '[It] must be repealed or amended substantially because we believe the media should not be regulated by the state or any government. The restoration of democracy has seen little change in the behavior of large sections of our media and individual journalists … as a result of the severe penalties.'

References

ABC News 2014, 'Fiji to set up media monitor ahead of election', 27 March. Viewed 9 December 2014 at www.abc.net.au/news/2014-03-26/fiji-media-monitor/5347638.

ABC Pacific Beat 2015, 'Fiji media changes not enough to lift censorship', 13 July. Viewed 2 December 2015 at www.abc.net.au/news/2015-07-13/fiji-media-changes-not-enough-to-lift-censorship/6614676.

Anneberg, M 2014, 'MIDA defends Bainimarama's "buckle up" billboard as within Fiji election rules', Pacific Scoop, 15 September. Viewed 12 December 2014 at pacific.scoop.co.nz/2014/09/mida-defends-bainimaramas-buckle-up-billboard-as-within-fiji-election-rules/.

Ben Zion, I 2014, 'Israel TV: UN had Qatar pay $25m ransom to free Golan peacekeepers', The Times of Israel [Online], 10 October. Viewed 16 December 2014 at www.timesofisrael.com/report-qatar-paid-nusra-front-25m-ransom-to-free-un-golan-hostages/.

Bhim, M 2015, 'FIJI: "Stifled aspirations": The 2014 general election under restrictive laws'. *Pacific Journalism Review*, vol. 21, no. 1, pp. 108–25. Viewed 2 December 2015 at search.informit.com.au/documentSummary;dn=244748207892188;res=IELHSS.

CCF (Citizens' Constitutional Forum) 2013, 'An analysis: 2013 Fiji Government Constitution'. Viewed 5 December 2014 at news.ccf.org.fj/wp-content/uploads/2013/10/CCFS-CONSTITUTION-ANALYSIS1.pdf.

Dateline Pacific 2014, 'Fiji Media Industry Development Authority pleased with industry', Radio New Zealand International [Audio interview], 10 January. Accessed 9 December 2014 at www.radionz.co.nz/international/programmes/datelinepacific/20140110.

Dixit, D 2010, *Dateline Earth: Journalism as if the planet mattered,* IPS Asia-Pacific, Bangkok.

Drageset, D 2013, 'New MIDA director attacks NZ, Australia for 'dictating' to Fiji media', Pacific Media Watch (PMW), 30 September. Accessed 9 December 2014 at www.pmc.aut.ac.nz/pacific-media-watch/fiji-new-mida-director-attacks-nz-australia-dictating-fiji-media-8422.

EFJ (European Federation of Journalists) 2014, 'EC First Vice-President backs journalists to defend quality journalism and reinstall journalism as a public good', European Journalists, 28 November. Accessed 14 December 2014 at europeanjournalists.org/blog/2014/11/28/ec-first-vice-president-backs-journalists-to-promote-quality-journalism-and-reinstall-journalism-as-a-public-good/.

Field, M 2013, 'Fiji TV editor "quits over criticism"', Stuff.co.nz., 19 June. Viewed 9 December 2014 at www.stuff.co.nz/world/south-pacific/8815729/Fiji-TV-editor-quits-over-criticism.

Fiji Sun 2014, 'Death threats for women journalists', 10 September. Viewed 5 December 2014 at fijisun.com.fj/2014/09/10/death-threats-for-women-journalists/.

Fijian Government 2010, 'Media Industry Development Decree 2010 [Decree No. 29 of 2010]', *Government of Fiji Gazette*, vol. 11, no. 69. Viewed 5 December 2014 at www.pmc.aut.ac.nz/sites/default/files/file_bin/201010/Decree%2029%20%20Media%20Industry%20Development%20Decree.pdf.

Fijian Government 2014, 'Electoral Decree 2014 [Decree No. 11 of 2014]', *Government of Fiji Gazette*, vol. 15, no. 28. Viewed 13 December 2014 at www.electionsfiji.gov.fj/wp-content/uploads/2014/03/Electoral-Decree-2014.pdf.

Fox, L 2014, 'Fiji opposition groups say intimidation, lack of coverage means September polls won't be free and fair', ABC News, 6 June. Viewed 11 December 2014 at www.abc.net.au/news/2014-06-05/an-fiji-opposition-groups-say-elections-won27t-be-free-and-fair/5501788.

HRW (Human Rights Watch) 2014, 'Fiji: Candidates' positions on rights in spotlight'. Viewed 12 December 2014 at www.hrw.org/news/2014/09/07/fiji-candidates-positions-rights-spotlight.

IFJ (International Federation of Journalists) 2014, 'IFJ condemns media blackout in Fiji', [Media release]. Viewed 13 December 2014 at www.ifj.org/nc/news-single-view/backpid/33/article/ifj-condemns-media-blackout-in-fiji-before-election/.

Loanakadavu, N 2013, 'Times fined $300,000', *The Fiji Times* [Online], 21 February 2013. Viewed 9 December 2014 at www.fijitimes.com/story.aspx?id=225792.

MIDA (Media Industry Development Authority) 2014, 'Local, international & freelance media registered for Fijian elections 2014 coverage as of 15/9/14' [Statement]. See also: '450 media workers to cover Fiji's 2014 election' (15 September 2014), *República*. Viewed 13 December 2014 at republikamagazine.com/2014/09/450-media-workers-to-cover-fijis-2014-election/.

Morris, R 2014, 'Fiji media regulation: Emerging from "worst of time" to "best of times"', *Pacific Media Centre Online* [Online], 1 December. Viewed 12 December 2014 at www.pmc.aut.ac.nz/articles/fiji-media-regulation-emerging-worst-times-best-times.

Morris, R 2015, 'Fiji media regulation: emerging from "worst of times" to "best of times"'. *Pacific Journalism Review*, vol. 21, no. 1, pp. 34–39.

Nandan, S 2014, 'Media freedom with integrity and ethics', *Pacific Journalism Review*, vol. 20, no. 2, pp. 17–22. Republished from *República Online*.

Narayan, V 2015, 'FIJI: Opposition MP's bid to repeal Media Decree defeated', 16 May. Viewed 27 June 2015 at www.pmc.aut.ac.nz/pacific-media-watch/fiji-opposition-mps-bid-repeal-media-decree-defeated-9276.

Narsey, W 2014, 'MIDA chairman changes his tune. Wadan Narsey on Fiji – for fairness and freedom' [Weblog], 19 November. Viewed 11 December 2014 at narseyonfiji.wordpress.com/2014/11/19/mida-chairman-changes-his-tune-19-nov-2014/.

PACMAS (Pacific Media Assistance Scheme) 2013, 'State of Media and Communication Report'. Viewed 11 December 2014 at www.pacmas.org/profile/pacmas-state-of-media-and-communication-report-2013/.

Parmar, S 2014, 'Ending a culture of impunity in Fiji', Human Rights Watch, 25 September. Viewed 12 December 2014 at www.hrw.org/news/2014/09/25/ending-culture-impunity-fiji.

PIR (Pacific Islands Report) 2014, 'Fiji yet to fully respond to UN Human Rights Review', Pacific Islands Development Program, East-West Centre, November 3. Viewed 11 December 2014 at pidp.eastwestcenter.org/pireport/2014/November/11-03-02.htm.

PMC (Pacific Media Centre Newsdesk) 2014, 'Fiji media blackout penalties "unduly harsh", says NZ news watchdog', *Pacific Scoop*, 15 September. Viewed 12 December 2014 at pacific.scoop.co.nz/2014/09/fiji-media-blackout-penalties-unduly-harsh-says-nz-news-watchdog/.

PMW8385 (Pacific Media Watch) 2013, 'Rights advocacy group has "grave concerns" over media freedom court case', 19 August. Viewed 12 December 2014 at www.pmc.aut.ac.nz/pacific-media-watch/fiji-rights-advocacy-group-has-grave-concerns-over-media-freedom-court-case-8385.

PMW8955 (Pacific Media Watch) 2014a, 'Don't use social media to incite violence, pleads MIDA chair', 10 September. Viewed 9 December 2014 at www.pmc.aut.ac.nz/pacific-media-watch/fiji-dont-use-social-media-incite-violence-pleads-mida-chair-8955.

PMW9034 (Pacific Media Watch) 2014b, 'MIDA accuses Al Jazeera and RNZ of racist reporting', 30 October. Viewed 12 December 2014 at www.pmc.aut.ac.nz/pacific-media-watch/fiji-mida-accuses-al-jazeera-and-rnz-racist-reporting-9034.

PMW9062 (Pacific Media Watch) 2014c, 'Media authority changes tune on "racism" allegation', 24 November. Viewed 12 December 2014 at www.pmc.aut.ac.nz/pacific-media-watch/fiji-media-authority-changes-tune-racism-allegation-9062.

PMW9104 (Pacific Media Watch) 2015, 'FIJI: Opposition calls for send to "siege" of media, repeal post-coup law', 15 January. www.pmc.aut.ac.nz/pacific-media-watch/fiji-opposition-calls-end-siege-media-repeal-post-coup-law-9104.

Prasad, Biman, 2015, 'Debate on motion to repeal or amend the Media Decree 2010', Speech by the opposition National Federation Party leader Professor Biman Prasad, 15 May. Viewed 26 June 2015 at www.pmc.aut.ac.nz/sites/default/files/file_bin/201505/NFP%20 LEADER%20-%20MEDIA%20DECREE%20MOTION%20 150515.pdf.

Pratt, RJF n.d., 'The Media Decree', [Discussion paper believed to have been written in 2011 by the former Executive Secretary of the Fiji Media Council and provided by him to the author in correspondence, 27 January 2015].

Robie, D 2009, 'Behind the Fiji censorship: A comparative media regulatory case study as a prelude to the Easter putsch', *Pacific Journalism Review*, vol. 15, no. 2, pp. 85–116. Viewed 9 December 2014 at www.pjreview.info/issues/behind-fiji-censorship-comparative-media-regulatory-case-study-prelude-easter-putsch.

Robie, D 2014a, 'Fiji pre-election 'politics' blackout stirs media protests, frustration', *Café Pacific,* 15 September. Viewed 12 December 2014 at cafepacific.blogspot.co.nz/2014/09/fiji-pre-elections-politics-blackout.html.

Robie, D 2014b, *Don't spoil my beautiful face: Media, mayhem and human rights in the Pacific*. Little Island Press, Auckland.

Romano, A (ed.) 2010, *International journalism and democracy: civic engagement models from around the world*. Routledge, London and New York.

RSF (Reporters Sans Frontières/Reporters Without Borders) 2014a, '2014 World Press Freedom Index'. Viewed 12 December 2014 at rsf.org/index2014/en-index2014.php.

RSF (Reporters Sans Frontières/Reporters Without Borders) 2014b, *Universal Periodic Review: Pacific Media Centre and RSF Written Submission*, UN Human Rights Council Universal Periodic Review – 19th session, 11 September 2014. Co-authors: Hélène Sackstein, Benjamin Ismail and Dr David Robie. Viewed 5 December 2014 at en.rsf.org/fiji-universal-periodic-review-pacific-11-09-2014,46934. html.

RSF (Reporters Sans Frontières/Reporters Without Borders) 2014c, 'Authorities ban all electoral coverage 48 hours ahead of historic poll', 16 September. Viewed 13 December 2014 at en.rsf.org/fiji-authorities-ban-all-election-16-09-2014,46965.html.

RSF (Reporters Sans Frontières/Reporters Without Borders) 2014d, 'Two women threatened during Fiji election campaign', 11 September. Viewed 9 December 2014 at en.rsf.org/fiji-two-women-journalists-threatened-11-09-2014,46928.html.

RSF (Reporters Sans Frontières/Reporters Without Borders) 2015, 'RSF World Freedom Index'. Viewed 2 December 2015 at index. rsf.org/#!/.

Singh, S and Prasad, B 2008, 'Media, democracy and development in Fiji: The last 20 years' [Special edition], *Fijian Studies: A Journal of Contemporary Fiji*, vol. 6, nos 1 & 2.

Slater, C 2014, 'Fiji election: Clear win for Bainimarama', *Whale Oil* [Blog], 18 September. Viewed 2 December 2015 at www.whaleoil. co.nz/2014/09/fiji-election-clear-win-bainimarama/.

Spasifik 2014, Spring, 'Setting the standard in student journalism', Viewed 16 December 2014 at www.spasifikmag.com.

Stewart, A 2014, 'Fiji's election: Fair and free?', *The Interpreter*, 11 September. Viewed 11 December 2014 at www.lowyinterpreter. org/post/2014/09/11/Fijis-Elections-A-step-forwards. aspx?COLLCC=2390445858&.

Vuru, A 2014, 'Relief as Fijian soldiers freed in Syria', *Mailife*. Viewed 16 December 2014 at www.mailife.com.fj/relief-as-fijian-soldiers-freed-in-syria/.

Walsh, C 2010, 'Political blogs on Fiji: A "cybernet democracy" case study', *Pacific Journalism Review*, vol. 16, no. 1, pp. 154–77. Viewed 12 December 2014 at www.pjreview.info/articles/political-blogs-fiji-cybernet-democracy-case-study-572.

Weaver, M 2014, 'Militant group releases UN peacekeepers held hostage in Syria', *The Guardian* [Online], 11 September. Viewed 16 December 2014 at www.theguardian.com/world/2014/sep/11/jabhat-al-nusra-releases-hostages-fijian-syria.

6

From the land to the sea: Christianity, community and state in Fiji—and the 2014 elections

Lynda Newland

Introduction

Much has changed since I left Fiji in December 2012, at a time when the Yash Ghai constitution was rejected by the government. A group led by the attorney-general, Aiyaz Sayed-Khaiyum, drew up a new constitution, notable for its affirmation of secularism, in 2013. The then president of the Methodist Church, Tuikilakila Waqairatu, began a review of the Methodist constitution to ensure that the church could not be used as a vehicle for political mobilisation, but passed away six months after his ordination in February 2014 (Rasoqosoqo 2013, 2014; Tawake 2013). In the lead-up to the general elections, Waqairatu's successor, Tevita Nawadra Banivanua, affirmed that ministers of the Methodist Church could no longer participate in politics without resigning from their positions (Talebula 2014). Outside the Methodist Church, debate about the significance of secularism for Fiji began to flow freely, reflected in an explosion of postings in the social media and Internet services, despite the restrictions on the regular media. The victory by Voreqe (Frank) Bainimarama and his FijiFirst party ensured that secularism in one of its forms was institutionalised, guaranteed by the Constitution.

In effect, the 2014 elections marked a threshold to a potentially radical transformation in the style of Fiji governance that the military government has developed since the 2006 coup. At the same time, the leadership of the Methodist Church, a key institution in which ethnic and religious nationalism has flourished in the past, has undertaken reforms begun by Waqairatu. In this chapter, I explore the religious climate in which Fiji's 2014 elections took place; and, in particular, I chart the relationship between the Bainimarama Government, the Methodist Church, and some of the other Christian churches to show the evolving politics of religion in Fiji. In doing so, I note the way the *vanua* (land and community) has come to be used in contemporary rhetoric; the continuing use of the motif of Exodus to describe Methodist Taukei experience, albeit in a theology that is shifting from the land (*vanua*) to the ocean (*moana*); and the fact that, although Christianity is diverse in Fiji, many Taukei Christians share conceptions about an active relationship between the Taukei community, church and the state.[1]

The Methodist Church of Fiji and the military government

At least since 1987 and until around 2009, the Methodist Church of Fiji represented the interests of a powerful section of the Taukei across most of the country. Broadly, these interests are commonly encapsulated in the formula known as 'the three pillars': *lotu* (denoting 'religion', particularly Methodism), *matanitu* (government and/or chiefly system) and *vanua* (the land and community) (Niukula 1994). *Lotu* and *vanua* are joined in idioms such as the nationalist maxim, *Noqu Kalou, noqu vanua* (My God, my land) (Ryle 2010; Tuwere 2002). The connection between God and the land is entrenched in the village

---

1 'Taukei' and 'Indo-Fijian' are the terms chosen for this publication. In 2010, it was decreed that indigenous Fijians be referred to as iTaukei (for its implications, see Newland 2013). The descendants of indentured labourers and other immigrants from India have variously been called Indo-Fijians and Fiji Indians, and since 2010 have been considered Fijians, but all these terms are inconsistently used, depending on the speakers and their contexts.

system, in which over half the Taukei population continue to live (Fiji Bureau of Statistics 2007).[2] Saturated with associations with land, the concept of *vanua* also signifies a community unified through kin ties and marriage rules, and connected with the land through *kava* ceremonies, agriculture and death rites.

From an early stage in the colonial history of Fiji, the church structure grew rather like a rhizome—from cell groups into districts under a connexional government (Baleiwaqa 2003), challenged only by the ancestral gods and Roman Catholicism, the latter which initially had little success (Kelly 1945). As the connexional government grew, Taukei nationalism was expressed through narratives about ancestral genealogies that came to be called the Kaunitoni Migration, and dissent from cult figures outside the church such as Navosavakadua and Apolosi Nawai, and their followers, who the colonial government frequently exiled and deported to other islands.

The Methodist Church of Fiji remained under British and then Australian administrative responsibility until the 1960s, when the administration was localised and the first local president appointed. As Taukei began to move towards the urban areas, the Methodist Church became the space in which politics were discussed (Halapua 2003). At the same time, indigenisation of the church was encouraged to reflect Taukei values and understandings of Christianity rather than Australian or European interpretations and despite the fact that the church also had an Indian Division (Tippett 1980). Although this indigenisation of the church aimed towards postcolonial self-determination, it also created the conditions through which conservative and traditionalist Taukei values would come to be used to mobilise support for the Taukei elite.

For the 20-year period after the church's independence in 1964, the presidents of the Methodist Church were moderates who endorsed ecumenism and multiracialism. They seemed to reflect a liberal mood in the church, to the extent of electing an Indo-Fijian president in 1977 (Weir 2015, p. 66). However, influenced by the politician Sakeasi

---

2   These figures are contentious given that the urban/rural divide is not clear in Fiji because many Taukei live in villages even within urban centres; mobility between rural villages and urban centres is high; local observations suggest that urbanisation has increased in the years since the 2007 census; and most Taukei identify themselves as belonging to the village of their ancestors even if they have not returned there for several generations.

Butadroka, and legitimated largely in relation to the strengthening political and demographic position of the Indo-Fijian population, Taukei nationalism grew increasingly strident. As has now been extensively documented, in 1987 Sitiveni Rabuka, a military colonel, overthrew the newly elected Indo-Fijian-dominated government led by Dr Timoci Bavadra, a Taukei commoner. Reverend Manasa Lasaro, a nationalist Methodist minister, led a parallel coup in the church and persuaded Rabuka to enact a Sunday ban that prohibited all commercial activities on Sundays, reflecting a transition to a particular kind of Christian state. Although the Sunday ban was eventually lifted, Rabuka became the Prime Minister of Fiji under the Constitution adopted in 1990 (e.g. Ernst 2004; Garrett 1990). He governed until 1999, when he lost the elections to the Indo-Fijian trade unionist, Mahendra Chaudhry.

Nationalist Taukei concerns centred on the theme of losing the land and with it the Taukei community's place in the world. The threat of losing the land was largely a fiction because Taukei land ownership was protected in the Constitution; but the idea of loss, combined with the two-fold meanings of *vanua* as land and community resonated deeply with many Taukei communities. Moreover, such concerns were preached from the pulpit in a direct analogy with the biblical teachings of Exodus and God's promise of land. One investigative documentary of the period shows Rabuka in his role as lay preacher, preaching both in English and Fijian from the book of Jeremiah:

> The words of Jeremiah the prophet, Lamentations Chapter 5. Remember oh Lord, what has happened to us. Look at us and see our disgrace. Our property is in the hands of strangers. Foreigners are living in our homes. Our fathers have been killed by the enemy and now our mothers are widows. Driven hard like donkeys or camels we are tired but are allowed no rest. (Rabuka in Walmsley 1987)

The use of Jeremiah reinforced the connection between *lotu* and *vanua* in a prophecy of loss—and, although land was a central concern, the prophecy was also about community and its relationship with God.[3] Implicit in the suggestion of community was the sense of an upset to Taukei tradition involving the correct ordering of the 'three pillars' of

---

3   Tomlinson discusses the Taukei sense of loss and diminishment in relation to the concept of *mana* on the island of Kadavu (Tomlinson 2006). In Suva, loss and diminishment has been associated directly with racial relations and contestation for political power and land.

Taukei society between *vanua, lotu* and *matanitu*. This order includes ideas about clear hierarchies from chiefs and churchmen down to the husbands and fathers of households; and about the attainments of a masculinity linked with a romanticised notion of the physicality of the Taukei warrior past and expressed through the *kava* ceremony, rugby and the norms of the patriarchal Methodist family, including adult heterosexuality and the obedience of wives and children to husbands, fathers and chiefs. In Rabuka's rhetoric, all this was threatened by a multiracial and multi-religious society.

A businessman, George Speight, led the next coup in 2000. While race was obviously a major issue, the 2000 coup also reflected the tensions between Taukei Christian churches, clans and institutions across Fiji. In response, the Methodist Church met with a number of Pentecostal churches after the coup to unify Fijians under an umbrella organisation called the Assembly of Christian Churches in Fiji (ACCF), with the vision of creating a Christian state (Newland 2006; 2007). In the ACCF version, Fiji is represented as a possession of God that would be treasured if ACCF members honoured and glorified Him by uniting and living in a correct relationship with Him (which is perceived in terms of loving and fearing God and being prepared to reconcile with each other) (Newland 2007, p. 306). Those who were not Christians were to be tolerated, providing they also lived by Christian values and acknowledged that they were guests in a Taukei country. Two implications of this theology stand out: the idea that the *vanua* was no longer simply a network of kin in a specific geographical area but was now considered concomitant with the nation-state of Fiji; and the legitimation of a racial hierarchy within Fiji in which Taukei continued to have paramountcy. Despite a greater tolerance of other races than was expressed in 1987, the ACCF leadership did not aspire towards any form of equity or equality with Hindu and Muslim Indo-Fijians, many of whom descended from the indentured labourers brought out from India in the 19th century. Likewise, secularism was not viewed as neutral because it challenged the Taukei nationalist ideas of paramountcy. This was legitimated by the notion that, if society is secular, God is absent (cf. Weir 2015).

In 2009, the Constitution was abrogated for the third time in 20 years, ostensibly to make way for the military's large-scale political, economic and social transformations. Three years later, a constitution commission led by academic Professor Yash Ghai wrote a draft constitution based on submissions from across Fiji.[4] While moderate Taukei argued for the retention of a Christian identity that tolerated others, many of the Taukei submissions showed a desire for a Christian state based on the patriarchal family form and on the continuation of Taukei paramountcy within the nation-state (Newland 2013). Although this was clearly an aggravation for Bainimarama and his government, the reasons the draft constitution ultimately proved unacceptable were because it required the Bainimarama Government to step down six months before the elections, it did not grant full and unconditional immunity, and court proceedings begun before interference from the regime could be revived (Narsey 2013).

In the meantime, the Bainimarama Government had begun court proceedings against the Methodist leaders, including the then president Tuikilakila Waqairatu and three former presidents well known for their ethno-religious nationalist inclinations: Ame Tugawe, Tomasi Kanailagi and Manasa Lasaro. They were charged for holding a meeting allegedly in breach of the Public Emergency Regulation in 2009. Where the position of various leaders of the Methodist Church had been ambiguous throughout 2012, Waqairatu realised that he had to counter the repressive tactics of the Bainimarama Government to avoid the church being deregistered. He began a review of the Methodist Church's constitution, which included the conditions that ministers must resign in order to contest elections and that no support for any coup would be tolerated (Rasoqosoqo 2013). From then on, Banivanua appeared in the media regularly to confirm that the Methodist Church would no longer play a political role or be aligned to any political party but would focus on the spiritual life of its members, family support groups and education. The church circuits were directed to avoid politics and to uphold the principle that church members had the right to join any political party. Church ministers who wanted to stand at the elections would be asked to resign but could reapply if they did not succeed at the elections (e.g. Bolatiki 2013; Tawake 2013). This attempt to engineer a massive top-down shift in Methodist nationalist thought failed to halt the court case, which was still in process in 2014 when Waqairatu passed away (Kate 2014).

---

4   For a discussion of this Constitution, see Kant & Rakuita 2014.

Although the church appeared to fully concede to the military government's demands, it was reported that 'while the church would be apolitical, they would make comments on some political decisions that affect the church' (Bolatiki 2013). In the lead-up to the 2014 elections, Banivanua confirmed in an interview that the church had to accept that Fiji was now defined as a secular state, but stated that they would continue to pursue their Christian principles in relation to the way that they viewed the governing of Fiji (Radio New Zealand 2014). These comments show that, despite the move away from direct political action, the leaders of the Methodist Church in Fiji continue to regard themselves as legitimate voices of 'the people' and in particular their congregations (which are predominantly Taukei), and therefore that they have a role in representing them in the political domain. On this point, the Methodist Church does not stand alone. As will become evident, many Christian churches share this idea. In fact, elsewhere, particularly among the priests and ministers who follow liberation theology from the Roman Catholic Church and the Presbyterian Church, it is termed 'the prophetic voice' (Newland 2006).

Religious advice to voters

In the lead-up to the 2014 elections, several churches in very different relationships with the government and representing very different interpretations of Christianity were reported as advising their congregations on how to vote, including the Roman Catholic Church in Fiji, the New Methodist Church, and the Seventh Day Adventists (SDA). The leaders of the first two of these churches had close relationships with the Bainimarama Government in the first three years or so after the coup, although for very different reasons (see Newland 2009, 2012). By contrast, in 2005 the general secretary of the SDA, Usaia Baravi, explained to me that the SDA remained completely separate from issues of the state (Newland 2006)—which was possibly a strategy to distance the church from George Speight, the leader of the 2000 coup and a member of SDA. Yet all these churches wanted their adherents to vote for a 'godly' government that would make decisions on the basis of the scriptures—despite the fact that each interprets the scriptures very differently and accords certain parts of the scriptures more important than others.

After the coup in 2006, the Roman Catholic Church in Fiji supported the military government and participated in its Charter in the hope that this was an opportunity to overturn deep-seated structures in Fijian society: in particular, to neutralise the racist aspects of Taukei religious ethno-nationalism, and to reduce exploitation and poverty, especially for Indo-Fijians who had faced mass expulsion from the land at the end of their tenancies or who made up a significant portion of the working poor (Newland 2009). This focus is consistent with the church's interest in liberation theology, a theology in which political activity is considered justified if it overturns exploitative structures in favour of the poor. However, the church faced some difficult moments when social justice appeared to become expedient to other interests in government decisions, which has given rise to a number of misunderstandings. Within the first year of his ordination, Archbishop Peter Loy Chong showed misgivings about the way the secularism of the Constitution was described in terms of ensuring that religion was a private matter (Chandar 2013). In the lead-up to the 2014 elections, he urged 'Catholics to make informed voting decisions for the betterment of the country' (Swami 2014). According to Chong, the church should be apolitical but also has the responsibility of informing its members to help them make wise decisions 'based on the Scriptures and the teachings of the Church' (Swami 2014). Clearly, Chong was concerned about the balance between church and state; and, in particular, any limitations that might affect Catholic religious practice.

Another church that had taken the stage from 2008 to 2009 was the New Methodist Church, a breakaway from the Methodist Church that quickly became Pentecostal in style. Due largely to the fact that the head of the New Methodist Church, Atunaisa Vulaono, was the brother of the then head of the police force, Esala Teleni, this church became aligned with the state in an attempt to convert the police force to Christianity as part of the fight against crime. For the military government, supporting this church had the advantage of undermining the hegemonic presence and public centrality of the Methodist Church. However, tensions rose over the New Methodist's evangelical activities, such as requiring police to perform on stage as part of its community outreach regardless of whether they were Christian or Hindu, the weekly evangelical sermons in the centre of Suva city, and the fact that a significant amount of the community policing budget was spent on these activities. Finally, the New Methodists fell out of favour with the government, but they continue to rally support from the youth (Newland 2012).

In April 2014, the New Methodists held a rally in Labasa that attracted 1,200 members drawn primarily from nine youth groups around the northern islands of Fiji. Vulaono gave a sermon, reminding 'church members of God's place in the September elections' (Taleitaki 2014). The report quotes him as saying:

'We need God before the upcoming elections; every district, province and the nation needs God's judgement as He alone knows best.'

He further said the general election needed God's intervention as He alone knew the future and what was good and best for Fiji.

The nation, he said, needed people to take the nation to greener pastures for the betterment of its people. (Taleitaki 2014)

Vulaono's statement clearly goes much further than asking its adherents to make a decision about voting for political candidates based on whether their policies are consistent with the teachings of the scriptures: it reflects the idea that God stands above the processes of democracy—in a way that does not sound very different from that promoted by the Assembly of Christian Churches in Fiji from 2001 to 2006 (Newland 2007). With God represented as guide and judge, Taukei are likened to the biblical Jews; but, here, God's intervention is required not for personal salvation but to save the nation. Given the intensity of the New Methodist Church's evangelical activity, it is clear that they do not envisage a multi-religious nation-state but one that is wholly converted to Christianity.

The Seventh Day Adventists (SDA) brought 150 female leaders together at a meeting in Suva to offer advice about voting. After being divided into small groups to pray, the women were read a letter from the church head, advising them against voting for relatives or for candidates on the basis of their or their party's work, but rather for the candidate who can champion God's will and ensure God's will is done on earth (*FijiLive* 2014). They were told to vote according to eight principles, which included striving to elect leaders who are led by God. Candidates who violated biblical commands about life, family, marriage and faith should be avoided. All members should vote in order to promote, protect and preserve godly government (*FijiLive* 2014). The letter continued:

> In our day and age, there are many who want to drive the name and message of Christ completely out of the public arena. Voting is an opportunity to promote, protect, and preserve godly government. Passing up that opportunity means letting those who would denigrate the name of Christ have their way in our lives. (*FijiLive* 2014)

Although SDA is a very different church from the New Methodists and has sought to separate its activities from politics, it is clear that they also seek a government that would promote the presence of Christianity in government, without which the people of Fiji would face a moral void.

While all three churches were advising their members to vote according to the scriptures, their intentions were very different. In the Catholic Church in Fiji, the scriptures were being interpreted from the perspective of liberation theology in an attempt to bring just social structures to the poor without racial prejudice. Secularism was a threat only if it limited the capacity of the church membership to publicly express their religion. By contrast, Vulaono's vision of Fiji is about making Fiji entirely Christian, therefore guaranteeing Taukei privilege—a vision very similar to that of the ACCF. Secularism would inhibit the capacity to evangelise and convert others. The SDA provides a third contrast because, as noted above, it has attempted to avoid any relationship with politics in the past, viewing it as a likely arena for the final deception of Satan (Newland 2006). However, in the lead-up to the 2014 elections, the SDA leadership was clearly seeking a champion of Christianity to reject secularism because it implied a moral void. Although these three visions are very different, the fact that they and possibly many more Christian churches in Fiji do distribute advice on voting shows that they view their churches as a space through which to reflect upon the government under which they live, and are actively working towards a government that reflects the values of these church communities as closely as possible.

Indeed, the Methodist Church was also, rather belatedly, reported as attempting to influence its adherents. After Bainimarama's government won the elections, the *Fiji Sun*—known to be the mouthpiece for the Bainimarama Government—claimed that a letter had been circulated to the divisions of the Methodist Church (with the exception of the Republic of Fiji Military Forces) circuit only a fortnight before the elections, instructing congregations to vote for the predominantly Taukei SODELPA (Social Democratic Liberal Party). According to this report, Iliesa Naivalu, the secretary of the Department of Christian Citizenship and Social Services of the Methodist Church, wrote the letter in Fijian asking the leaders of the division to advise members to 'think before you vote. Don't be swayed by the look of the party and the candidates. Don't be swayed also by the developments carried out and the promises made on what they would do if elected to govern' (Bolatiki 2014). The letter strongly opposed Fiji becoming a secular state instead of a Christian state and asked for the return of the Ghai constitution, which it considered as the voice of the people. It also claimed the church was concerned with the deterioration of the Taukei position in state bureaucracy, including the weakening of Taukei Affairs, the cessation of the Great Council of Chiefs, and changes in leadership and representatives on the Taukei Affairs Board and, finally, the redistribution of scholarships. As many of these issues were the same as those in SODELPA's manifesto, the other major party contesting the elections, Bainimarama accused SODELPA of lying and dictating to congregations what they should believe in (Bolatiki 2014).

Banivanua, now the President of the Methodist Church, responded not by publishing the letter but by posting an open letter on the church's blogsite.[5] Explaining that he was unaware of the letter's contents until the media response, Banivanua pointed out that the Department of Christian Citizenship and Social Issues was established to provide members with information about the church's position on current issues. The issues raised in the letter were based on resolutions that had been deliberated and voted on at the 2014 Methodist Annual Conference. They needed to be disseminated so that members could reflect on them before they voted. Banivanua further explained that, although Naivalu was writing in a theological context rather than a political and adversarial one, an internal policy for communication

---

5   Rather strangely to the outsider, the letter begins by welcoming Jewish and Hindu adherents and their festivals. There are very few Jews in Fiji, although a number of Christian sects claim they are descended directly from the Lost Tribes of Israel and many Taukei certainly view the Israelites romantically (see, e.g. Karavaki 2014). The inclusion of both Jews and Hindus in the same welcome suggests that he was welcoming both Taukei and Indians.

would be introduced (Banivanua 2014a).[6] He then noted that a policy on multi-faith worship had not yet been developed as the church did not want to compromise on doctrinal beliefs and tradition. He finished with:

> The Church is beginning her new exodus, our *Lako Yani Vou* [new Exodus], just as our nation is embarking on a new democracy. Just as we pray for our nation and our government, we seek your prayers for us. (Banivanua 2014a)

By drawing on Exodus and Jeremiah, who also spoke of a new exodus or covenant, Banivanua depicted a new order in which church and state have been separated and in which the leaders and their communities had to find their own ways.

The letter was also posted on Facebook, to which Nikotemo Sopepa, Moderator of the Presbyterian Church of Fiji, replied:

> This time-round the church should not be intimidated by the State but speak what is true, what is democratic (voices of the people). I believe the State also needs to be educated on the role of the church in the community. We attend not only to the spiritual welfare of the community we serve, but also the whole sphere of their living (political included). If the church fails to do this, it will lose its calling to serve the community. I agree that Church and State must be separated, but i [sic] totally disagree with the State trying to intimidate the church through/by coercive means – that is not democracy. (Sopepa 2014)

This comment was 'liked' by Pacific Youth Council and Pacific Conference of Churches, among others, and reflects the idea that Christian churches have a role to play as representatives of their communities is widespread among Taukei. Moreover, this role is viewed to be necessarily political, whether that is represented in terms of social justice for the many (the Roman Catholic view) or the legitimation of the moral right of an indigenous community (the nationalist Methodist view).

---

6   The Methodist leadership had declined an invitation to an Interfaith Thanksgiving Service organised by the PM's Office on the release of the 45 Fijian UN peacekeepers who had been held hostage by an al Qaeda-related organisation. Banivanua explained that, as this service was to be held on the day before the elections, Methodist leaders were concerned because it 'may be construed as a political event' (Banivanua, 2014a).

However, of concern to any government that attempts to promote a plural society in Fiji, the call for a Christian state or a godly government or even a government based exclusively on Christian principles is also a call for the state to be run by the Taukei and not Hindu or Muslim Indo-Fijians. That almost all Taukei are Christian, that Taukei are a majority in Fiji, and that this Christian message was propagated throughout the Christian churches suggests that this is more than a passing concern.

SODELPA, Christianity and the elections

Although the leaders of the Methodist Church of Fiji knew that their public face had to be apolitical and that they could not be seen to be aligned with any one political party, political parties did not necessarily share the idea that church and state should be separate. SODELPA, headed by Ro Teimumu Kepa,[7] represented itself as the legitimate successor of SDL (Soqosoqo Duavata ni Levenivanua or United Fiji Party)—the party that was elected and ousted from government in 2006 (SODELPA 2014a, p. 45). SDL had been sympathetic to the notion that Fiji should be a Christian state and that the Taukei should retain a privileged position in the governance of the state, and SODELPA retained these ideas, although with some contestation from younger members.

In fact, there were at least two contrasting positions on the ideal relationship between church and state in Fiji, both of which have been published on SODELPA's Facebook page. The first, which appeared on 18 July 2014, has been shared and remains there still. In it was a set of bullet points that noted the 2013 Constitution declared Fiji a secular state, which therefore signified the Constitution is a godless Constitution that has ignored the role of Christianity in the development of Fiji (SODELPA 2014b). SODELPA was concerned with the teaching and practice of religious faiths in schools and especially about school prayer and similar controversies about religious devotions during government functions (SODELPA 2014b). When this statement was posted it attracted 24 'likes' and it received another 61 'likes'

7   Ro Teimumu Kepa was Deputy Prime Minister for the SDL government prior to the 2006 coup. She is also paramount chief of the Burebasaga confederacy and Catholic, but retains strong links with the Methodist Church.

THE PEOPLE HAVE SPOKEN

on a shared version. Almost all appeared to be from Taukei. A small number commented that the secular state was the thin end of the wedge and would lead to legalising same sex marriage; that, under Sayed-Khaiyum's influence, the state was becoming Muslim; and that Fiji's situation could be likened to biblical Israel when Muslims demolished the holy temple of Jerusalem. All of these comments reflect views associated with nationalist Taukei Methodism.

A second posting on 22 August reflected a very different perspective. In this posting, the argument made was that:

> SODELPA constitution and Manifesto do not call for a Christian State. What we say is that as a government, we will conduct ourselves based on Christian principles and values. These are values shared by all the world's great religions. We are commanded to love our neighbours and do to others as we would have them do to us. We are required to forgive and to be merciful. We must care for the poor, the sick, the homeless, the forgotten and those in need. We must seek truth and social justice. These are the principles and values by which we shall govern. (SODELPA 2014c)

The posting goes on to say that all religious groups should be free to practice their faith without fear or intimidation and that the Christian values of the party makes it more sensitive to respecting the values of others, thus reflecting the idea that Fiji draws its strength from the rich variety of traditions, languages and cultures of its communities (SODELPA 2014c). This post received 79 'likes'. Evidently, this posting suggests some diversity in the views of the SODELPA membership, albeit, perhaps too liberal for the mainstay of the party as it no longer appears on the official SODELPA Facebook page. The views espoused here match the first part of the SODELPA manifesto (also available online), which claims it will guarantee:

- The freedom, equality and dignity of all individuals as fellow citizens,
- The freedom and dignity of all religions and religious denominations;
- The equality and dignity of all communities, their freedom to promote their languages and customary practices, and the protection through appropriate legislation of their cultural heritage and intellectual property ... (SODELPA 2014a, p. 5).

However, the second part of the manifesto reverts to strongly nationalist Taukei interests, revealing a desire to reinstate the Great Council of Chiefs and the institutions for Taukei land. Clearly, the SODELPA leaders intended to focus on attaining the support of the nationalist Christian Taukei, but knew that would not be enough to win the elections.

As a government supporter, the *Fiji Sun* is known to be a vigilant critic of nationalist Taukei values. For instance, it reported that SODELPA member Semesa Karavaki proposed in Parliament that government should fund the teaching of the Ten Commandments in school, which, he argued, would end crime and all other social ills (Tuwere 2014).[8] On the one hand, although reminiscent of the New Right in the USA, the notion of teaching the Ten Commandments in school is not terribly extreme for Taukei Christians, because meetings in government departments in Fiji have often begun with Christian prayers. On the other hand, if the secular state might choose to remove prayers and religious teaching from schools, there was another issue of concern for SODELPA. Many Taukei schools in Fiji are private, religious schools (Methodist, Catholic, SDA, Pentecostal, etc.). If the government enforced the secular state, it was feared that the government would also then enforce a secular curriculum in these religious schools (SODELPA 2014a), to which SODELPA was unequivocally opposed.

If SODELPA seemed to be promoting the nationalist Taukei vision of a Christian Fiji, members of the Bainimarama Government have also attracted accusations of religious and communal favouritism, contrary to its aim of providing equal opportunities across social and ethnic division. Allegations have included the question of whether the Attorney-General, Aiyaz Sayed-Khaiyum, took out massive loans to support his brother's move to head the Fiji Broadcasting Corporation (Lal 2012). Rumours also targeted Muslim businessmen, alleging they had roles in the coup (Bola-Bari 2014). Certainly, the government's

---

8   A further example of the extent to which Karavaki identifies with such values can be found in his video on YouTube, *Noqu Kalou, Noqu Vanua*, which opens with a graphic showing a red line being drawn from Israel directly to Fiji (Karavaki 2014), a reference to the narrative of the Kaunitoni Migration that claims Taukei travelled from somewhere in Africa, possibly from the Holy Lands, to Fiji by canoe, and which suggests that Karavaki identifies strongly with nationalist Taukei Methodism.

post-election gift of FJD$12,000 towards a Muslim priest's house in Labasa (Drauna 2015) ignored the way that public perception might construe such a gift in terms of religious and therefore racial bias.

In this way, the intention to increase the distance between church and state in Fiji has been fraught with difficulties because not only do many people share the view that religious institutions should represent their adherents but also because government representatives frequently belong to religious communities they feel obliged to support in patron–client styles of relationship, or at least are represented as doing so.

Where the land ends and the sea begins …

Two years before the elections, the Fiji National Rugby League posted a message to Facebook that showed the extent to which the old maxims had retained their power. Simply by translating *Noqu Kalou, Noqu Vanua* as 'My God, my country' (Fiji National Rugby League 2012), the conception of the *vanua* was being used in such a way that its meaning had expanded from the description of a kin group the size of several villages to the borders of the nation-state.

Yet, the fact that SODELPA attracted less than 50 per cent of the Taukei vote in 2014 (Ratuva, this volume) suggests that the nationalist voice had been neutralised on the national stage quite effectively. Were Taukei voters turning away from SODELPA because of its support for Taukei institutions such as the Great Council of Chiefs and the protection of Taukei land, which is indicative of this nationalism? Certainly, the suggestion that increasing numbers of Taukei are rejecting nationalism has been posited as a reason for the Methodist Church of Fiji losing adherents (Weir 2015), but it is difficult to verify. The decline in Methodist Church numbers made the agenda of the 2014 conference, where it was recorded that membership had declined by 1,788 people in the year from 2013 to 2014 (Methodist Church in Fiji 2014). Although this is only a decline of 0.9 per cent (from 200,565 to 198,777), it appears that the Methodist Church is losing ground to other Christian denominations (Weir 2015). Yet, although Pentecostal churches offer profoundly different theologies to those of the Methodist Church, many retain conceptions of the paramountcy of the Taukei in the Fiji nation-state, Christianity's role in state affairs, and conservative forms of male leadership, Christian marriage and family. Therefore, conversion to Pentecostal Christianity is not by itself a convincing indicator that Taukei are rejecting the values underpinning nationalism.

A more likely reason for SODELPA's failure at the elections was that it reflected its failure to appeal to a broad section of the electorate. The manifesto *Reclaiming Fiji* attempts to channel and mobilise the resentments of all those who had been threatened and coerced since the military's takeover in 2006, including nationalist Taukei, Catholics, pro-democracy supporters, and feminist activists. However, this was a difficult, perhaps impossible, challenge because ultimately SODELPA's central party focus was to support the Taukei institutions of governance and land, which lie in opposition to other interests motivated by democracy and/or women's rights. Despite claims to the contrary, the nationalist vision excludes other races and other religious persuasions from holding full rights as equal citizens in nationhood. In addition, in spite of the fact that SODELPA's leader is a woman, the nationalist vision positions women without chiefly titles structurally as second to men at work and in their marital homes, and excludes homosexuals and transgender citizens. Further, even within the Taukei community that espouses nationalism, there are tensions about exactly what the ideal relationship between the *vanua*, *lotu* and *matanitu* should be (cf. Ryle 2010).

Taukei nationalism, whether in SODELPA or the Methodist Church, sits in opposition to what Weir calls 'universalism' (which, I would argue, refers to a liberal set of values, most of which originated in so-called Western countries) (Weir 2015). The inconsistencies in the SODELPA manifesto reflect the struggle among and between village-level notions of Methodism and international ideas of Methodism as they play out at the national level. However easy it is to support one side of the debate over the other, any solution for the Taukei community must lie, not in repression of the other side, but in a synthesis between indigenous and international ideas (in all their diversities) in a style particular to Fiji.

This is perhaps one of the undercurrents of a distinctive turn in current Methodist theology, away from the *vanua* and towards the *moana*, the ocean. From Epeli Hau'ofa's recasting of the Pacific Islands from specks in the sea to 'a sea of islands' (Hau'ofa 2008) to a rising interest in the

Pacific-designed and built double-hulled sailing boat or *drua*,[9] and the realisation that Pacific Islanders must face the destruction created by rising sea levels and climate change (Halapua 2008), theologians from many of the Pacific mainline churches are now turning to remembrances of the early sailors and their navigation of the ocean for new possibilities of hope and pride.

The new Exodus of the Methodist Church of Fiji

Central to the nationalist rhetoric was the notion that Fijians were like the Hebrews cast from their lands as depicted in Exodus and Jeremiah.[10] As President-elect of the Methodist Church of Fiji, Banivanua continued using these ideas, but central to his conception of the new Exodus facing the Methodist Church of Fiji is a sense of reflection:

> Moses speaks to the people of Israel as they prepare to enter the 'Promised Land' and asks them to look back at their 40-year journey through the wilderness and from being a rag-tag group of oppressed people to becoming a nation on the move, people who have made a collective covenant with God. (Banivanua 2014b)

After taking office as the President of the Methodist Church of Fiji in January 2015, Banivanua's ideas about the church's new exodus, *Na Lako Yani Vou*, were further elaborated at a meeting a couple of months later:

> For me one of the main questions that we should ask was: Why did God allow this to happen to a church that God had called to bring Christianity to this land in 1835?

> Like that pre-Exodus time, the Israelites were going through very difficult times at the hands of the Egyptians. Likewise in the pre-Babylonian exile period the Jewish people went through some very difficult times as well. Both these events were going on without the full knowledge of the Israelites of God's intention.

---

9   For example, seven drua were built in Auckland, New Zealand, for different trusts around the Pacific to encourage Pacific Islanders to continue or to revive their traditional boatbuilding and navigational skills (Pacific Voyagers n.d.)

10   See Newland 2015 for the development of this rhetoric.

> I believe that the same situation, faced by Israelites in the Exodus and after the Exile, is now faced by the Methodist Church in Fiji. (Baghwan 2015)

Here, Banivanua is appealing to the same community who felt they were losing their place in the nation-state in 1987 and 2000, but he consistently uses the notion of Exodus to reflect on the changes that need to come about in the Methodist Church, saying, 'the time had come to do some reordering of society and help people called Methodists in Fiji to renew, recreate, reinvent and rebuild, God's church' (Baghwan 2015). Central to this vision is ecumenism between Christian churches and building relationships with the Hindu and Muslim communities. He focuses on restoring 'a right relationship between us and God, a relationship based on love. The Methodist Church's building of relationships is part and parcel of our new journey, the *Lako Yani Vou*. It is part of our calling' (Baghwan 2015).

As part of this revised rhetoric, Banivanua introduces a new concept of an inclusive *vanua*:

> In this process of rebuilding relationships, the church's relationship with the *vanua* continues to be one we value and need to strengthen …

> At the same time we are called to practise love in a radical way that impacts the *vanua*. As Christian Fijians we need to be inclusive our understanding of the *vanua* to include all the other ethnic groups that live in the *vanua*.

> My vision is that the Methodist Church's relationship-building process must be one that engages not only with government or a certain community but engages with everybody in Fiji. (Baghwan 2015)

In adapting some of the nationalist language to his own rhetoric, Banivanua is attempting to write over previous ideas of exclusiveness, to appropriate nationalist language in a different direction while (re-)creating a vision that Methodist adherents can identify with. At the same time, it is a more inclusive vision that attempts to unify the rural, the urban and the international notions of Methodism. While Banivanua's vision of the new Exodus redefines the *vanua* as multiracial and multi-religious, extending beyond the Taukei, the *vanua* is still grounded firmly in Taukei conceptions of the world.

However, it is a stride away from the ethno-religious nationalism of the coups in 1987 and 2000, and of the government's policies prior to the 2006 coup.

How convincing Banivanua is to the adherents of the Methodist Church of Fiji is yet to be seen. Given the postings on the Methodist Church's blogsite, there remain tensions within the church about teachings with regard to homosexuality and family form. This indicates that, although it might appear that the Methodist Church has been transformed, coming to a consensus on how the church community can suitably relate to the wider world may be more complicated. The new Exodus, then, is a fragile process.

In another shift in theology, if the land is still in sight, it is no longer the place from which decisions are made:

> The *drua* is ready, the map is ready, the winds are blowing. All that is needed now is for the crew to commit to the journey and follow their captain in this bold journey. (Baghwan 2015)

Again, the use of old images and language in this way is a tentative one. While drawing on the romance of the *drua*, the ocean-based journey has been used by nationalist Methodist clans in the Kaunitoni Migration, the narratives that talk of ancestors arriving from foreign lands by sea in canoes. Can the redeployment of this imagery erase and/or redirect the old meanings? Is a theology of the ocean already too reminiscent of other interests or does it represent the hope of new directions?

Acknowledgements

This paper was written at the University of St Andrews, which provides a considerable distance for my own reflection on the nine years I spent lecturing out of the University of the South Pacific in Fiji, during which I experienced the atmosphere of Suva for a year in 2001 and from 2005 until 2012. Thanks to Steven Ratuva for giving me this opportunity to reflect on more recent events.

References

Baghwan, James 2015, 'Let's mend bridges', *Fiji Times* [Online], 11 March. Viewed 13 July 2015 at www.fijitimes.com/story. aspx?id=297753.

Baleiwaqa, Tevita 2003, *Rerevaka na kalou ka doka na tui: Fear God and Honour the King: The Influence of the Wesleyan Methodists on the Institutions of Fijian Identity*, Unpublished PhD thesis, The Australian National University, Canberra.

Banivanua, Tevita 2014a, 'Statement to the media', 25 September, methodistfiji.blogspot.com.au and on Facebook. Viewed 13 July 2015 at www.facebook.com/permalink.php?id=432821093498034 &story_fbid=640634679383340.

Banivanua, Tevita 2014b, 'Fiji Day message', 7 October. Viewed 13 July 2015 at methodistfiji.blogspot.co.uk/search?updated-max=2014-12-01T22:22:00%2B13:00&max-results=7&start=7&by-date=false.

Bola-Bari, Vuniwaqa 2014, 'Keep religion out, Sareem tells politicians', *Fijilive*. Viewed 13 July 2015 at fijilive.com/news/2014/07/keep-religion-out-sareem-tells-politicians/58414/.

Bolatiki, Maika 2013, 'Methodist Church says "no" to politics', *Fiji Sun* [Online], 21 June. Viewed 2 February 2015 at fijisun.com. fj/2013/06/21/methodist-church-says-no-to-politics/.

Bolatiki, Maika 2014, 'Church disappoints PM', *Fiji Sun* [Online] 25 September. Viewed 2 February 2015 at fijisun.com.fj/2014/09/25/ church-disappoints-pm/.

Chandar, Reginald 2013, 'Be responsible, religious leaders told', *Fijilive,* 21 September. Viewed 13 July 2015 at fijilive.com/.

Drauna, Peni 2015, 'New Quarters For Priest', *Fiji Sun* [Online], 7 January. Viewed 2 February 2015 at fijisun.com.fj/2015/01/07/ new-quarters-for-priest/.

Ernst, Manfred 2004, *Winds of change: Rapidly growing religious groups of the Pacific Islands*, Pacific Conference of Churches, Suva.

Fiji Bureau of Statistics 2007, 'Census of Population and Housing'. Viewed 2 February 2015 at www.statsfiji.gov.fj/index.php/2007-census-of-population.

Fijilive 2014, 'Women, church cautioned ahead of election', 9 September. Viewed 29 November 2015 at fijilive.com/m/newsdetails.php?cat=1&id=58878.

Fiji National Rugby League 2012, [Facebook Post] 8 June. Viewed 13 July 2015 at www.facebook.com/Fijibati/posts/159707494161503.

Garrett, J 1990, 'Uncertain sequel: The social and religious scene in Fiji since the coups', *The Contemporary Pacific*, vol. 2, no. 1, pp. 87–111.

Halapua, Winston 2003, *Tradition, lotu, and militarism in Fiji*, Fiji Institute of Applied Studies, Nadi.

Halapua, Winston 2008, 'Moana methodology: A way of promoting dynamic leadership', *Talanoa Oceania*. Available at sites.google.com/a/nomoa.com/talanoa/Home/papers-presentations/halapua—moana.

Hau'ofa, Epeli 2008, 'Our sea of islands', in E Hau'ofa, *We are the ocean: Selected works*, University of Hawaii Press, Hawai'i.

Kant, Romitesh and Rakuita, Eroni 2014, *Public participation & constitution-making in Fiji: A critique of the 2012 constitution-making process*, State, Society and Governance in Melanesia Discussion Paper 2014/6, pp. 1–19. Viewed 2 February 2015 at digitalcollections.anu.edu.au/bitstream/1885/12254/1/Kant%20%26%20Rakuita%20Public%20participation%202014.pdf.

Karavaki, Semesa Druavesi 2014, *Noqu Kalou, Noqu Vanua*, 7 September. Viewed 2 February 2015 at www.youtube.com/watch?v=k-xk6i2eeIA.

Kate, Talebula 2014, 'Court told of the Reverend Waqairatu's death', *Fiji Sun* [Online], 19 February. Viewed 2 February 2015 at fijisun.com.fj/2014/02/19/court-told-of-the-reverend-waqairatus-death/.

Kelly, Charlotte 1945, 'The Catholic Church in Fiji 1844–1944', *An Irish Quarterly Review*, vol. 34, no. 135, pp. 361–68.

Lal, Victor 2012, 'The Kaiyyum's $22 million bank loan to set up FBC TV', Coupfourpointfive, 1 July. Viewed 2 February 2015 at www.coupfourandahalf.com/2012/07/khaiyums-22million-bank-loan-to-set-up.html.

Methodist Church in Fiji 2014, *Resolutions from the 2014 Conference.* Viewed 13 July 2015 at www.methodistfiji.org/2014-conference-resolutions.html.

Narsey, Wadan 2013, 'Why the Fiji regime rejected the draft constitution', in Sam Roggeveen (ed.), *The Interpreter*, Lowy Institute for National Policy, Sydney. Viewed 2 February 2015 at www.lowyinterpreter.org/post/2013/01/15/Why-the-Fiji-regime-rejected-the-draft-constitution.aspx?COLLCC=4154162473&.

Newland, Lynda 2006, 'Fiji', in Manfred Ernst (ed.), *Globalization and the re-shaping of Christianity in the Pacific Islands.* The Pacific Theological College, Suva, pp. 317–89.

Newland, Lynda 2007, 'The role of the Assembly of Christian Churches in Fiji (ACCF) in the 2006 elections', in Jon Fraenkel and Stewart Firth (eds), *From election to coup in Fiji: The 2006 campaign and its aftermath,* ANU E Press and Asia Pacific Press, Canberra. Available at: epress.anu.edu.au/wp-content/uploads/2011/05/ch23.pdf.

Newland, Lynda 2009, 'Religion and politics: The Christian churches and the 2006 coup in Fiji', in Jon Fraenkel, Stewart Firth and Brij V Lal (eds), *The 2006 military takeover in Fiji: A coup to end all coups?* ANU E Press, Canberra. Available at: epress.anu.edu.au/wp-content/uploads/2011/02/ch091.pdf.

Newland, Lynda 2012, 'New Methodism and old: Churches, police and state in Fiji, 2008–09'. *The Round Table: The Commonwealth Journal of International Affairs*, Special Edition, vol. 101, no. 6, pp. 537–55.

Newland, Lynda 2013, 'Imagining nationhood: narratives of belonging and the question of a Christian state in Fiji', *Global Change, Peace & Security*: formerly *Pacifica Review: Peace, Security & Global Change*, DOI:10.1080/14781158.2013.784247.

Newland, Lynda 2015, 'The lost tribes of Israel – and the genesis of Christianity in Fiji: Missionary notions of Fijian origin from 1835 to cession and beyond', *Oceania*, Special Edition, Lynda Newland and Terry Brown (eds), vol. 85, no. 3, pp. 256–70.

Niukula, Paula 1994, *The three pillars: The triple aspect of Fijian society*, Christian Writing Project, Suva.

Pacific Voyagers n.d., 'General Overview', Pacific Voyagers. Viewed 13 July 2015 at pacificvoyagers.org/vaka-moana/.

Radio New Zealand 2014, 'Fiji's Methodist Church takes new approach', 27 August. Viewed 13 July 2015 at www.radionz. co.nz/international/programmes/datelinepacific/audio/20147334/fiji%27s-methodist-church-takes-news-approach.

Rasoqosoqo, Losalini 2013, 'Strong stand: Church warns ministers about politics, coups', *Fiji Sun* [Online], 29 August. Viewed 2 February 2015 at fijisun.com.fj/2013/08/29/strong-stand/.

Rasoqosoqo, Losalini 2014, 'Reverend Waqairatu dies aged 66', *Fiji Sun* [Online], 12 February. Viewed 2 February 2015 at fijisun. com.fj/2014/02/12/reverend-waqairatu-dies-aged-66/.

Ryle, Jacqueline 2010, *My God, My land: Interwoven paths of Christianity and tradition in Fiji,* Ashgate Publishing Co, Surrey and Burlington.

SODELPA 2014a, *Reclaiming Fiji: The Manifesto of Sodelpa*. Viewed 2 February 2015 at sodelpa.org/SODELPA-manifesto-LR.pdf.

SODELPA, 2014b, [Facebook Post], 18 July. Viewed 2 February 2015 at www.facebook.com/sodelpa/posts/1397324750488161.

SODELPA, 2014c, 'Statement No 21: SODELPA's position on matters misrepresented by the media'. Viewed 2 February 2015 at fijitoday. wordpress.com/2014/08/22/statement-no-21sodelpas-position-on-matters-misrepresented-by-the-media/ and Viewed 2 February 2015 on Facebook at www.facebook.com/707325785971101/photos/a.70 7329135970766.1073741828.707325785971101/731218353581844/.

Sopepa, Nikotemo 2014, [Facebook Comment]. Viewed 2 February 2015 at www.facebook.com/permalink.php?id=432821093498034 &story_fbid=640634679383340.

Swami, Nasik 2014, 'Think before you vote', *The Fiji Times* [Online], 18 July. Viewed 13 July 2015 at www.fijitimes.com/story.aspx?id=274655.

Talebula, Wati 2014, 'New Methodist president in August', *Fiji Sun* [Online], 9 May. Viewed 2 February 2015 at fijisun.com.fj/2014/05/09/new-methodist-president-in-august/.

Taleitaki, Siteri 2014, 'New Methodists rally in the north nation needs god for the betterment of its people: Rev Vulaono', *Fiji Sun* [Online], 28th April. Viewed 2 February 2015 at fijisun.com.fj/2014/04/28/new-methodists-rally-in-the-north-nation-needs-god-for-the-betterment-of-its-people-rev-vulaono/.

Tawake, Salaseini 2013, 'Methodists: No politics', *Fiji Sun* [Online], 8 January. Viewed 2 February 2015 at fijisun.com.fj/2013/01/08/methodists-no-politics/.

Tippett, Alan R 1980, *Oral tradition and ethnohistory: The transformation of information and social values in early Christian Fiji 1835–1905*, St Marks Library, Canberra.

Tomlinson, Matt 2006, 'Retheorizing mana: Bible translation and discourse of loss in Fiji', *Oceania*, vol. 76 no. 2, pp. 173–85.

Tuwere, Iliesa S 2002, *Vanua: Towards a Fijian theology of place*, Institute of Pacific Studies, University of the South Pacific and College of St John the Evangelist, Suva.

Tuwere, Josua 2014, 'Money for the church?' *Fiji Sun* [Online], 4 December. Viewed 2 February 2015 at fijisun.com.fj/2014/12/04/money-for-church/.

Walmsley, Claire 1987, *Paradise in Peril* [Documentary], Reporter: Martin Young, BBC TV.

Weir, Christine 2015, 'The 2014 Fiji elections and the Methodist church', *The Round Table: The Commonwealth Journal of International Affairs*, vol. 104, no. 2, pp. 165–75.

7

Native land policy
in the 2014 elections

Sefanaia Sakai

Introduction

One of the most debated issues prior to the September 2014 elections in Fiji was the security of Taukei land. This resulted from uncertainty about the implications of the many changes the Bainimarama Government had introduced since it took control of the government after the 2006 coup. In response, the political parties included policies on land issues in their manifestos. This chapter begins by examining the way in which land issues were addressed by the two major parties: the Social Democratic Liberal Party (SODELPA) and the FijiFirst Party. SODELPA promised to roll back Bainimarama's reforms, while FijiFirst proposed to further improve access to and utilisation of native land. The other political parties adopted a moderate position on land in the hope that the contradictory views espoused by the two major parties would be to their advantage. The chapter aims to analyse the extent to which the land issue, and the rhetoric of the leading parties, was a factor in the election result.

The 2014 general elections

After eight years of political uncertainty, the 2014 September elections restored democratic rule in Fiji, much to the relief of the people of Fiji as well as others in the region. Despite some criticisms,[1] the elections were labelled as free and fair by the Multinational Observer Group (MOG). FijiFirst won a landslide victory, polling 59.2 per cent of the total votes, dispelling any hope of a coalition government expected by some political analysts. The voting age was reduced from 21 to 18 years, and 84.6 per cent of Fiji's 591,101 registered voters participated in the 2014 general elections (Fijian Elections Office 2014).

There had been much speculation by various observers about the possible outcome of the elections, although former vice president and high court judge Ratu Joni Madraiwiwi noted the difficulty of knowing what voters were actually thinking ahead of the polls. The fact that the elections were being held under a new constitution, and with new parties competing for the first time, together with the fact that it had been eight years since the last elections, made it almost impossible to use past trends as a basis for judging the outcome in September 2014. Even so, land had been a particularly sensitive issue in all elections since independence in 1970, and it was reasonable to expect that the radical changes made to Taukei land policy under the Bainimarama regime prior to the elections might result in a backlash against FijiFirst among Taukei voters, with SODELPA as the main beneficiary. SODELPA certainly promoted the view that the changes to native land laws would bring social, economic and cultural disaster to the Taukei.

At least part of the problem surrounding the election hype over land issues was due to ignorance on the part of Taukei landowners regarding their legal rights, which made them easy prey to fearmongering propaganda, as had occurred in previous elections. As Lal (1988, p. 81) noted, the Alliance Party, which had formed the government in Fiji since independence, exploited 'the land fear strategy' against the newly formed Fiji Labour Party in the 1987 general elections.

---

1   See 2014 Electoral Commission Report. One of its recommendations concerns the need for changes to relevant sections of the 2013 Constitution, the Electoral Decree and the Political Parties Decree to allow good governance in the election process.

Chiefs, custom and land

Official records show the Taukei owned about 91 per cent of the land while freehold and crown land made up approximately 6 and 3 per cent of the remaining land respectively (TLTB 2014, p.8). A significant difference between customary Taukei land tenure compared to western systems is its communal ownership, which is held in accordance with customs and traditions. Individual Taukei do not have legal title to native land but each individual is registered under a *mataqali* (clan) which is the legal land owning unit, as stated in the Native Land Act 1961. The *mataqali* can neither sell land to outsiders nor grant private property rights to individual members. In practice, each *mataqali* is entitled to a share of the land that constitutes the *vanua* or village. In pre-contact time, however, all land belonged to groups of Taukei, although land tenure systems varied throughout the islands. The *Tukutuku Raraba*[2] recorded by various Native Land Commissions (NLCs) demonstrated that precolonial customs were far from homogeneous. Various groups of Taukei were frequently displaced, their composition was fluid, and hierarchy varied considerably by region (France 1969; Nayacakalou 1975; Ravuvu 1998).

Customary views on land transcend the tangible representation of resources. This contributed to the Taukei's resolve to protect their land from alienation. Like other Taukei scholars, Tuwere (2002, p. 36) reaffirms that for Taukei, land, spirit and people are integral to the *vanua*,[3] and the components are inseparable. Thus the *vanua* is seen as a 'social fact' that holds the Taukei together and gives it meaning (Tuwere 2002). This view incorporates a host of spiritual values as well as more practical aspects of land ownership and use. In earlier periods, the idea of a sacred tie was often emphasised by the spokesmen representing their *vanua* when giving evidence to the Native Land Commission (NLC) on landownership and occupation (France 1969, p. 10). Narration would include tribal origins linked to a known god in a given area. Consequently, Taukei land tenure practices were

---

2   Oral traditions of the landowning units and individuals regarding historical accounts such as initial land settlement, ownership, distribution and occupation.

3   The *vanua*, for Taukei, literally means 'land', but it encompasses a holistic meaning attached to it which includes the Taukeis' identity, resources, culture and spiritual being.

formulated in what Malinowski referred to as 'codification of belief' (cited in France 1969, p. 10). It is because of the strength of this value system that land is not seen as a commodity (Boydell 2005).

Although traditional land tenure systems were varied and flexible, colonial order required a certain uniformity throughout the islands and so Sir Arthur Gordon, the first colonial governor, instituted a formal native land tenure system that could be applied in all parts of the island group. In addition to introducing a certain degree of uniformity where it had not previously existed, the system was designed to protect indigenous land and the way of life from the greed of white settlers (France 1969, p. 107). However, some scholars have argued, and rightly so, that the colonial policy of protecting Taukei also impeded their socioeconomic progress (Boydell 2005; Lawson 1996; Nayacakalou 1975).

Another important point to note is that although Taukei land was protected, the need to develop a plantation economy required some flexibility, some modifications in the system, and so the leasing of native land for agricultural purposes was introduced. In 1936, Ratu Sir Lala Sukuna, the first indigenous Native Land Commissioner, together with the Great Council of Chiefs (GCC) determined that all land not required for the sustenance of Fijian owners was to be made available for national development through native land leases. A Native Land Trust Board (NLTB) was established in 1940 to administer and protect native land. In the process, chiefs recommended to the colonial administration that land policies not only safeguarded land ownership but also secured their positions in a changing society. As a result, chiefly control became an integral part of the colonial native land tenure system, which included the distribution of wealth from land development.

Fijian chiefs, who were regarded as anointed by God, obviously occupied a special position in traditional Fijian society, being given precedence, loyalty, obedience, authority, privilege and respect (Nayacakalou 1975, p. 81). But their primary role was to look after the welfare of the people and to safeguard resources and ensure distribution, such that every member of the group had access to land. Surprisingly, historical records show that prominent chiefs actually sold large areas of land, thereby contravening their traditional roles as custodians of ancestral land. For instance, Derrick (1968, p. 185) writes that in Vanua Levu, the second largest island of the Fiji group, land sales were assumed to be the prerogative of the high chiefs and few dared to question them.

As with the land tenure system, the role of chiefly authority was reconfigured and codified by the colonial government. Under the separate Fijian Affairs Board, Taukei were made to live as a communal group under traditional leaders whose privileges and status were increased and secured, while the land rights of individuals and small groups were submerged in *mataqali* groups, restricting the free transfer of land between groups and individual in times of need (Tupouniua, Crocombe & Slatter 1980, p. 33). Ravuvu (1998, p. 129) explains that land which was once considered by the people of the village to provide them with various needs for their daily lives had been made sole property of a particular *mataqali*. The method of allocating land rights introduced by the colonial government were, as noted above, much more rigid and as a consequence often failed to meet the needs of village life (Ravuvu 1998).

As for the high chiefs, their positions were firmly entrenched during colonial rule through the Native Regulations. This was very unlike pre-contact times, when inefficient leaders could be wiped out by stronger and more efficient leaders, especially during tribal wars (Tupouniua, Crocombe & Slatter 1980, p. 33). Consequently, Fijian individuality was suppressed under many self-serving traditional leaders whose claim to office rested on nothing more than the accident of birth. Any attempt to break away from this bondage was firmly suppressed under the new powers given to chiefs under the Native Regulations.

Fiji's history also shows lack of commitment by Taukei political leaders to implement positive legislative changes to meet the changing needs of society. Nayacakalou (1975, p. 5) discussed the dilemma facing Fijian leaders regarding the preservation of Fijian culture, including the system of land tenure and management. If any advocated radical change they could attract accusations of being anti-Taukei; on the other hand, if they emphasised the importance of maintaining traditional (or neo-traditional) ways, they were accused of being reactionary.

This dilemma remained a serious problem in the post-independence period, especially whenever issues concerning Indo-Fijian farmers and their need for secure leases were raised. The chiefs represented themselves as the only ones capable of ensuring that Indo-Fijians did not take over Taukei land altogether, although this was never a real possibility, either legally or politically. This was in addition to the constant emphasis on the notion that there is a sacred, unbreakable connection between land, chiefs and the *vanua*. These notions were featured prominently in post-independence election rhetoric aimed at Taukei voters. In the 1987 elections, for instance, a prominent Alliance politician of chiefly status blamed the Labour–National Federation Party coalition for trying to meddle with the scared ties between the *turaga* (chiefs) and the *vanua*. A warning was issued concerning the dire consequences for the future of Taukei (Lawson 1996, p. 50). One chief stated that 'the *Turaga* and the *Vanua* were one – one could not exist without the other – the chiefs were a bulwark of security for all and the custodians of Taukei identity, land and culture' (Lawson 1996).

The political triumphs and failures of the architect of the 1987 coups, Lieutenant-Colonel Sitiveni Rabuka, were tied to how Taukei regarded him as protector of Taukei interests, including land. In the aftermath of the 1987 coups, he was seen as the champion of Taukei rights in the face of alleged threats to land, identity and the entire edifice of Taukei tradition (Lal 2000; Lawson 1996). But this was to change when Fiji returned to democratic rule. Lal (2000, p. 326) notes that when Rabuka's Soqosoqo ni Vakavulewa ni Taukei (SVT) party went into coalition with the largely Fiji-Indian National Federation Party to form a coalition prior to the 1999 general elections, many Taukei voters deserted him and his party because he was seen as betraying Taukei interests and Taukei political control.

With respect to the 2000 coup, Boydell's (2005) analysis suggests that one reason for the 2000 civilian coup was a growing concern among Taukei about land security under the Chaudhry Government, especially when it appeared that the government wanted to legislate to allow access to unused native land for development without considering the welfare of Taukei landowners. With these factors in mind, the issue of Taukei insecurity (whether based on real threats or fabrications) needs careful analysis and understanding, especially by non-Taukei, for many Taukei will view them with suspicion in matters concerning land.

Land security issues in the 2014 elections

Given this background, it is no surprise that the issue of land was one of the most contested campaign issues prior to the 2014 elections, as evident in the party manifestos, opinion polls, policies and land decrees. The SODELPA and FijiFirst manifestos, as set out in Table 1, reflect contrasting positions on land protection and land innovation, although both claimed to be advocating both objectives.

Table 1: SODELPA and FijiFirst manifestos on native land

	SODELPA	FijiFirst
Land Policies	Uphold Native Land Act 1997 Constitution entrenchment provision on Native Land Act. Revise the equal distribution policy. Abolish the Land Use Decree. Revise the Surfing Decree. Land protection as in the 1997 Constitution.	Uphold Native Land Act 2013 Constitution. Continue with Land Use Decree and equal distribution policy. Uphold the Surfing Decree. Land Protection as in the 2013 Constitution. FJD$10 million to help Land Owning Unit (LOU) develop land.
Great Council of Chiefs	Re-establish the GCC.	Abolish the GCC
Secular State	Secular state gives lesser value towards Christian role in Fiji.	Support secular state as part of equal citizenship.
Constitution	Revise 2013 Constitution with inclusion of the 1997 Constitution.	Uphold the 2013 Constitution.
iTaukei Land Trust Board	Restructure and keep as the legal custodian of native land as institution.	Restructure and drive for economic development for the betterment of iTaukei and Fiji.
Squatter Settlements	Provide affordable housing.	Squatters on native land given residential 99-year leases with LOU approval.

Source: Derived from the manifestos of SODELPA and FijiFirst, 2014.

On land policy, SODELPA promised to facilitate consultation regarding the 2010 Leases and Licences Regulations amendment and to immediately abolish the 2010 Land Use Decree if elected to government. It also said it would uphold the ILO (International Labor Organization) Convention 169 and the 2007 UN Declaration on the Rights of Indigenous Peoples[4] to strengthen opposition to the 2013 Constitution.

---

4   This declaration, while accepting the fundamental equality of all peoples, nevertheles notes that many indigenous peoples the world over have suffered marginalisation through colonialism, and recognises the need to respect and promote the rights of indigenous peoples affirmed in historical treaties and other agreements with the state.

FijiFirst's manifesto built on their existing policies, which they claimed fostered inclusive growth for all Fijians. As for land issues, the party pledged to uphold the Land Use Decree and provide financial support for Land Owning Units (LOUs) who wished to develop their land. Additionally, they promised to provide a 99-year residential lease to squatters residing on native land with the approval of LOUs. Other parties such as the National Federation Party (NFP)[5] and the People's Democratic Party (PDP) adopted a balanced approach regarding changes to native land legislations, arguing that proper mechanisms should be followed and native land ownership should be protected. The NFP for instance, pledged to include the entrenchment clause in the 2013 Constitution for native land legislation and would not exercise the power of 'compulsory acquisition' of native land as stated under Section 27 of the 2013 Constitution (NFP 2014, p. 19). The party clearly supported SODELPA's stance that land issues and Taukei institutions needed wider consultation rather than the non-consultative approach taken by the regime.

The Tebbutt opinion poll in August 2014 showed that 74 per cent and 16 per cent of registered voters considered land issues as very important and quite important respectively.[6] This was across all age groups, both genders and all ethnicities in both the Central and Western divisions of Fiji. Interestingly, only 25 per cent said they understood land issues quite well, while 83 per cent said they would like to know more about the subject (Vakacolo 2014). As noted above, native land protection is extremely important for indigenous people for a variety of reasons; not least, because in a competitive world it is the only resource that provides a sense of social, political and economic security. However, Taukei land rights are in fact protected under the 2013 Constitution as well as under two sets of native land legislation introduced by the Bainimarama regime in 2010. These will now be examined in greater detail.

---

5   The National Federation Party is the longest-surviving Indo-Fijian dominant party since independence and, like SODELPA, would adopt a consultative approach regarding land issues and reinstatement of the GCC if it won the elections.
6   Tebutt poll conducted on 1,047 registered voters between 4 and 6 August. The poll asked: 'How important is the land ownership issue to the nation? How well would you say that you understand the current land ownership issues that are being discussed? And how interested are you to learn more about land ownership issues?'

In 2010, the Bainimarama Government amended the Leases and Licenses Regulations of the Native Land Act to ensure equal distribution of lease money to *mataqali* members. The amendment was introduced in line with a government policy of inclusiveness and designed to address inequality among Taukei landowners. Wealth from the use of Taukei land through leasing has been substantial, but had not been distributed on an equal basis. According to the iTaukei Land Trust Board (TLTB, formerly the Native Land Trust Board or NLTB), the total lease income distributed to LOUs has increased from FJD$24 million in 2000 to FJD$64 million in 2014 (TLTB 2014, p. 11). For the first time, under the new equal distribution policy, chiefs and commoners within a *mataqali* would share the economic gains from the use of their *mataqali* land equally (see hypothetical scenario Figure 1). Before the amendment, the TLTB usually deducted 25 per cent as an administration fee and also to assist the TLTB to generate development projects on Taukei land. There were also three categories of chiefs who received the largest share of the lease money under the old distribution system: *turaga ni vanua* (village chief) received 5 per cent, *turaga ni yavusa* (tribal chief) received 10 per cent, and *turaga ni mataqali* (clan chief) received 15 per cent. Often a single chief would receive the full 30 per cent entitlement because he was holder of all three titles and belonged to the clan whose land was leased for development. The remaining 45 per cent was shared by the rest of the *mataqali* members. In 2013, the Bainimarama regime also reduced the TLTB share from 25 per cent to 10 per cent, putting an emphasis on the TLTB self-funding its own operation rather than relying so heavily on deductions from lease money.

The equal distribution policy has also contributed to the reduction in the number of registered disputes over chiefly titles in the country in 2013 and 2014. For example, the Native Lands Commission received three chiefly titles dispute cases in 2014 compared to 13 recorded cases in 2013. The commissioner attributed this decline to the implementation of the equal distribution policy by the Bainimarama Government (FBC 2014). However, the validity of this analysis could be substantiated only after in-depth research on the issue of equal distribution and titles disputes.

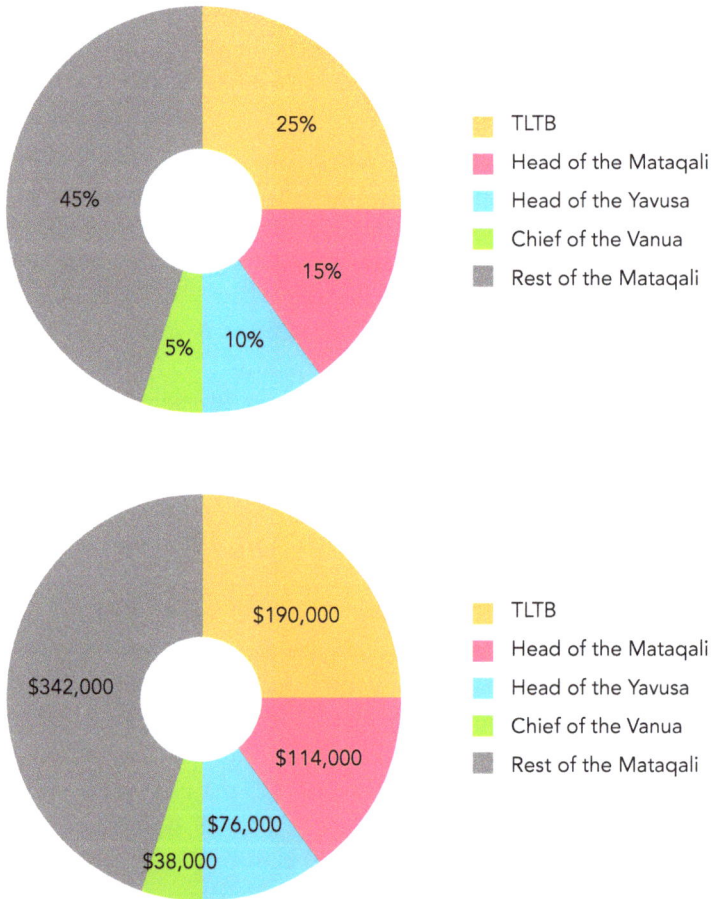

Figure 1: Old distribution policy FJD$760,000: A hypothetical scenario

Source: Sakai 2014, presentation at Tahiti PIPSA conference.

Returning now to the responses by political parties: SODELPA portrayed these reforms as detrimental to the livelihoods of Taukei and a violation of indigenous rights. From the outset, it must be noted that SODELPA had attempted to use land security issues and also the abolition of the GCC in 2012 (through the Taukei Affairs Revocation Regulation), which put an end to the GCC's 136 years of existence, as a trump card to attract Taukei voters in its 2014 election campaign (Fraenkel 2014, p. 2). Bainimarama had questioned the GCC's relevance to the country's contemporary political structure and criticised the institution as being not only highly politicised but also irrelevant in an era that championed the equality of Fiji's citizens (Gonedua 2012). Another issue for SODELPA was the ban placed on the Methodist Church's annual national conference under the Public Emergency Regulations. SODELPA, in opposing the restrictions on church activities, attempted to appeal to the largely Methodist Taukei voters. Indeed, many Methodist Church followers had previously formed a substantial part of the support base of SODELPA's immediate predecessor, the Soqosoqo Duavata ni Lewenivanua (SDL) party, which had been overthrown while in government in 2006 (see Newland, this volume). Finally, in early 2013 the Bainimarama Government withdrew all ethnic-based scholarships, including the Fijian Affairs Scholarship, which had served to promote education for Taukei students at the expense of other ethnic groups.

With respect to land policy, SODELPA claimed that the equal distribution of lease monies was not conducive to the traditional livelihood of Taukei. SODELPA leader Ro Teimumu Kepa, a high chief and beneficiary of the previous system of distribution, explained that chiefs, as heads of the *mataqali* and *yavusa*, had responsibilities to the *vanua* and their larger shares would cater for major obligations. Deposed SDL Prime Minister Laisenia Qarase, while campaigning for SODELPA, invented his own version of redistribution when replying to a question that the author posed during the SODELPA campaign in Wainivula, Suva. He said that the party would let the provincial council decide on the fate of the equal distribution policy in consultation with the people. This was clearly different from Ro Teimumu's position that SODELPA would revert to the old system.

These contradictory views became counterproductive to the party's campaign before the elections.[7] First, in advocating the old distribution system, Ro Teimumu was condoning inequality among Taukei, using facile cultural justification. What the party overlooked was that many chiefs in Fiji did not receive lease money yet still fulfilled their obligations to the *vanua* successfully because communalism and reciprocity were crucial values of Taukei culture.

---

7   SODELPA, through Qarase, had given a few contradictory views such as on land and the interpretation of the secular state during the 2014 election campaign, which may have dissuaded people from voting for the party.

The old distribution policy actually contributed to inequality and the marginalisation of ordinary Taukei in their traditional villages; and they never questioned it because of the belief that it was an essential part of Taukei culture. It must be noted that the chief's lease allocation was a private entitlement and he was not obliged by law to spend or redistribute his share of lease monies on traditional obligations. Those chiefs in receipt of land monies had benefited from a land policy that had its origins in the colonial order, which contributed to some chiefs becoming individualistic and very wealthy while ordinary Taukei remained disadvantaged despite also being owners of an important communal resource.

In advocating a policy of equal citizenship, Bainimarama criticised the chiefly institution as promoting inequality amongst the Taukei community by holding on to privileges bestowed, not by tradition, but by colonial laws. In the past several decades, neither the GCC nor political leaders had taken any steps to reform land policies to benefit all Taukei. Despite promises by previous Taukei-led governments such as the SVT and SDL to improve Taukei welfare, the socioeconomic situation of most Taukei continued to deteriorate.[8] Narsey (2008, p. vii) suggests that the proportion of Taukei living in poverty in 2000 was about 49 per cent in early 2000, although that could have increased after the 2006 coup because of the initial economic downturn.

It can be argued that to change something that benefits the majority of Taukei landowners through fair distribution would be unethical. In the hypothetical scenario illustrated in Figure 2, for instance, under the equal distribution policy, the FJD$760,000 revenue from the leased land is distributed to two recipient groups, the TLTB (FJD$76,000) and *mataqali* (FJD$684,000), with the latter figure being distributed equally to all members. Thus if the *mataqali* has 300 members, each one will receive FJD$2,280, including women and children. It is then the prerogative of the landowners to decide what to do with the income. For instance, even with the new policy in place, some landowning units may have a consensual agreement that the heads of *vanua*, *mataqali* and *tokatoka* continue to receive their normal shares, or at least a higher proportion than other *mataqali* members, as a reward for good leadership prior to the amendment. However, governance at

---

8   See Scarr 1999.

village level is not necessarily inclusive and the consensus reached may not take into account the views of women and youth, who usually remain silent in community discussions.

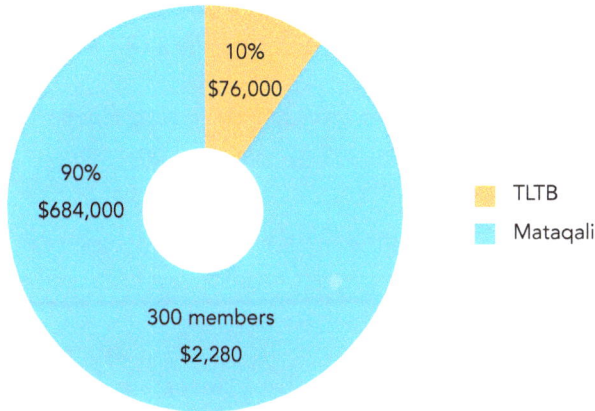

10%
$76,000

90%
$684,000

TLTB
Mataqali

300 members
$2,280

Figure 2: New equal distribution share FJD$760,000: A hypothetical scenario

Source: Sakai 2014, presentation at the Tahiti PIPSA conference.

Following the reforms, there has been no major resistance to the changes made by the Banimarama government, except from SODELPA. However, silence on these matters does not mean acceptance of the policy changes. Many Taukei feel constrained in articulating their views publicly on many political issues for cultural reasons (Madraiwiwi 2014; Nabobo et al. 2005). While silence is part of custom, Taukei support for the interim government may have also contributed to a subdued response.

Another contested issue prior to the elections was the 2010 Land Use Decree, a policy framework that aims to facilitate productivity of unused native and crown land. Under the decree, unused native land would be deposited in a Land Bank provided that 60 per cent of the *mataqali* members consent. Once the land is designated and deposited, the government would find potential investors who would be sub-lessees and would develop the land according to the provisions of the lease agreement. SODELPA had publicly campaigned against the decree, arguing once again that it would erode Taukei rights. SODELPA pointed out that there was one clause in the decree that removed the right of native land owners to seek redress in a court or tribunal. The party had mainly used a Fiji-based study and its own legal expertise to highlight the weaknesses of the decree. This study (see Dodd 2012) provided a detailed analysis of the legal implications of allocating Taukei land under the Land Use Unit, which included unchallenged legal power allocated to government to control native land for the duration of lease.[9] It is argued that the Land Use Decree would weaken the LOU's decision-making process and dispute-settlement capacity once the land was designated and the negotiation grace period of five years had lapsed, giving the government and investors total control of native land.

In its media release on the issue, SODELPA noted its reservations regarding the process of achieving majority consent and the confusion between individual rights and group rights regarding native land protection under the Land Use Decree.[10] The party also noted that the decree did not protect Taukei land from alienation as in other past constitutions and its real intention was to allow foreign investors easy access to native land on 99-year lease terms, and this effectively alienated the land for up to four generations.

In paving the way for this decree one necessary step had been the abrogation of the 1997 Constitution, which allowed the Bainimarama regime to abolish the GCC. Under the 1997 Constitution, the GCC had constitutional power to stop any amendments regarding any parliamentary proposal that might lead to possible alienation of Taukei land. An additional measure was the weakening of the structure of the TLTB board,[11] to which, under the 1997 Constitution, the GCC appointed the majority of members.

It is indeed possible that the Land Use Decree will facilitate land alienation because the LOU, once the lease has expired, may not have the financial capacity required to compensate investors for any general improvement to the land that has occurred during the leasing period. On another issue related to land use, SODELPA argued that the 2010 Surfing Decree did not obligate any investors to compensate the relevant LOU for the use of traditionally owned fishing grounds belonging to Taukei for leisure activities such as surfing, therefore removing potential

---

9   See clause 15(1) of the 2010 Land Use Decree.
10   See SODELPA 2013.
11   The prime minister becomes board chair and appoints at least three members of the board.

revenue sources for Taukei landowners. Another general criticism that could be made of the Bainimarama regime's approach with respect to all these policies is that good governance processes, which include public participation and consultation, were not followed.

The controversial land decree, in particular, provided the basis for a political agenda for SODELPA to launch its election campaign against FijiFirst, despite the latter's popularity in many provinces around the country. The party's strategy focused on the need to protect native land and other Taukei institutions in its effort to appeal to Taukei voters, who make up around 58 per cent of the population. Unfortunately, the ethnic approach employed by SODELPA backfired, as many undecided voters from all ethnicities found FijiFirst's liberal manifesto more appealing than SODELPA's conservative approach. For many people it seemed that what mattered was the 'real' development approach taken by the Bainimarama Government for those who needed it most— the poor, women and children, and rural dwellers. The issue of land insecurity was cushioned by the fact that the Bainimarama campaign seemed to convince many Taukei voters that their land was effectively secured under the 2013 Constitution. In fact, the Land Use Decree was an alternative lease arrangement available for LOUs to utilise unused land, with landowners receiving 100 per cent of the lease revenue.

These policy changes, however, still needed wider national consultations to prevent confusion and possible confrontation amongst landowners. Furthermore, the debate about the Land Use Decree did cause uneasiness amongst many Taukei because of the vague and selective explanations offered by both SODELPA and FijiFirst. The common response from FijiFirst to questions about native land was simply that Taukei land was protected by the Constitution. On the other hand, SOLDELPA emphasised the notion of land alienation and raised the spectre of Taukei becoming landless in their own country. The debate therefore left many Taukei voters confused and feeling that 'we don't know who is telling the truth'. Even so, it is clear that most ultimately placed their trust in FijiFirst.

Part of the problem was that among candidates of both parties there was a lack of understanding about the details of the new land decree, with FijiFirst candidates simply declaring in response to questions that 'Taukei land is safe'. In Wainivula, Suva, a FijiFirst candidate responded abusively when he was questioned by the author about the detailed provisions in the Land Use Decree and the possibility that it might lead to a *de facto* alienation of native land. As a result, this candidate was expelled from representing the party. Two other candidates and current ministers in the then interim government were present but could not answer the questions either. In Nasole, Suva, a FijiFirst candidate could not answer the question regarding a Land Use Decree provision concerning a landowner's right to take the government to court in the event of a dispute. The answer to this question, according to Bainimarama, is that the government may be challenged in court if fewer than 60 per cent of the LOU members consented to allocating the land under the Land Bank (FBC TV 2014).

The 2014 elections results

Issues concerning land insecurity, which should have been SODELPA's political trump card, appear to have failed to gain much appeal during the 2014 elections, even though the party got the great majority of its votes from among Taukei. For ordinary Taukei, acquiring basic needs and making progress were more important and many believed that their customary land was safe. The 2014 general elections results indicated that voters in many of the 14 provinces of Fiji supported FijiFirst, except for Lomaiviti, Kadavu, Lau and Rewa, which voted predominantly for SODELPA (see Figure 3).

The official result shows 56.5 per cent of the total rural votes went to FijiFirst, with a majority of votes from key provinces such as Ba, Ra, Nadroga-Navosa and Natasiri. These provinces constituted major areas of native leased land for commercial agriculture, tourism, mining and housing. In Ba province alone, the total number of tourism leases on native land by foreign investors is 41, three times more than other provinces (TLTB 2012, slide 7). More generally, Bainimarama's popularity stretched nationwide, accounting for 202,459 votes. In Yasawa for instance, 29 per cent of the 46 per cent vote for FijiFirst went to Bainimarama personally (see Figure 4).

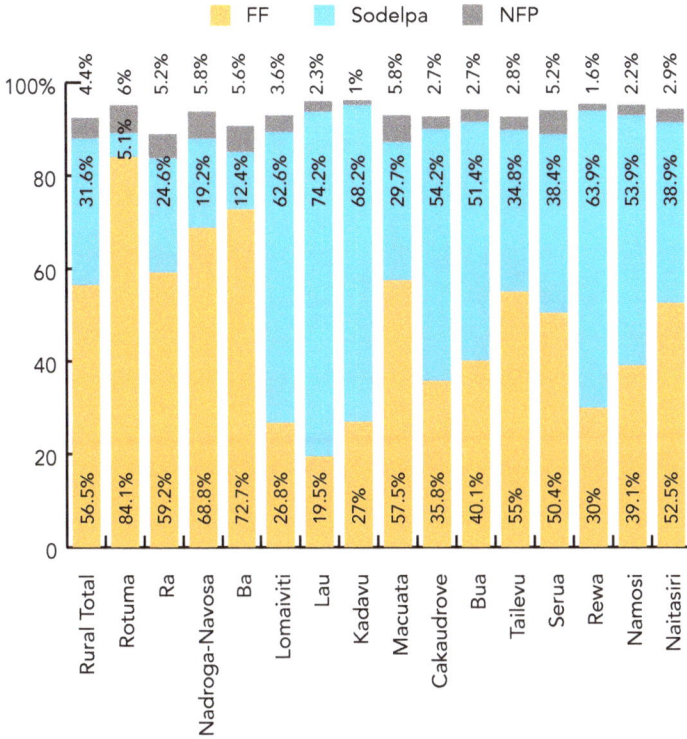

Figure 3: Rural party votes according to province: Fiji 2014 national elections
Source: Nakagawa 2014.

Given these results, it is evident that Taukei voters favoured the changes initiated by Bainimarama for the benefits they appear to have delivered to ordinary LOU members. Ethnic-based voting seemed to have lost its appeal, although whether this remains the case in future voting behaviour remains to be seen. Traditional ties among chiefly families between the provinces remain an important factor in Taukei voting behaviour, as demonstrated in the provinces of Rewa, Cakaudrove and Namosi in 2014. Given that their paramount chiefs were SODELPA candidates, and all won seats in the elections, these provinces remain a stronghold for SODELPA. Lau province, home to some of Fiji's most important statesmen including Fiji's longest-serving prime minster, Ratu Sir Kamisese Mara—a close relative of SODELPA leader Ro Teimumu Kepa—saw some of the highest voting figures for SODELPA (74.2 per cent).

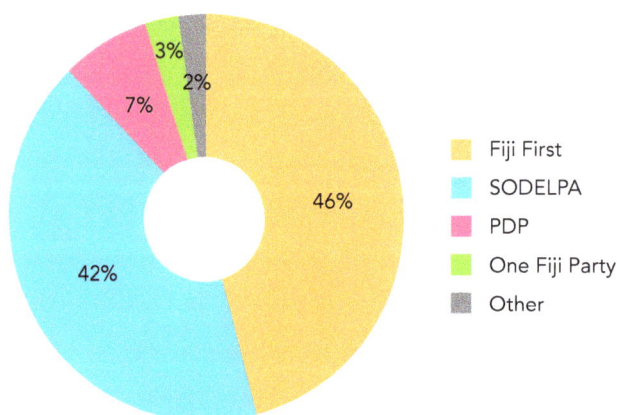

Figure 4: Total votes (%) in Yasawa by political parties
Source: Nakagawa 2014.

All Fijians will no doubt assess FijiFirst's performance over the next four years, but for Taukei one focus will be on how matters develop in relation to land, especially how the new land use decree is applied. Land is a highly sensitive issue and has the potential to inflame passions and tensions. In its current form, the decree may prove problematic, as it does not provide an avenue for redress of land issues.

Conclusion

Land issues may have had some impact on the results of the 2014 elections, but the concerns expressed by SODELPA in their campaign were not sufficiently persuasive among Taukei, let alone other communities, to give SODELPA victory in the elections. It seems that Taukei voters, who outnumber all other ethnic groups in terms of voting power, considered other basic matters such as education, water, electricity and other infrastructure as more important than land. In addition, the equal distribution policy gave FijiFirst an advantage, as many LOU members whose lands are leased received economic benefits denied under the old system. In the shorter term, this policy can deliver positive benefits to many more Taukei because it alleviates marginalisation and inequality within the Taukei social structure and potentially can improve the standard of living for all Taukei—rural and urban dwellers alike—if the proceeds are better utilised. It has also contributed to the reduction in the number of registered disputes over chiefly titles in the period 2013–14. These improvements may therefore alleviate the perceived insecurities and fear of land alienation that has caused so much political instability in the past. At the same time, perceptions concerning the possibility of future Taukei land alienation need to be clarified. There is also a need to change the current use of newly earned revenue from land from mainly basic consumption to long-term investments to sustain Taukei livelihoods while avoiding land insecurity in the future.

The Land Use Decree offers an alternative lease tenure system for Taukei to develop their land to earn good returns. It encourages innovative land utilisation for the Taukei themselves apart from leasing it to non-Taukei enterprises. It facilitates use of idle Taukei lands for commercial revenue-generating purposes and provides secure access to land to non-Taukei entrepreneurs over a longer period of time. Under this decree, the government also provides technical and financial support for LOUs that allocate their land under the newly created Land Bank to encourage Taukei entrepreneurship. However, the issue of control specifically awarded to the Prime Minister as well as the Minister of Lands within this legislation needs to be rethought to allow LOUs to make their own decisions. This will also help alleviate fears concerning possible alienation.

Finally, what more needs to be done regarding land issues for Taukei in Fiji and their impacts on future general elections? There needs to be wider consultation on the land decrees and policies regarding native land. Awareness about indigenous rights regarding land and innovative commercial programmes to increase productivity benefiting the communities also needs attention and support. The provision of relevant infrastructural and financial support for land development is crucial. The adoption of new methods for commercial ventures for Taukei, such as being core partners in business rather than just being recipients of lease money, needs to be encouraged. By the same token, effective commercial partnerships with non-Taukei entities with business acumen should be sought, built and maintained for the success of any Taukei entrepreneurship; and all such efforts need to be sustained until Taukei can operate independently. Taukei landowners will achieve a greater sense of security once they comprehend the implications of land legislation and feel the tangible benefits flowing from the use of their land. Well-informed Taukei will also not be misguided by fabricated threats frequently used by politicians in the past to generate fears about land insecurity. Even so, there may well be ongoing debates regarding traditional social structures and identity, especially with respect to chiefly institutions. The greater equality now enjoyed by Taukei under the new policies may well serve to undermine the traditional social structure and its place in contemporary Taukei society.

References

Boydell, S 2005, 'Secure land tenure in the South Pacific Region – Developing tool kit', in *Expert Group Meeting on secure land tenure: 'new legal frameworks and tools'*, 8–9 December 2005, UNESCAP, Bangkok.

Derrick, RA 1968, *A history of Fiji Vol 1*, Government Press, Suva.

Dodd, MJK 2012, *Reform of leasing regimes for customary land in Fiji*. MA thesis, University of Otago, Otago.

FBC (Fiji Broadcasting Commission) 2014, *Radio Interview Na Vakekeli Program*, 16 July.

FBC TV (Fiji Broadcasting Commission TV) 2014, *Straight Talk Program*, 8 September.

Fijian Elections Office 2014, *2014 Election Result*, Ministry of Information, Suva.

Fiji Electoral Commission 2014, *Annual Report*, Fiji Electoral Commission, Suva.

Fraenkel, J 2014, 'Reflecting on the 2014 general election', *Fiji Times*, 22 September.

France, P 1969, *The Charter of the Land*, Oxford University Press, London.

Gonedua, M 2012, 'Decree abolishes Fiji's GGC', *Pacific Island Report*, 14 March.

Lal, BV 1988, 'Before the storm: An analysis of the Fiji general election of 1987', *Journal of Pacific Studies*, vol. 12, no. 1, pp. 71–96.

Lal, BV 2000, 'Rabuka of Fiji: Coups, constitutions and confusion: Review and Reflections', Review of *Rabuka: No Other Way: His Own Story* by Eddie Dean & Stan Ritova; and *Rabuka of Fiji: The Authorised Biography of Major-general Sitiveni Rabuka* by John Sharpham, *The Journal of Pacific History*, vol. 35, no. 3, pp. 319–26.

Lawson, S 1996, *Tradition versus democracy in the South Pacific*, Cambridge University Press, Oxford.

Madraiwiwi, J 2014, 'Analysis: where parties going?', *Fiji Sun* [Online] 28 August. Viewed 7 January 2015 at fijisun.com.fj/2014/03/31/ratu-joni-madraiwiwi-analysis-where-parties-going/.

Nabobo, U, Baba, T and Anai, M 2005, *Pacific Education; Issues & Perspectives*, University of the South Pacific, Suva.

Nakagawa, H 2014, 'Analysis of Fiji's general election 2014 by region and urban/rural division', School of Government, Development and International Affairs Writers' Workshop on the 2014 General Election, 22 November 2014, University of the South Pacific.

Narsey, W 2008, *The quantitative analysis of poverty in Fiji*, Vanuavou Publications, Suva.

Nayacakalou, RR 1975, *Leadership in Fiji,* Institute of Pacific Studies, University of the South Pacific, Suva.

NFP (National Federation Party) 2014, *Our People's Future Manifesto 2014 General Elections*, NFP Suva.

Ravuvu, A 1998, *Development or dependence,* Institute of Pacific Studies, University of the South Pacific, Suva.

Sakai, S 2014, 'National governance on native land its impact on the livelihood of the iTaukei', in Pacific Island Political Studies Association Conference, 3–7 July, University of French Polynesia, Tahiti.

Scarr, D 1999, 'Communalism and a Constitution: Fiji's General Election of 1999', *Journal of Pacific History*, vol. 34, no. 3, pp. 253–58.

SODELPA 2013, 'A new type of Land Alienation? Indigenous Fijian Land and Government Constitution', media release No. 10/2013 (August).

TLTB (iTaukei Land Trust Board) 2012, Presentation to the Executive Management Board. Unpublished, 20 December, TLTB Boardroom, Nadi.

TLTB (iTaukei Land Trust Board) 2014, 'TLTB's achievement 2008–2014', *Na I Rogo,* vol. 3, no. 3, pp. 1–12.

Tupouniua, S, Crocombe, R and Slatter C (eds) 1980, *The Pacific Way*, South Pacific Social Sciences Association, Suva.

Tuwere, I 2002, *Vanua: Towards a Fijian theology of place*, Institute of Pacific Studies and College of St John the Evangelist, Suva.

Vakacolo, S 2014, 'Majority want to know more about our land', *Fiji Times.* 30 August.

8

Fiji elections and the youth vote—token or active citizenship?

Patrick Vakaoti

Introduction

The 2013 Constitution, particularly its provision reducing the voting age to 18 years, helped propel young people into the political limelight. Traditionally and historically, young people in Fiji have often been left out of structures of political decision-making at the local and national levels (Vakaoti 2013). During the September 2014 general elections, young people between the ages of 18 to 35 years constituted about 40 per cent of the electorate (Round 2014b). As a result, political commentators asserted that young people held the balance of power. Given the absence of relevant voter information, the influence of young voters on the election outcome is difficult to establish. This is complicated by the fact that young people are not a homogenous group. It is evident that the majority of registered young voters exercised their right and voted in the 17 September 2014 elections, embracing the democratic opportunity to elect parliamentary representatives.

Given the dearth of published sources on young people's democratic participation, specifically voting in Fiji, the discussion in this chapter uses as a backdrop the Citizen's Constitutional Forum's (CCF)

2014 report, 'Young People and Democratic Participation in Fiji' (Vakaoti 2014). The report, hereafter referred to as the CCF Youth Democratic Participation survey, uses the concept of generation to explore young people's understanding of democratic participation and the influences on their political involvement in the lead-up to the 17 September general elections. Of particular interest for this chapter are the findings of the report relating to young people and electoral and constitutional reform, which looked specifically at young people's responses to questions on political parties, politics and voting.

This chapter is divided into five sections. The first section explores the rationale for reducing the voting age to 18 years and makes the point that voting is only one part of active citizenship. The second section looks at the support provided to young people by the government, political parties, civil society organisations (CSOs) and the media. The third section considers the impact of the youth vote, with the fourth section suggesting ways youth stakeholders discussed in section two can support young people's democratic participation that extends beyond voting. The chapter concludes with a caution to stakeholders, particularly the government, about its promise to accord young people equal civil and political rights.

Engaging young people: 2013 Constitution

The reduction of the voting age from 21 to 18 years was one of the non-negotiable principles[1] of the 2013 Constitution. This decision appeared to align with the minimum voting age of 18 years in countries like Australia, New Zealand and the United Kingdom.[2] In Fiji, reasons for the reduction in the voting age are vaguely expressed in government statements such as 'Government has recognized the need to empower and involve youths in decision making and has reduced the voting age to 18 [years]' (Fiji Government Online 2014) and 'Fiji's Constitution … provides for greater civil and political rights to youths through reduction of the voting age from 21 to 18 years ensuring their say in

---

1   Other non-negotiable principles and values include a common and equal citizenry; a secular state; the removal of systematic corruption; an independent judiciary; elimination of discrimination; good and transparent governance; social justice; one person, one vote, one value; the elimination of ethnic voting and proportional representation.

2   This criteria is assessed with other criteria, particularly that around residency status.

the political life of the nation' (Fiji Government Online 2013). It could be argued that this position reflects the government's mantra of 'a common and equal citizenry, a common identity and a level playing field on which every citizen can excel' (Online Editor 2014).

The reduction in the voting age was received with mixed reactions. Political parties like the Fiji Labour Party (FLP), People's Democratic Party (PDP) and the Social Liberal Democratic Party (SODELPA) welcomed this change (Gibson 2014b; Baines 2013; Round 2014a). Fifty-four per cent of respondents in the CCF Youth Democratic Participation survey also supported this change, with the view that young people at 18 years are mature enough to vote. On the other hand, 41 per cent of young people in the survey believed that the voting age should be retained at 21 years. The main contention was that young people were not consulted about this decision. According to Vakaoti (2014, p. 37) focus group participants in the survey argued that:

> young people are being manipulated, a government tactic to generate support given its knowledge about the significance of the youth vote … [Focus group participants] in Nadi argued that the government was drawing from developed countries where many young people are independent. They added that the Fiji situation is different as many young people continue to depend on their parents who at the same time can influence a young person's voting behavior.

Despite this contention, young people actively and excitedly took to the polls. This was evident in the CCF Youth Democratic Participation survey, where 67 per cent of participants were identified as having registered to vote, 61 per cent of whom intended to vote (Vakaoti 2014). This suggests that many young people were excited by the prospect of voting, many for the first time (Ewart 2014). The nature of young people's political participation in the lead-up to the elections can be examined based on their engagement in political party campaigning, CSOs voter awareness and training and media engagement.

Young people and the elections: Preparedness and support

According to Esser (2007, p. 1195), 'voting is still the most basic and arguably most important democratic act … it is an essential part of political socialization, a cornerstone of democratic stability …'. The importance of voting assumes that as a result of preparedness and education, voters will make an informed decision on Election Day. In Fiji's case, this was questionable. The CCF Youth Democratic Participation survey identified that only 29 per cent of young people felt they 'most probably' understood the voting system, whilst 40 per cent stated they had 'no understanding' at all. This limited understanding raises questions about young people having the ability to make informed choices. The majority of those who felt they had 'no understanding' were between the ages of 17 and 23 years and were first-time voters (Vakaoti 2014). This lack of understanding and awareness demonstrates the underpreparedness of young voters. This is of concern because it was considered that the young people's votes held the 'balance of power'.

In the lead-up to the elections the government, through the Fiji Elections Office (FEO), CSOs, political parties and the media, engaged in voter education and awareness. This section discusses activities directed at young people by the various stakeholders.

Ministry of Youth and Sports and youth voter awareness

The government's role in supporting young and first-time voters was restricted to awareness of the electoral process. Whilst the Ministry of Youth and Sports pledged to support young voters, its assistance was guided by what was provided by the FEO (Vukailagi 2014a). The FEO was commended for this role and its conduct of the elections resulted in the Multinational Observer Group endorsing the polls as being credible (Radio New Zealand International 2014). In June 2014, the government, through the Ministry of Youth and Sports, convened a youth conference for over 500 young people from across Fiji. Participants discussed 'issues relating to health, the environment, sports and human rights' (Fiji One 2014). It is unclear whether, even if the intention was to have a multiplier effect, gatherings such as this are enough to assist young people critically engage with issues that affect their lives.

Political parties: Attracting the youth vote

Political parties and, particularly, independent candidate Roshika Deo[3] were actively seen to include young people in the election process. The National Federation Party (NFP), hosted three youth-specific mini conferences and a national conference to deliberate on issues to be considered in the party manifesto (Vukailagi 2014b). In addition, the party's youth wing president was a member of the party's management board. The party also fielded young candidates in the general elections. The FLP, despite its historical rivalry with the NFP, did not appear to have an active engagement with young people; its party president, Mahendra Chaudhry, was also the 'youth' spokesperson (Anthony 2014). However, the FLP nominated Laisa Bale as its official youth candidate.

The SODELPA, although dominated by seasoned Taukei politicians and adults, courted young supporters. The SODELPA Youth Council president expressed the following view: 'we feel that all political parties have started working with young people … that's an important shift in terms of party politics and it's important that they incorporate young people into their work' (Tokalau 2014). The involvement of young people in the SODELPA party, either as volunteers and campaigners or as executive members, was magnified because of the use of social media. The SODELPA National Youth Council Forum (SODELPA Youth) manages a Facebook page[4] where it posts and generates conversation about social and political issues it deems significant. The party manifesto dedicates a section to young people. The content was derived from a youth vote survey coordinated by SODELPA Youth (Swami 2014). The party fielded some young candidates, one of whom, Mosese Bulitavu, is a current parliamentarian.

---

3   The 17 September elections were contested between seven political parties and two independent candidates, Umesh Chand and Roshika Deo.
4   For a detailed view of SODELPA Youth activities see www.facebook.com/sodelpayouth.

Newer parties, such as the PDP and One Fiji Party (OFP), also appealed to young people during the build-up to the elections. The PDP president, Lynda Tabuya, who self-identified as a young person, labelled her party as offering a 'new brand of politics', particularly for women, young people and minority groups (Doviverata 2014). The PDP, in supporting young people's direct involvement in the party, had them represented in its management board and also had a mandated 30 per cent representation of women and young people on its branch committees. OFP, led by an articulate lawyer and young aspiring politician, Filimoni Vosarogo, released thematic social contracts or manifestos, one of which focused specifically on 'igniting young people'.[5] The influence of OFP on young people is unknown; however, their policies proposed to support the future participation of young people through life skills training and the convening of a Youth Parliament, a popular structure for youth deliberation and debate in the past.

'Be the Change Campaign', the movement behind independent candidate Roshika Deo, was the only political entity that ran a youth-led and youth-focused election campaign. Roshika Deo mobilised her supporters predominantly via political discussions on Facebook and, in the lead-up to the elections, organised pocket meetings. Limited funding hindered her goal of visiting as many geographical locations as possible. 'Be the Change' ran a successful campaign influencing and including young people in its membership drives, community visits and pocket meetings (Gibson 2014a). Unlike political parties, Roshika Deo concentrated on developing young people's political consciousness and addressing structural barriers like patriarchy, ageism and gender inequality. In Fiji, this campaign approach, although necessary, is up against well-resourced parties campaigning on addressing developmental issues and providing for a secure future.

FijiFirst (FF), the party of the incumbent Bainimarama Government, which had governed Fiji since 2006, did not appear to have specific policies targeted at young people. Instead, it employed the discourse of inclusivity, hosting 'family fun days' in Fiji's main centres and advertising its pragmatic developmental approach during the campaign period (Tolley 2014). The rhetoric of equal citizenry and developmental

---

5   For more details on One Fiji Party's manifesto see www.onefiji.org.fj/.

assistance in the form of infrastructure development, free schooling and school bus fares, scholarships and subsidised electricity and water won favour with adults and young people alike.[6] For young people concerned about completing school and finding employment, FijiFirst offered an element of stability and continuity, even if their track record of adherence to democratic principles was questionable. It could be argued that the reduction of the voting age to 18 years was a calculated decision, given the Bainimarama Government's appeal for a new brand of politics and the many policies and forms of assistance that directly impacted on first-time voters. Whilst the influence of FF on young people is real, it is imperative that young people are supported as active citizens and not used as a political ploy in between elections and during the next elections.

Civil society organisations and youth engagement

CSOs also played a role in preparing and supporting young people's democratic participation. Local CSOs like the CCF, Fiji Women's Rights Movement (FWRM) and the Fiji Women's Crisis Centre (FWCC), which were critical of the government, banded together under the Fiji NGO Coalition for Human Rights. Despite working in a restrictive environment, these organisations persisted with their human rights and democratisation work in communities. Many young people became directly or indirectly involved in these activities.

The government's decision to commence constitutional consultations and eventually to hold elections was welcomed by CSOs. The CCF supported communities with constitutional consultation submissions and an awareness on the 2013 Constitution. The FWRM was instrumental in the formation of the Fiji Young Women's Forum (FYWF),[7] which worked to help young women with minimal or no understanding of democracy realise their responsibility as citizens and what this means in practice. The FYWF hosted two forums

---

6   For details of FijiFirst's manifesto see fijifirst.com/our-manifesto/#toggle-id-7.
7   The forum was co-convened by the FWRM, the Emerging Leaders Forum Alumni (ELFA), Generation Next (GenNext), the Young Women's Christian Association (YWCA) and the Diverse Voices for Action (DIVA).

with an ensuing outcome statement and declaration,[8] and produced a publication entitled 'My Guide to Voting'. The outcome statement, declaration and the guide to voting booklet addressed the passivity that characterised the spaces of young people's involvement. Through these activities, the FYWF critically connected its members to their lived realities and the importance of aligning this with the democratic structure and leadership the young women wish to see in post-election Fiji.

The United Nations Development Programme (UNDP), through its Strengthening Capacities for Peace and Development (CPAD) project, complemented the work of CSOs during the constitution consultation process. The CPAD project was intended to 'generate interest in the constitution making process and enhance understanding of why the constitution is important to the everyday lives of all Fijians' (Saune & Murdock 2013, p. 3). The project provided assistance through funding and support of other capacity-building strategies that allowed communities to openly and safely discuss issues they wanted reflected in the Constitution. Of the 146 funding applications received, 114 groups and organisations received funding. A notable number of these were youth groups or organisations that worked with specific youth-based interest groups (Saune & Murdock 2013).

The project found that despite the challenges of working with marginalised groups like women and young people, many organisations succeeded in developing participatory spaces specifically for them. As a result, many youth groups were able to make submissions on the Constitution, some using creative mediums. This exercise offered young people the opportunity to be meaningfully engaged and to understand the issues experienced in their communities (Saune & Murdock 2013). This awareness was intended to assist young people make an informed choice at the polls.

---

8   For details of the outcome statement and declaration see www.fwrm.org.fj/index.php/news/media-releases/2013/318-fiji-young-women-s-forum and www.fwrm.org.fj/index.php/news/media-releases/2014/330-young-women-s-declaration.

The media and young voters

The media, both traditional outlets and the Internet, were also active in the lead-up to the elections. Traditional media (radio, television and newspapers) continued to be the main sources of political information, a view supported by respondents in the CCF Youth Democratic Participation survey. The Internet is gaining popularity and as access increases many people, particularly the young, will opt for the Internet as their source of information. In the lead-up to the elections, social media was labelled the 'Fiji election battleground' (Round 2014b), because political parties and politicians took to social media as an alternative campaign strategy. Social media was used to address time and resource constraints as well as young people's lack of engagement in traditional party politics. Social media became particularly useful for young activists and politically conscious young people in an environment where the traditional media was restricted. Active political engagement on social media became the domain of urban, educated young people, perhaps those who needed the least convincing when it came to voting. The extent to which social media influenced the election outcome is unknown because it is highly likely that family and friends would have been influential, particularly for undecided young voters.

Did the youth vote matter?

In the lead-up to the 17 September elections, confident sentiments were expressed about young people's influence on the election outcomes. The May issue of the *Republika* magazine had the headline 'Fiji votes: youth hold the balance of power' on its cover. In its feature article, Kelvin Anthony, a youth activist, wrote, 'when the counting of votes is completed after Wednesday 17 September elections, a lot will hinge on the contributions of young people who form the majority of the voters' (2014, p. 17). Similar sentiments were echoed until the eve of the elections. Days away from the elections, academic Steven Ratuva asserted that young people's votes would decide the election outcomes (Wilson 2014). Did young people's votes actually decide the election outcomes?

This question is difficult to answer because the elections office provided neither figures nor analysis on voting characteristics, apart from the total votes cast at polling stations and total votes attained by political parties, party candidates and independents. One observation was clear: young people were not voting for young candidates. As an example, independent candidate Roshika Deo, who ran an overwhelmingly youth-centred campaign, attracted only 1,005 votes,[9] far fewer than the over 14,000 likes on her Facebook campaign page and the required minimum threshold for a seat in parliament. Whilst this demonstrated that virtual support does not necessarily translate into actual votes, it also showed that young people exist as a diverse group and thus voted accordingly.

In an election where young people's votes were the centre of discourse within government, non-government and media circles, exit polls would have been useful to offer indications of voter demographic characteristics. Available analysis of voter behaviour has been limited to understanding voting along ethnic lines (Ratuva 2014). The characteristics of votes by young people are subsumed within these analyses. Given the overwhelming support for FF, which campaigned mostly on development and 'bread and butter' issues, it is not difficult to suggest that the majority of young people voted on the basis of securing their well-being. This is fairly consistent with the results of the CCF Youth Democratic Participation survey, in which most of young people identified, in order of priority, employment (43 per cent), education (37 per cent) and transport (11 per cent) as issues that would influence their vote (Vakaoti 2014).

Ethnic analysis of voter behaviour in the elections is useful, and in the absence of comprehensive demographic voter behaviour information young people are easily included in this analytical frame. Whilst this approach reflects the government's position on doing away with ethnic compartmentalisation, it fails to give due consideration to young people and their priorities and preferences. If the pre-government rhetoric of doing away with 'old politicians and politics' should become reality, it could ensure that voting behaviour is transparent, particularly for understanding young people, whose generational influences

9 For detailed election results see the Supervisor of Elections report available at www.electionsfiji.gov.fj/.

166

are markedly different from those of their parents and other elders. Despite this reality, a bigger challenge lies with sustaining democratic support for young people into the post-election period and beyond.

Supporting active citizenship for young people

Voting is just one way of demonstrating active participation. The challenge for Fiji lies in supporting democratic structures at every level of society that meaningfully include young people. Whilst there are many structural and historical barriers, Fiji's return to parliamentary democracy offers hope that Fijians are aware of the future they want. Young people will significantly contribute to building on this vision and must be accorded an equal opportunity and provision of resources to do so. Stakeholders are equally critical in this process.

The role of government

Whilst it is difficult to assess the government's role in supporting the democratic participation of young people before the elections, performing this role in the post-election period is critical. The Ministry of Youth and Sports has the necessary structure and geographical reach to achieve this. Perhaps what is required is a reorientation of its focus from one of futurity and governmentality to one that considers the diverse realities and needs of young people (Vakaoti 2012). A national youth conference like that which was held in June 2014 could be made an annual event. In addition, the Ministry should consider reintroducing a national youth parliament as a way of connecting potential young leaders to decision makers and structures that facilitate their work.

Government has at its disposal the education system, where active and democratic citizenship could be introduced into the curriculum. It is imperative that Fiji's young people understand the country's socioeconomic and political history in order to make critical and informed decisions about their future. Discussion on topics like voting and the Constitution should be introduced in both primary and secondary schools. Participants in the CCF Youth Democratic Participation survey suggested that the best way of receiving political information in the future would be through citizen education in schools. Doing this will ensure 'a seamless transition from learning about democracy to putting such knowledge into practice' by the time one is 18 years of age (Youth Citizenship Commission 2008, p. 17). Universities would be expected to continue with this tradition, though this would be somewhat challenging given the recent experience where the University of the South Pacific in the period following the December 2006 coup had political debates and free thinking restricted as a result of a 'culture of political convulsion' (Lal 2004; Vakaoti 2012). Given Fiji's return to 'democracy' and healthy competition between the three universities in Fiji, there is optimism that critical young minds will continue to be cultivated at these institutions.

The role of political parties

Historically, the involvement of young people in party politics has been minimal. Results of the CCF Youth Democratic Participation survey reflects this reality. Of the 201 young people who participated in the survey, 90 per cent stated that they did not belong to a political party. This could in part be explained by the absence of party politics since 2006 and to the historical tendency of political parties to exclude young people from party machinery and processes. Young people's involvement in youth wings of the now disbanded Alliance Party, the waning FLP and the rejuvenated NFP were often regarded as tokenistic.[10]

The test of young people's sustained involvement in political parties will be seen in the period between elections. Parties like the NFP, PDP and SODELPA should continue to support the representation of young people on their management board, ensuring that their interests are considered and discussed at the decision-making level. This might be a point for consideration by parties that currently do not have such representation. It is also important that there are clear pathways within political parties for young people who aspire to move beyond being mere members, campaigners and volunteers. Parties serve

---

10   There are isolated cases where youth wings have been meaningfully involved and influential. Prior to 2006, the FLP's National Council, comprising 42 members, included a youth representative (Pareti & Frankel 2007). It is likely that a lone youth individual would have little influence on party deliberations and decisions (Vakaoti 2012). Lal (2010), writing about Jai Ram Reddy, alluded to the influence of the NFP Youth Wing in the removal of the party leader in the mid-1980s.

as ideal breeding grounds for future election candidates, politicians and leaders. Senior party officials and leaders could act as mentors to support this process. The members of the young people's Fiji Youth for Democracy (FYD) movement echo similar sentiments:

> FYD believes that political parties are crucial for the long-term development in transitioning societies like Fiji … Without well-functioning parties, governments and legislatures will have little chance of representing the wider society in a meaningful and effective way. Parties form a bridge between government and society, both in the ways they translate society's demands into political ideas and programs and in the way they hold government to account on society's behalf. (Scoop 2014)

The role of civil society organisations

Between 2006 and 2014, CSOs provided the 'voice of reason' in an environment devoid of basic democratic activities and processes. This role should continue into the post-election period. It is encouraging that the FYWF organised its third forum in November 2014 to discuss lessons learned from young women's political participation during elections and strategise for effective ongoing lobbying of decision makers. It is likely that other CSOs have plans of this nature in place for the future. The role of CSOs in this area need to be supported because they are effective spaces where young people can pursue issue-based interests and have direct experiences of different aspects of democratic participation.

Youth-led initiatives

Fiji is beginning to see an increase in youth-led organisations, active in the areas of mental health, gender discrimination and the creative arts (Vakaoti 2012). The lead-up to the 17 September elections brought to the fore young political activists like Roshika Deo of 'Be the Change Campaign' and youth-led organisations like the FYWF. The FYD movement, another youth-led organisation, was established in early

2013 by a group of youth activists. The focus of FYD has been to generate critical conversations around the constitutional development process and related democratic issues.[11]

A noticeable trend with youth activists and organisations is their use of social media. Whilst the use of social media appeals to technologically savvy young people, it also addresses issues related to limited funding and technical assistance required to support the work of these organisations. Alternatively, it could be just that as members of this generation young people find that social networking and social media better serve their purpose. The FYD, for instance, exists as a virtual organisation with an active Facebook page[12] and Twitter account.[13] Given that Internet penetration in Fiji stands at about 30 per cent, it is likely that the group is able to garner support only in areas with Internet accessibility, most certainly in urban areas. Whilst the confidence of these young people and their social media strategies ought to be noted, their connection to the wider youth audience is yet to be realised. As Fiji transitions into democracy and the media environment progressively becomes free, young people will perhaps be able to complement their virtual activism in bolder and more visible ways.

Conclusion

The elections brought a semblance of democracy to Fiji. The polls were declared to be credible by the Multinational Observer Group, a government was sworn in and parliament is back in session following an absence of seven-and-a-half years. Fiji has returned to the fold, reinvited into the Pacific Islands Forum and readmitted into the Commonwealth; and in November 2014 hosted the Indian Prime Minister, Narendra Modi, and the Chinese President, Xi Jinping. These visits and developments signal that Fiji is well on its transitional path to democracy.

---

11   In 2013, the FYD organised four panel discussions at the University of the South Pacific on the Constitution, democracy, reflections on the 26th anniversary of the first coup in 1987 and extractive industries and livelihoods.

12   See www.facebook.com/FijiYouthForDemocracy.

13   See twitter.com/FijiYouth.

Whilst government institutions appear to be fully functioning and diplomatic relations have been re-established, the government must deliver on its promise of granting young people greater civil and political rights. It must ensure that it has mechanisms and structures in place to consolidate the different ways in which young people participate and become involved in politics. The government's policy of generating a knowledge-based society must also include supporting young citizens to develop the critical ability to relate their issues and circumstances to decision-making structures at both the local and national level. CSOs also play a significant role in this process and must be encouraged to enter into dialogue with relevant government departments to deliver this opportunity for young people.

Young people from the age of 18 years were accorded the right to vote in the elections. Political parties and CSOs were active in this process. Community-based organisations supported the voter registration and awareness and education process, whilst political parties engaged young people directly as campaigners and volunteers, as members of management committees and as election candidates. Apart from traditional political campaigning and pocket meetings, social media became a vital part of engaging young voters with Internet connectivity. The influence of social media on voters, let alone young voters, is variable. A knowledge gap exists in relation to the use of social media for active political engagement and influence in Fiji. An understanding of this would assist those intending to digitally engage young voters in the next elections.

Regardless of intentions and speculations about the reduction of the voting age, young voters as active citizens must not rest on their laurels. They should, both in their youth sub-groups and as a collective, hold the government accountable to its promise of inclusivity and equality. Engaging in this process will give a sense of purpose to their vote on 17 September. Their collective strength, perhaps missing in the 2014 elections, could possibly be realised in the 2018 elections. A government that ignores the concerns of Fiji's growing and engaged population of young people does so at its peril.

References

Anthony, K 2014, 'Young Blood: Fiji's young people hold the key to the election result, but do they know and will they use it?' *Republika*, May issue.

Baines, M 2013, 'Fiji's PDP supportive of constitution – but wants to fix laws', Radio New Zealand International, 28 August. Viewed 20 November 2014 at www.radionz.co.nz/international/pacific-news/218895/fiji's-pdp-supportive-of-constitution-but-wants-to-fix-flaws.

Doviverata, R 2014, 'Lynda Tabuya Up for the Task', *Fiji Sun* [Online], 5 May. Viewed 20 November 2014 at fijisun.com.fj/2014/05/05/lynda-tabuya-up-for-the-task/.

Esser, F 2007, 'Comparing Young Voters' Political Engagement in the United States and Europe', *American Behavioral Scientist*, vol. 50, no. 9, pp. 1195–213.

Ewart, R 2014, 'Fiji's young people excited to be voting for the first time', *Radio Australia*, 16 September. Viewed 21 November 2014 at www.radioaustralia.net.au/international/radio/program/pacific-beat/fijis-young-people-excited-to-be-voting-for-the-first-time/1368559.

Fiji Government Online 2010, *Announcement on the Constitutional Consultations Process*. Viewed 25 August 2014 at www.#ji.gov.&/Media-Center/Speeches/PM-BAINIMARAMA---ANNOUNCEMENT-ON-THE-CONSTITUTIONAL CONSULTATIONS-PROCESS.aspx.

Fiji Government Online 2013, '*Fiji Country Statement on ICPD Programme of Action – Sixth Asia and Pacific Population Conference*'. Viewed at 20 November 2014 at www.fiji.gov.fj/Media-Center/Speeches/Fiji-Country-Statement-on-ICPD-Programme-of-Action.aspx.

Fiji Government Online 2014, '*Ministers urges youths in Ba to vote*'. Viewed 16 November at www.fiji.gov.fj/Media-Center/Press-Releases/MINISTERS-URGES-YOUTHS-IN-BA-TO-VOTE.aspx.

Fiji One 2014, *'Youths to converge in Suva for conference'*, 19 November. Available from fijione.tv/youths-to-converge-in-suva-for-conference/.

Gibson 2014a, 'Youths join 'change' campaign', *Fiji Times* [Online], 21 April. Viewed 16 November 2014 at www.fijitimes.com/story. aspx?id=266230.

Gibson 2014b, 'Youths role vital in election', *Fiji Times* [Online], 16 June. Viewed 20 November 2014 at www.fijitimes.com/story. aspx?id=271581.

Lal, B 2004, 'Laucala Bay' in B Lal (ed.), *Pacific Places, Pacific Histories*, University of Hawaii Press, Honolulu.

Lal, B 2010, *In the eye of the storm: Jai Ram Reddy and the politics of postcolonial Fiji*, ANU E Press, Canberra.

Online Editor 2014, 'Fiji PM Bainimarama delivers his promise to the world', Pacific Islands News Association, 28 September. Viewed 20 November 2014 at www.pina.com. fj/?p=pacnews&m=read&o=1545660808542882f682f626c8834d.

Pareti, S and Fraenkel, J 2007, 'The strategic impasse: Mahendra Chaudhry and the Fiji Labour Party', in J Fraenkel and S Firth (eds.), *From election to coup in Fiji: the 2006 campaign and its aftermath*, Asia Pacific Press and ANU E Press, Canberra.

Radio New Zealand International 2014, 'Fiji elections deemed credible', Radio New Zealand International, 19 September. Viewed 20 November 2014 at www.radionz.co.nz/international/pacific-news/254975/fiji-elections-deemed-credible.

Ratuva, S 2014, 'A symbol of hope – reflections on the Fiji election', *Pacific.Scoop*, 17 October. Viewed 20 November 2014 at pacific. scoop.co.nz/2014/10/a-symbol-of-hope-reflections-on-the-fiji-election/.

Round, S 2014a, 'Fiji Sodelpa pushes youth voter registration', Radio New Zealand International, 13 March. Viewed 16 November 2015 at www.radionz.co.nz/international/programmes/datelinepacific/audio/2588748/fiji-sodelpa-pushes-youth-voter-registration.

Round, S 2014b, 'Social media becomes Fiji election battleground', Radio New Zealand International, 25 March. Viewed 7 January 2015 at www.radionz.co.nz/international/programmes/datelinepacific/audio/2590200/social-media-becomes-fiji-election-battleground.

Saune, N and Murdock, J 2013, *Supporting Community Outreach for the Constitutional Development Process Project Report*, UNDP, Suva.

Scoop 2014, 'Fiji Youth for Democracy critical over interim Regime', *Scoop*, 29 July. Viewed 16 November 2014 at www.scoop.co.nz/stories/WO1307/S00644/fiji-youth-for-democracy-critical-over-interim-regime.htm.

Swami, N 2014, 'SODELPA's youth wing discusses manifesto', *Fiji Times* [Online], 27 July. Viewed 22 November 2014 at www.fijitimes.com/story.aspx?id=275543.

Tokalau, T 2014, 'People, parties trying to get the youth vote', *Fiji Times*, 17 February. Viewed 20 November 2014 at www.fijitimes.com/story.aspx?id=260226.

Tolley, P 2014, 'Fiji First stages big rally in Nausori', Radio New Zealand International. Viewed 20 November 2014 at www.radionz.co.nz/international/pacific-news/254512/fiji-first-stages-big-rally-in-nausori.

Vakaoti, P 2012, 'Mapping the landscape of young people's participation in Fiji', SSGM Discussion Paper 6, pp. 1–19.

Vakaoti, P, 2013 'Young people's participation in Fiji: Merits, challenges and the way forward', *Asia Pacific Viewpoint*, vol. 54, no. 1, pp. 77–90.

Vakaoti, P 2014, *Young People and Democratic Participation in Fiji*, Citizens Constitutional Forum, Suva.

Vukailagi, D 2014a, 'Youth ministry encourage first time voters', *Fiji One*, 28 April. Viewed 15 November 2014 at fijione.tv/youth-ministry-encourage-first-time-voters/.

Vukailagi, D 2014b, 'NFP urges youth to make their votes count', *Fiji One*, 26 July. Viewed 16 November 2014 at fijione.tv/nfp-urges-youth-to-make-their-votes-count/.

Wilson, C 2014, 'Youth votes will decide elections: Ratuva', *Fiji One*, 7 September. Viewed 15 November 2014 at fijione.tv/youth-votes-will-decide-elections-ratuva/.

Youth Citizenship Commission 2008, *Old enough to make a mark? Should the voting age be lowered to 16?* Youth Citizenship Commission, London.

9

The Fiji military and the 2014 elections

Jone Baledrokadroka

Introduction

The role of the military in Fiji's politics over the last 27 years has been decisive. Four military coups followed by democratic elections have indelibly shaped Fiji's political landscape. Held under the 2013 Constitution imposed on Fiji by the Bainimarama regime, Fiji's September 2014 elections were hailed by the coordinator of the Multinational Observer Group as 'broadly reflecting the will of the people' (Goledzinowski 2014). The readiness of the international community to sanction the polls after eight years of authoritarian rule underscores the pragmatism of realpolitik as also shown by the people of Fiji,[1] whose acquiescence to military intervention is now a hallmark of politics in the country. At the October 2014 swearing in of the new parliament after eight years of dictatorship, the 10 democratically elected former military officers, including several other members of FijiFirst (FF), all wore regimental neckties. In a sense, this display

---

1   In projecting forward the 2007 census percentages to September 2014, indigenous Fijians would make up 62 per cent and Indo-Fijians 34 per cent of the 591,101 registered voters.

of solidarity symbolised the pervasiveness of the Fiji military's political power.[2] Against this broad background, this chapter analyses the role of the military and its impact on the election outcome.

The most likely scenario is that former coup leader, and now elected Prime Minister, Frank Bainimarama, will be around for another four years until the 2018 elections—a total of 12 years in power. But the military is likewise destined to remain close to the centre of power. Bainimarama has certainly learnt from the past political mistakes of his military predecessors, Sitiveni Rabuka and Epeli Ganilau. Both former commanders made the miscalculation; it seems, of relinquishing their military command and basing their political ambitions on civilian political institutions. Rabuka used the Great Council of Chiefs to patronise his political party, the Soqosoqo ni Lewe ni Vanua iTaukei (SVT), and sanction his nationalist agenda. Insidious Taukei infighting involving its elite and fringe nationalist groups during Rabuka's prime ministership led to his downfall and the dismantling of the SVT. Ganilau, with the patronage of president and father-in-law Ratu Sir Kamisese Mara and Methodist reformists, formed the Veitokani Lewe ni Vanua Party (VLV) in 1999 and later in 2006, with business elites, cobbled together the moderate National Alliance Party. Both parties failed to draw mainstream Indo-Fijian or Taukei support. In Fiji's polarised ethnic politics Ganilau's elitist moderate alignment probably led to his demise and later falling out with Bainimarama. Ironically Ganilau, on venturing into politics, had chosen Bainimarama as his successor. Ever since, many senior officers have been purged or compelled to resign due to the personalised and political orientation of the commander.

Military's ethnic paradox

At the outset, the Achilles heel of Bainimarama and his officer elite's policy to reform Fiji's divisive communal society into an all-inclusive state based on civic nationalism lay in the exclusive ethnic makeup of

---

2   The 10 former military officers that make up the 33-member FijiFirst Party parliamentary members in government are V Bainimarama, T Natuva, J Konrote, P Tikoduadua, I Tuitubou, I Seruiratu, J Cawaki, N Rika, S Vunivalu and S Korolavesau. Incidentally, the opposition SODELPA Party has five former military officers in I Tikoca, V Tagivetaua, S Matanitobua, K Kiliraki and J Dulaki, accentuating the influence of the military in national politics as a whole.

the military. After eight years of espousing the values of multiracialism over ethno-nationalism, the military remains overwhelmingly an indigenous Fijian institution, with all its Taukei shibboleths. The reason for this ethnic disparity perhaps is historical, but the fact that the military regime overlooks this national political paradox whilst simultaneously dismantling other Taukei institutions is an oddity. Given Fiji's *vanua* politics, it is arguable that Bainimarama has created a super fourth Taukei confederacy using the military, which sits above the three neo-traditional confederacies. Perhaps herein also lies the inherent institutional character flaw that apparently triggers the military to intervene in Fiji's ethnically based politics. I suggest that the ethnic homogeneity of the Fijian military, unlike the heterogeneous makeup of its Melanesian counterpart in Papua New Guinea, is decisive in fostering the coup phenomenon.

Bainimarama has openly engaged in national politics, using the advantages of his military position. He later rationalised his actions by claiming that 'only the military can bring about real political change'. This became a political mantra that appears to have gone down well among youthful voters who, in spite of numerous claims against the regime of human rights abuse, see in Bainimarama's strongman persona the necessary political catalyst for bringing about a multiracial Fiji. His muzzling of nationalist elements within the Methodist Church has also proved effective in dampening ethno-nationalist fervour and engendering a more universalist orientation in the Methodist hierarchy (Weir 2014).

By cleverly co-opting receptive serving military officers, Bainimarama enticed a clique of officers with accelerated promotion and handsome salary increases that have enabled him to build a strong political base while using the military as a nation-building institution. This developmental face of the military, spearheaded by the Engineer Rural Development Unit, Trade Training School and National School cadetship program, have been effectively propagandised by the Ministry of Information and its proxy media outlets such as the *Fiji Sun* newspaper and FBC TV to great effect. On the darker side, Bainimarama has used the institution as a coercive political tool to great effect and, with his protégé Brigadier Mosese Tikoitoga, continues to do so subtly.[3] This patron–client relationship is the mainstay of the FF in spite of Tikoitoga's assurance that in future the military will be strictly 'politically neutral'. Hence the big question remains: will Fiji's third transition to democracy follow the Burmese model, where the military remains entrenched in the new democratic government, or evolve similarly to the Indonesian model where military influence is increasingly precluded in place of civilian democratic rule? I argue that the military's role as rationalised by the 2013 Constitution leaves the door ajar for further political intervention in the new democratic Fiji. This ambiguity in the military's constitutional role points ominously to a military that will remain a political force for at least the next decade.

Open List Proportional Representation and the advantage of incumbency

With an 84 per cent voter turnout on Election Day, the newly instituted open list proportional representative system, on the face of the polling results, favoured Bainimarama and his incumbent military regime's FF, which won 59.2 per cent of the popular votes. In a post-election review, Fraenkel (2014) stated that some of the major characteristics of the new electoral system were:

a. the reduction of the voting age from 21 to 18 years, which accounted for some 28 per cent of registered voters;

b. the eligibility of dual nationality and overseas permanent residence registered voters, which accounted for 7,186 votes or 1.4 per cent of the total votes cast;

c. the 5 per cent threshold of votes to gain a parliamentary seat, thus handicapping smaller parties and independent candidates;

d. the abolishing of communal constituencies; and

e. a single national constituency.

---

3   Master Joseva Bilitaki's much publicised allegation of being assaulted by military intelligence officers after sending angry text messages to Bainimarama around election time was dropped by the Director of Public Prosecutions for lack of evidence.

Invariably, the pre-election advantage of incumbency favoured Bainimarama's FF. The persecution of the opposition, especially former prime ministers Laisenia Qarase and Mahendra Chaudhry, the exorbitant civil servant pay rises and the vote-buying manifesto promises effectively foiled the opposition democratic front's late run in mustering voter support. Bainimarama's provoking rhetoric, bordering on political blackmail of 'you vote for me and there will be no coup', had its marked effect on voters. Furthermore, with half the population hovering on or beneath the poverty line, many voters were swayed by bread and butter issues as exemplified in the FF manifesto's promises of 'free water and milk'.

When all is said and done, the elections were the essential first step towards parliamentary democracy and the opening up of the political space that had been muted by draconian decrees in the previous eight years. Sceptics had serious doubts, given Bainimarama's track record, that the elections would eventuate. That it did take place on a relatively free and fair basis is a credit to the much maligned Fiji Elections Office and the Supervisor of Elections, although in the week before the elections Bainimarama's bombastic 'Suva will not burn again' statement, alluding to the 2000 Speight crisis, was political 'dog whistling' at best. In addition, the military's highly visible 'public exercises' in the week leading up to the elections almost certainly influenced undecided and impressionable youth voters as to who was the ultimate guarantor of public safety.

In military parlance, the Bainimarama regime had fought its opponents 'on ground of its own choosing'. The shaping of the 2014 elections 'battlefield' was cleverly executed, as in any well-constructed military-based process. The opposition parties were 'fixed' and 'channelled' by the obstacles on the 'killing ground' well before the battle began. The high hurdles set by the election decree for political parties and candidates ensured an uneven playing field in the pre-election period. Scott MacWilliam, an election observer, had even suggested that a bigger victory margin would have been achieved by FijiFirst if a 48-hour election media blackout had not been decreed. This is because of the party's huge undeclared donor-funding from businesses, which could have been deployed to ramp up its propaganda until polling hour, especially as the regime was well in control of the media industry.

Prior to the elections, Brigadier Tikoitoga's odd public comments further compounded the public's fears that the military would not remain neutral should Bainimarama lose the elections. The spectre of ethno-nationalism was incessantly invoked by Bainimarama while Tikoitoga harked back to the 2000 coup, thus subtly reminding the public of Bainimarama's artfully airbrushed 'saviour' role. Interestingly, among coup-prone states, only Fiji's military have conducted coups to avert perceived ethnic conflict. In Fiji's case, the contentious anti-ethno-nationalism rhetoric effectively justifies and may prolong the military's role in politics. With an ethno-nationalist Social Liberal Democratic Party as the principal opposition, Bainimarama can further strengthen the justification for the military's hardnosed approach via its proxy—FijiFirst.

The ethnic Gordian knot and the 'Glorious Revolution'?

Has the past eight years of Bainimarama's military authoritarian rule, as symbolised by the abolition of communal constituencies, cut through the Gordian knot of 'old' ethnic politics and its multi-complex issues? Coup apologist Graham Davis (2014), like many of his ilk, was enthralled with the result and went so far as to proclaim Bainimarama's decisive election victory as a 'glorious revolution' in which 'he took a sledge hammer to the entire political edifice, smashed it to smithereens and then set about rebuilding Fiji into a modern nation-state that has been transformed almost at every level'.

In spite of Davis's enthusiastic endorsement, Bainimarama's legacy and performance as Prime Minister and Minister of Finance remains debatable. One serious concern has been highlighted by members of the UN Human Rights Council (UNHRC), meeting in October 2014, who found the 2013 Constitution seriously flawed and recommended a commission to undertake its comprehensive review. There were 137 other recommendations that were brought to the attention of Fiji's high-powered delegation of eight senior government members to Geneva, headed by Attorney General Aiyaz Sayed-Khaiyum. Robert Jackman, in comparing the performance of military regimes, had found that 'military governments have no unique effects on social change, regardless of level of economic development' (quoted in

Perlmutter 1981, p. 118). The Auditor General's report from 2007–13 tabled in parliament stated that 'it has become abundantly clear there has been widespread abuse of public funds and blatant disregard of fundamental financial procedures'. Independent economist Professor Biman Prasad puts economic growth annually from 2006–13 on average at a paltry 0.1 per cent GDP. Furthermore, Janowitz states that in measuring overall economic development, the experience of military regimes is hardly impressive (Janowitz 1964, p. 79). The lack of public transparency and accountability in the last eight years due to authoritarian rule has indeed produced a society numbed by false 'feel good' propaganda churned out by a controlled and muted media industry.

Outspoken economist Professor Waden Narsey conservatively puts the total loss of potential GDP from 1987 to 2010 at close to FJD$10 billion as a result of Fiji's coups. The revelation of the released Auditor General's report is damning on the regime, and indeed the military, under Bainimarama. During the 2006–07 budget period, an unauthorised FJD$45.5 million was incurred by the military. What has played a major role in the survival of the Bainimarama regime has been the political support of superpower China. In the eight years of its authoritarian rule, in spite of the economic and political sanctions imposed by the West, the Bainimarama regime was able to resist the call for a prompt return to democracy because of Chinese economic aid and trade (Radio NZ 2014b). Indeed, much self-praise was generated by the Bainimarama regime due to its public infrastructure development record. Furthermore, Chinese President Xi Jinping's visit to Fiji after the elections, where he also met with leaders of Samoa, Vanuatu, Niue, Tonga, Federated States of Micronesia, Cook Islands and Papua New Guinea, underscores Beijing's backing of Fiji's new standing in the region.

Perlmutter, writing in the Cold War era prior to the rise of China, asserted that 'many observers may have been mistaken in attributing unique political skills to the military, whether directed toward progressive or conservative ends' (Perlmutter 1981, p. 117). Given that there are seven handpicked former senior military officers in Bainimarama's cabinet, it will be a challenge for them to display the independent and rigorous thinking vital to a transparent democratic society.[4] The optimistic prognosis of a progressive military promoting social change does not stand up to empirical analysis either. In their examination of whether policies that favour the military reduce the risk of coups, Collier and Hoeffler 'have found if anything, their effect was perverse: high military spending may even increase the risk of coups' (Collier & Hoeffler 2005, p. 2). The Fiji military's overspending record and expansion in non-core defence roles since the first coup in 1987, and after the coups of 2000 and 2006, verifies this assessment. By 2005, Bainimarama had developed a political agenda. This was clearly evident in Bainimarama's opposition to the Qarase government's National Security White Paper of that year. Obviously, the Qarase government saw the insolent military commander as a thorn in its side and was trying to get rid of him in early 2004 at the end of his contract. Bainimarama was adamant that any reform under the Qarase government would weaken the institution through a reduction in budget, retrenchment and more civilian control of the military. Under pressure from Bainimarama, the paper was shelved. The military's corporate power had won out.

A key question arising from this is how has this corporate identity developed over the years? Former vice president Ratu Joni Madraiwiwi, at a recent post-election symposium, warned that any dialogue with Bainimarama or the military as to its future role will have to be handled very carefully for obvious reasons (Radio NZ 2014a). As argued in a previous analysis (Baledrokadroka 2012a, p. 105), Fiji's participation in UN peacekeeping since 1978 has given the military an inflated corporate image that is now manifest in its perceived role of political conflict mediator.

Fijian peacekeepers in the UNDOF Golan Heights hostage crisis

In the lead-up to the elections, a number of Fijian soldiers serving with the UN Disengagement Observer Forces (UNDOF) were captured and held hostage by the jihadist al-Nusra group on the Golan Heights. This threatened to undermine Bainimarama's political campaign and split military solidarity. Questions were raised as to the wisdom of

4   The seven former RFMF officers included in the 20-member FF cabinet are V Bainimarama, T Natuva, J Konrote, P Tikoduadua, I Tuitubou, I Seruiratu and J Cawaki.

deploying Fijian soldiers to the Golan when other nations such as Austria, Japan, Croatia and the Philippines were withdrawing their contingents due to the highly dangerous civil war in Syria that had spilled onto the Golan. As argued earlier (Baledrokadroka 2012b, p. 105), Fiji's international peacekeeping has become a determining factor, with unintended consequences for the internal stability of the nation. This role has justified an oversized military with a similarly disproportionate share of the national budget. Even though the soldiers were released unharmed on the eve of the elections through the diplomatic negotiations of Qatar, Fiji's proud international peacekeeping image was tarnished. Arguably, Fiji's policy of providing soldiers on demand for UN peacekeeping missions unwittingly provides the military with its expanded political role. At the time of writing, 1,100 or a third of the military's 3,300 regular forces soldiers are on active duty with international peacekeeping forces.[5] An additional force of 5,000 active territorial and reservist soldiers, topped up by an annual recruitment of 300, provide peacekeeping replacements on six-monthly rotations. Hence, many youths see the military as a means of highly rewarding overseas employment. In spite of criticism during the Golan hostage crisis, Brigadier Tikoitoga revealed that Fiji was being invited by the UN Department for Peacekeeping Operations (UNDPKO) to provide more peacekeepers for UNDOF. After the Golan hostage crisis, the purchase of six 105 mm howitzers to upgrade obsolete artillery is also seen as a call by UNDPKO for Fiji to upscale its peacekeeping force protection armaments, given the high risk level in the volatile Southern Syrian border region with Israel. This FJD$10.2 million acquisition was carried out on the unilateral authority of Bainimarama as Minister of Finance.

Coup culture calculus

The National Federation Party leader, Tupou Draunidalo, has asserted:

> The coups in our country do not occur as an extension of widespread and sustained public disaffection. They occur after private and secretive consultations amongst private individuals, who then find the requisite personality in the military to carry out the coup. (Draunidalo 2014)

---

5   This consists of 339 all ranks with MFO Sinai, 270 all ranks with UNAMI Iraq and 500 all ranks with UNDOF Golan Heights.

This resonates with Samuel Finer's disposition/opportunity calculus to explain military intervention in Fiji's politics (Finer 1962, p. 140). Finer identifies the disposition of the military elite, which is bound to its corporate and individual interests, as the push factor. The pull factor is the military's opportunity to intervene when a weakening of public support for government has occurred. In applying the calculus in the Fiji coups context, it can be seen that these push-pull factors of political forces were present. The coalescence of the political Taukei Movement with Rabuka prior to the 1987 coup, and with Speight and Taukei political elites prior to the 2000 overthrow of the coalition government led by the Fiji Labour Party's Mahendra Chaudhry, and Commodore Bainimarama's plotting with politicians, community leaders and legal experts prior to the 2006 coup, substantiates Finer's coup theory.

Unfortunately, the role of the military as set out in the 2013 Constitution does not promote a coup-free future, thus raising questions about the political intentions behind it. The document states that '[t]he role of the Republic of Fiji Military Forces is to ensure at all times the security, defence and well-being of Fiji and all its residents'. This clause can be used by the military to justify intervention in a political crisis. The appointment of the commander of the Republic of Fiji Military Forces by the Prime Minister, as prescribed in the Constitution, may encourage partiality in what should essentially be a politically neutral office.

Conclusion

According to renowned Chinese strategist Sun Tzu: 'He will win who, prepared, takes his opponents unprepared'. Bainimarama had boasted before the elections that his FijiFirst party would win 50 seats. While the military regime and its proxy political party enjoyed the advantages of incumbency, the opposition parties were hobbled by unrealistic deadlines and decrees. Other tactics deployed by Bainimarama included handouts and civil service pay increases on the one hand and threatening rhetoric on the other. These factors, combined with the new national single constituency system, clearly favoured FijiFirst. Fraenkel (2014) also contends that the new open list system handicapped opposition parties, as candidates were also competing against each other for votes to ensure a seat in parliament. He further suggests that the ethnic cleavage of the past was still a feature of the 2014 elections. Even though the new electoral system was designed to eradicate this colonial legacy, old habits of thought and political behaviour die hard and it will take at least another generation for ethnic politics to be expunged, if they ever are.

While some, such as Madraiwiwi, see the election outcome as a significant step to a coup-free future despite these problems (Radio NZ 2014a), others are convinced that the legitimation of Bainimarama's party through the polls means that the coup culture remains firmly embedded. Draunidalo (2014) rightly contends that 'it would now appear to military personnel back home that Fiji likes to endorse coup makers and/or their proxies at the polls. Crime and treason certainly pays'. In explaining how civilian support coalesces around coup makers in Fiji, Draunidalo is critical of coup apologists, especially legalists and academics. She echoes Finer's coup theory, in which opportunists unite with the military, as brashly stated by another 18th-century military commander: 'I begin by taking. I shall find scholars later to demonstrate my perfect right' (quoted in Draunidalo 2014).

In summary, this chapter has addressed, if not answered, two sets of key questions. First, has the election result under the new Constitution finally eradicated Fiji's coup culture, or does it provide encouragement for future extra-legal political putsches? Second, will the military in Fiji hold to its constitutionalised political role, or will it retreat from politics and adopt a neutral philosophy as promised by Brigadier Tikoitoga? Certainly, the ethos of an essentially apolitical role needs to be strongly inculcated into the military officer corps. The arrival after the elections of British Army officers to conduct training in military leadership and other subjects seems to auger well for a return by the RFMF to its core professional role. Furthermore, balancing the ethnic makeup of the military with Indo-Fijians will also send a signal that the FijiFirst government is genuine in creating an all-inclusive multiracial state. This is part of the equation for a stable democracy. The other part of the equation is to ensure that political elites do not coalesce with the military elite at critical junctures of political tension. Meanwhile, in the transition to democracy post elections, Professor Brij Lal's quip that the 'military will remain the unseen elephant in the room' is quite apt. The absurdity of the military as both agent and client of its patron, Bainimarama's FijiFirst government, whilst claiming to be the final guarantor of national security, remains a paradox.

References

Baledrokadroka, J 2012a, 'The unintended consequence of Fiji's international peacekeeping', *Security Challenges*, vol. 8, no. 4, Summer.

Baledrokadroka, J 2012b, 'Sacred king and warrior chief: The role of the military in Fiji politics', Unpublished PhD thesis, SSGM, The Australian National University, Canberra.

Collier, P and Hoeffler, A 2005, *Coup traps; why does Africa have so many coup d'Etats?* University of Oxford Press, Oxford.

Davis, G 2014, 'The New Democracy Begins', *Grubsheet*, 22 September. Viewed 19 November 2014 at www.grubsheet.com.au/the-new-democracy-begins/.

Draunidalo T 2014, 'Fiji return to democracy: The 2014 elections and the coup culture', SSGM Workshop, 5 November 2014, The Australian National University, Canberra.

Finer, SE 1962, *The man on horseback: The role of the military in politics*, Pall Mall Press, London.

Fraenkel, J 2014, 'Fiji return to democracy: The impact of Fiji's switch to open list proportional representation, an analysis of the September 2014 elections', SSGM Workshop, 5 November 2014, The Australian National University, Canberra.

Goledzinowski, A 2014, 'Fiji Return to Democracy: Conduct of 2014 Fiji Elections', SSGM Workshop, 5 November 2014, The Australian National University, Canberra.

Janowitz, M 1964, *The military in the political development of new nations*, University of Chicago Press, Chicago.

Perlmutter, A 1981, *Political roles and military rulers*, Routledge, London.

Radio NZ 2014a, 'Fiji elections 'significant step' to coup free future', 20 November. Available at www.radionz.co.nz/international/pacific-news/259832/fiji-elections-'significant-step'-to-coup-free-future.

Radio NZ 2014b, 'More Chinese Aid to Fiji 'people focused', 24 November. Available at www.radionz.co.nz/international/pacific-news/260140/more-chinese-aid-to-fiji-'people-focused'.

Weir, C 2014, 'Fiji return to democracy: The election and the Methodist church', SSGM Workshop, The Australian National University, Canberra

10

The genesis of the Social Democratic Liberal Party: A struggle against the odds

Pio Tabaiwalu

Introduction

Fiji's political landscape has been shaped along a fractured fault line between the country's two main communities: indigenous Fijians and Indo-Fijians. This legacy of Fiji's colonial past has dogged the country since independence in 1970. The Indo-Fijians are descendants of Indians brought to the colony as indentured labourers by Britain, the then colonial power, to develop a plantation economy. Indo-Fijians came to dominate the economy, arousing resentment from indigenous Fijians. There was increasing fear amongst indigenous Fijians, many of whom lived in semi-subsistence communities, that the Indo-Fijians would ultimately acquire political dominance as well.

This difficult relationship has been the cause of much political upheaval, beginning with the military *coup d'état* of 14 May 1987 that resulted in the overthrow of the elected government of Prime Minister Timoci Bavadra, the deposition of Elizabeth II as Queen of Fiji, and the declaration of a republic, ending the monarch's reign in Fiji. This was followed by a second coup on 28 September 1987. Both military actions were led by Lieutenant Colonel Sitiveni Rabuka, then third in command of the Royal Fiji Military Forces.

The Fiji coup of 2000 was a complicated affair involving a civilian, George Speight, backed by hard line indigenous Fijian nationalists against the elected government of Prime Minister Mahendra Chaudhry on 19 May 2000.

The latest coup was carried out by military commander Commodore Frank Bainimarama, who seized power on 5 December 2006 from elected Prime Minister Laisenia Qarase.

Overview of the conflict

The 2006 military coup had its origins in the coup of 2000 led by civilian George Speight. The 2000 coup was aimed at the multiethnic government led by Mahendra Chaudhry. After Bainimarama declared martial law and resolved the crisis by force, an interim government was sworn in, headed Laisenia Qarase. Laisenia Qarase and his colleagues in the interim government went on to form the Soqosoqo Duavata ni Lewenivanua (SDL) party and won the elections in 2001 and 2006. Commodore Bainimarama had often said that forming a political party was not part of his 'understanding' with members of the Interim Civilian Government when they were installed. Many commentators have cited this as the beginning of the falling out between Qarase's SDL party and Bainimarama. The SDL had also introduced parliamentary bills that provoked the displeasure of the military.

Three were three bills that were especially contentious to the military and opponents of the SDL government: the Reconciliation Tolerance and Unity Bill (RTU), the Qoliqoli Bill and the Land Tribunal Bill. Perhaps the most significant of these was the RTU bill, which would grant an amnesty to some of those involved in or being investigated for involvement in the coup of 2000.

Relations between the Qarase Government and the Republic of Fiji Military Forces (RFMF) deteriorated from then on. Qarase and his ministers made several attempts to remove the Commander from office: by offering him a diplomatic posting in 2001 and later by resisting the renewal of his contract, and finally by advising the president to remove him. None of these attempts succeeded.

Political commentators have pointed out that the 2006 military coup was the culmination of the personal ambition of Bainimarama for political leadership. Coupled with this was his attempt to suppress allegations of the misuse of military regimental funds, and his role in the deaths of Counter Revolutionary Warfare Unit (CRW) soldiers who were involved in a mutiny against him in November 2000. Fiji's former police chief, Andrew Hughes, had also launched an investigation into Commodore Bainimarama for alleged sedition after he threatened to overthrow the elected government of Qarase. All these precipitated Commodore Bainimarama's actions against Qarase and his government.

The 2006 general elections once again illustrated historical voting patterns along ethnic lines, with over 80 per cent of the popular vote and all 23 seats reserved for indigenous Fijians going to the SDL, and a similar percentage and all 19 seats reserved for Indo-Fijians going to the Fiji Labour Party (FLP). Overall, the SDL won 36 seats, the FLP won 31 seats and the remaining seats were shared by the United People's Party and independent candidates. The SDL victory must have intensified Bainimarama's resolve to carry out the military coup.

Commodore Bainimarama carried out his coup on 5 December 2006 after months of public vilification of Prime Minister Qarase and of the SDL government.

Bainimarama had supposedly invoked special powers under the Constitution and was using them to dismiss Qarase. On 4 January 2007, executive authority was returned to the President Ratu Josefa Iloilo and Dr Senilagakali resigned as interim prime minister. Ratu Josefa declared his support for the military takeover although he had earlier condemned it as illegal. He then appointed Bainimarama as interim prime minister and also announced the formation of an interim government to lead the country to fresh elections.

The genesis of the Social Democratic Liberal Party

Under the Political Parties (Registration, Conduct, Funding and Disclosures) Decree 4 2013, the previously registered political parties had 28 days to re-register. Each political party had to collect 5,000 signatures with allocations from Fiji's Central, Western, Northern and

Eastern administrative divisions. Previously a party only required 180 members to become registered. The membership threshold was a major challenge to the SDL Party.

The more sinister provision of the decree was a requirement that all political parties be named in English rather than Fijian. The SDL Party was keenly aware that the regime wanted to eradicate the party, evidenced by Bainimarama's strong disapproval of SDL policies and a personal falling out with the ousted prime minister, Laisenia Qarase. The provision of the decree to change the name of all parties into English was seen by the party as a direct means to deregister the SDL.

The party hierarchy had initially made a decision to contest the elections as a practical means of moving the country to democratic rule. Rather than changing its name, the SDL Party wound itself up and reformed as the Social Democratic Liberal Party (SODELPA) in order to retain the SDL acronym. However, a subsequent amendment to the Political Parties Decree banned the use of the acronyms of deregistered parties. It was evident that the regime did not want the SDL to exist even as an acronym. However, the decree allowed the use of abbreviations; the party resorted to the abbreviation SODELPA to register as the Social Democratic Liberal Party. The party applied for registration on 26 February 2013, and was registered on 3 May 2013. But the regime had achieved its aim to deregister the SDL Party.

The party was led by Ro Teimumu Kepa as its president and drew up a new constitution. Its stated vision was based on the following:

- commitment to the promotion of peace, stability and economic prosperity and to pursue a policy of dialogue and negotiation at all times to achieve peaceful solutions to Fiji's challenges;
- totally rejecting the notion that such solutions can be reached through acts of violence, force, intimidation and illegality;
- that Fiji's progress must be founded on the rule of law, parliamentary democracy, equity, and social justice for all our people; and
- that the strength of the nation comes from the strength of its component communities and individuals (SODELPA 2013a, p. 2).

There was a strong commitment from party officials to state categorically in its Constitution the principles of good governance and transparency and to assure all communities that the party embraced and respected the basic rights and freedoms of other communities. It has the following in its aims and objectives:

- to establish a peaceful, caring and prosperous nation;
- to unite the citizens of Fiji and to represent them and their interests fully and with integrity;
- to uphold Christian values and principles and to respect the beliefs and values of other religious faiths;
- to protect, enhance and promote the economic, social and human development of all communities and to secure their future in the Fiji Islands;
- to associate with and/or collaborate with other political parties in order to create an association/alliance for national unity and to promote nation-building;
- to provide the nation with good, honest, dedicated, transparent and competent government and to serve it with devotion;
- to provide policies that prevent all corrupt practices and behaviour; and
- to facilitate and foster positive economic and social development, sustained economic growth and development of all our communities (SODELPA 2013a, p. 2).

From its inception, SODELPA had striven to be attractive to other communities than the Taukei only, knowing that the future of any major political party depended on its cross-ethnic national appeal. This proved to be very difficult, as many perceived SODELPA as just a reincarnation of the SDL and its ethno-nationalist policies. This also became a rallying point for Bainimarama, who frequently referred to party officials as 'old politicians with the same old ideas'.

An important objective of the SODELPA Constitution was the protection and enhancement of the rights of indigenous Fijians, as contained in the United Nation Declaration of the Rights of Indigenous Peoples (UNDRIP) and the International Labour Organization Convention No. 169 on Indigenous and Tribal Peoples. This generated strident views within the party as a consequence of provisions in the 2013 Constitution and specific decrees that were perceived as deliberate attempts by the regime to weaken the rights of indigenous Fijians, especially their group rights to their ancestral land. This was best illustrated in the party manifesto as follows:

> To the indigenous Fijians land is not just an economic commodity. It is part of culture, kinship and group identity. That is why the Fijians cling so fiercely to their land ownership. The Bainimarama-Khaiyum constitution does not reflect this indigenous attachment to their land.
>
> Their claim that Fijian land has greater protection than before is a lie. Its protection has been weakened. In fact there was no reference at all to native land in the first draft of their constitution. It was left out completely. This caused great fear and uncertainty among landowners. It was only when supporters of SODELPA began to speak out that Bainimarama-Khaiyum decided to include specific reference to native land in their constitution. Without the SODELPA protests they would likely have enacted their supreme law with no special reference to native land. (SODELPA 2013b, p. 89)

The draft constitution by the Yash Ghai Commission that was scrapped by the regime also included a list of protected laws: iTaukei Lands Act (Cap 133), iTaukei Land Trust Act (Cap 134), Rotuma Lands Act (Cap 138), Banaban Lands Act (Cap 124) and Agricultural Landlord and Tenant Act (Cap 270). All these safeguards were not in the constitution drafted by the Bainimarama regime. Instead, in the 2013 Constitution indigenous Fijian land ownership was simply placed alongside a list of provisions in the Bill of Rights. However, section 6 of the Bill of Rights permits rights to be limited and therefore changed. All these rights listed can be subjected to limitations. These developments were of grave concern to traditional stalwarts of the party, who feared a gradual deterioration of the entrenched rights of indigenous Fijians.

Furthermore, since the coup of 2006 the military regime had systematically dismantled and weakened the native Fijian Administration (Matanitu Taukei) and the laws that govern it, which has caused further disaffection among indigenous Fijians. This is clearly reflected in the following decrees:

- the Fijian Affairs Great Council of Chiefs (GCC) Regulation Decree of 2007 to suspend the GCC;
- the GCC Amendment Decree of 2008 to terminate GCC nominees to the Fijian Affairs Board, to be replaced by government appointees;

- the Fijian Affairs (Provincial Councils) amendment regulation of 2008 to terminate attendance at Provincial Councils of educated urban indigenous Fijians;
- the Fijian Trust Fund (Amendment) (No. 2) Decree 2009 to remove authority of the chiefs from appointing members to the Fijian Trust Fund Board and substituting it with government appointees;
- the Native Land Trust Act (Amendment) (No. 31) Decree 2009 to amend Section 3 of that Act to remove the appointing authority of the chiefs to the Native Land Trust Board and its replacement by the government appointees;
- the Native Land Trust (Amendment) Regulation of 2010 that terminated the share of royalty income for the chiefs;
- the Mahogany Industry Development Decree (No. 16) of 2010 that terminated iTaukei Land Trust Board's (TLTB) power and authority over mahogany leases on native land and the power to negotiate financial return on mahogany plantations and its replacement by a Mahogany Industry Council headed by Prime Minister Voreqe Bainimarama;
- the Regulation of Surfing Areas Decree (No. 35) of 2010 that terminated control of surfing areas by iTaukei and their trustee TLTB, vesting all rights in the government;
- the Native Land Trust Act (Amendment) (No. 31) Decree 2010 to terminate reference to indigenous 'Fijians' to be replaced by the label 'iTaukei' and application of the label 'Fijian' to all citizens of Fiji without consideration of the views, and consent of, the indigenous Fijian;
- the Native Land Trust (Amendment) (No. 32) Decree 2010 to amend Section 3 of that Act to vest control of that institution in the minister, who replaces the president as representative of the chiefs and customary landowners; and removing chiefly representation to the board, replacing it with the government and prime minister as sole appointing authority;
- the iTaukei Land Trust (Amendment) (No. 20) Decree 2012 to amend Section 19 of that Act to remove the GCC as authority to determine customary ownership and its replacement with government authority;
- the iTaukei Affairs (Amendment) (No. 22) Decree 2012 to amend Part 2 of that Act to remove and terminate the existence of the GCC;

- the iTaukei Trust Fund (Amendment) Decree (No. 23) of 2012 that terminated the GCC administrative power of the Fijian Trust Fund;

- the Land Use Decree (No. 36) of 2010 that gave to the prime minister unfettered power to designate native land to a land bank, to be administered by the Land Use Unit and Director of Lands;

- the Native Land Trust (Amendment) Decree (No. 20) of 2010 that terminated the GCC's authority over extinct *mataqali* land;

- the Native Land Trust (Amendment) Decree (No. 20) of 2012 that terminated the power of the GCC to determine customary ownership of extinct *mataqali* land;

- the iTaukei Trust Fund (Amendment) (No. 23) Decree 2012 to remove any reference to the GCC and the need to provide for its financial autonomy;

- the Unit Title (Amendment) Decree (No. 38) of 2013 that removed the restriction of that Act on native land.

The 2013 Constitution had further weakened indigenous Fijian group rights; there is no reference to the Deed of Cession and its historical significance, as in the 1997 Constitution. The Deed of Cession was for many indigenous Fijians the basis on which they could rightly claim their inheritance as first inhabitants, including their inalienable rights to their traditional lands and resources.

Moreover, the 1970 and 1997 Constitution had special entrenched provisions, providing extremely strong safeguards for indigenous Fijian, Rotuman and Banaban landownership. These constitutional provisions laid down very detailed and entrenched procedures for altering the following: the Fijian Affairs Act; Fijian Development Act; Native Lands Act; Native Lands Trust Act; Rotuma Act; Rotuma Lands Act; Banaban Lands Act; and the Banaban Settlement Act. These entrenched provisions are no longer in the 2013 Constitution.

There is also no provision in the 2013 Constitution on customary law and customary rights, which were provided for in the 1997 Constitution as group rights. This would have allowed the application of such laws in the proper maintenance and observance of customary practices.

The 1997 Constitution stated as follows:

Customary laws and customary rights

186. (1) The Parliament must make provision for the application of customary laws and for dispute resolution in accordance with traditional Fijian processes.

(2) In doing so, the Parliament must have regard to the customs, traditions, usages, values and aspirations of the Fijian and Rotuman people.

(3) The Parliament must make provision granting to the owners of land or of registered customary fishing rights an equitable share of royalties or other moneys paid to the State in respect of the grant by the State of rights to extract minerals from the land or the seabed

(Fiji Constitution 1997, Section 186)

Coupled with the above, the military regimes took control of all companies established under Fiji's semi-autonomous native administration (Matanitu Taukei), including Fijian Holdings Limited and the Native Land Trust Board, the government agency that administers native land (SODELPA 2013b, p. 38).

The above actions by the regime were perceived by SODELPA as a deliberate attempt by the regime to regress indigenous rights. This suppression of the communal group rights of indigenous Fijians, for the creation of a progressive nation-state, is clearly espoused by the military regime's Attorney General Aiyaz Sayed-Khaiyum in his unpublished thesis. In his conclusion Khaiyum states as follows:

Therefore cultural autonomy must have a sunset clause. Its prolonged continuation will place a stranglehold on the very members it seeks to protect and it will concomitantly disallow the critical cultural space in which a just, vibrant and coherent nation-state can flourish while embracing diversity. (Sayed-Khaiyum 2002, p. 69)

But such impositions will not create a stable and lasting solution to Fiji's long-term stability as a multicultural nation. As Jon Fraenkel states, 'It is inconceivable that an assault on the institutions of indigenous Fijian post-colonial rule will yield a viable future for that country' (Fraenkel 2014, p. 1).

This will be a major challenge in the years ahead as SODELPA tries to reconcile its traditional base voters, who perceive the threat to the deterioration of their rights as indigenous people on the one hand, and the need to address the social and economic needs of a new, more urbanised voter on the other.

In addition, the voting age was reduced to 18 years, which has its own political dynamic. Many young voters will have not voted before and many are divorced from the traditional sentiments about indigenous concerns such as the GCC or land rights. For them, bread and butter issues, access to education and job opportunities are critical factors. As Jon Fraenkel states:

> The main opposition party, SODELPA, chose to campaign—as Laisenia Qarase did in 2001 and 2006—by appealing mainly to the indigenous Fijian community on issues such as hostility to the dissolution of the Great Council of Chiefs and threats to indigenous Fijian land ownership. These issues struck a chord amongst older ethnic Fijian voters, but they carried little weight among the younger generation. With the voting age reduced to 18, these voters held sway in 2014. (Fraenkel 2014, p. 1)

In examining the new voting system and the demographic distribution, SODELPA party officials were always aware that they could not win the elections alone. They needed the other opposition parties to win some of the seats, with the intention of going into a coalition to form a government. Contrary to Fraenkel's observation, SODELPA also had economic, social, governance and bread and butter issues in its manifesto. The pliant media had become a propaganda tool for the regime and SODELPA could not get its other progressive messages across.

The restrictive political environment

Although Voreqe Bainimarama stepped down eventually from leadership of the army, before the general elections it was evident that Fiji was still governed by a military-backed dictatorship. The promulgation of restrictive decrees placed severe limitations on the ability of political parties to launch their political campaigns.

For instance, the Political Parties Decree stated that a person who had been convicted and imprisoned for an offence for a period of six months or more in the last five years cannot be a party official. This effectively ruled out Qarase, who had served a year-long prison sentence after he was convicted for offences committed before he was prime minister. The same provision later ruled out Mahendra Chaudhry, the FLP leader. The decree also banned trade union officials from being political party officials; many commentators believed this provision targeted union officials like Felix Anthony (National Secretary of the Fiji Trades Union Congress) and Attar Singh (General Secretary of the Communications, Mining and General Workers Union), who had shown keen interest in contesting the elections. An amendment to the decree also nullified the candidacy of Anare Jale, a strong and popular candidate for SODELPA, and unfairly disqualified some opposition party candidates because they had been overseas for more than 18 months prior to the writ of elections. The party perceived all these restrictive sections of the decree as an attempt by the regime to weaken prominent opposition figures at the polls.

Increasingly, within the regime decisions were made by a few, there was no consultation with political parties and information was published through the pliable media. Repressive and undemocratic decrees were promulgated, such as the State Services (Amendment) Decree 2000; Public Order Amendment Decree 2012; the Media Industry Development Decree 2010; the Political Parties (Registration, Conduct, Funding and Disclosures) Decree 4 2013; the anti-worker and anti-union Essential National Industry (Employment) Decree 2011; Regulation of Pension and Retirement Allowances Decree 2009; and the Compulsory Registration of Customers for Telephone Services Decree 2010. These decrees placed severe limitations on activities that would provide for more transparent democratic processes to ensure free and fair elections.

The muzzling of the media

The media industry had been under severe censorship since the military coup of December 2006. The people saw for themselves the pervasive damaging influence of the Media Decree on the quality and content of what was reported. Many journalists spoke of the self-censorship in the newsroom. The net effect is that what eventually came out as news was heavily truncated and edited by regime lackeys. There were many complaints lodged with the Media Industry Development Authority (MIDA) by concerned citizens and SODELPA party officials, but nothing eventuated. There was also growing unease that MIDA may have been unduly influenced by the regime due to its lack of response to the pro-regime propaganda and the suppression of opposition views.

Section 22 of the Media Industry Development Decree states that content must not include material, which is (a) against the public interest or order; (b) against the national interest; or (c) creates communal discord. This provision effectively regulated how the media generated its news and in many instances was selectively interpreted by the regime.

The heavy penalties for a breach of the decree also placed undue pressure on the media to exercise self-censorship. Upon conviction for any breaches of the media code, a media organisation could be fined FJD$100,000; a publisher/editor FJD$25,000 and/or two years imprisonment; and a journalist or media FJD$1,000 and/or two years imprisonment.

A free and fair media without the restrictive and selective interpretations of the Media and MIDA Decrees was essential to balanced reporting in terms of the opposition parties getting their views and opinions to the general public.

This lack of media coverage proved to be a crucial factor in the overall performance of the opposition parties at the polls, including SODELPA. They were simply shut out of the media, and with less visibility and coverage it was always going to be an uphill battle for them.

A system of elections to suit the FijiFirst Party

It became quite clear to SODELPA that the system of elections that was imposed on the country by the regime would favour Bainimarama's FijiFirst. The system of voting is prescribed in the 2013 Fiji Constitution as follows:

53. (1) The election of members of Parliament is by a multi-member open list system of proportional representation, under which each voter has one vote, with each vote being of equal value, in a single national electoral roll comprising all the registered voters and

(3) A political party or an independent candidate shall not qualify for any seat in Parliament unless the political party or the independent candidate receives at least 5% of the total number of votes cast. (Fiji Government 2013)

SODELPA was supportive of a multiple constituency system that would allow representations in specific constituencies and allow voters to cast their votes along party lines. But the regime had chosen a single national electoral roll—a system that would ultimately benefit it.

Furthermore, the rejection by Bainimarama of the Yash Ghai draft should be seen in the context of the overall election strategy of FijiFirst and its performance at the polls. As explained by Wadan Narsey:

First, the Ghai draft electoral system had four constituencies (the divisions), apparently a trivial difference, but it would have limited Bainimarama to appear on the ballot paper for only one constituency and hence strictly limited his personal vote appeal. All other FF candidates in the other three constituencies would have had to struggle for votes against other competitors, instead of riding on Bainimarama's coat-tails.

Second, the Bainimarama government would have had to resign six months before the election. This would have prevented Bainimarama and his ministers from using taxpayers' funds and donor-funded projects, right up to polling day, in blatant and very successful vote buying.

Third, Bainimarama would not have had the complete control over the media through their restrictive media decrees (including the Media Industry Development Authority – MIDA) to obtain maximum political mileage for themselves, while criticising and ruthlessly suppressing opposition parties.

Fourth, to obtain immunity, Bainimarama and his coup collaborators would have had to express remorse for specific actions for which they wanted immunity, with clearly negative consequence for their image with voters. (Narsey 2004, p. 1)

Apparently, the Yash Ghai draft constitution was discarded and a new one manufactured to put in place the most conducive electoral system to win the elections for Bainimarama's intended party.

The electoral decree came out in March 2014, although the regime had earlier promised that it would be ready by December 2013. The lateness of the electoral decree, which took an inordinately long time to draft, was another ploy by the regime to restrict the time for other political parties to prepare for elections.

The decree also had provisions that were clearly against free and fair elections. SODELPA had conveyed the following issues to the Electoral Commission:

- party symbols to be part of the ballot paper and candidates be grouped together under their respective party symbol instead of just having the numbers of the candidates;
- adequate training to be provided for party officials and agents;
- examination of the role of media and their self-induced censorship as a consequence of the restrictive provisions of the Media Industry Development Decree;
- allow more public political rallies, the number of which was limited by the Public Order Amendment Decree;
- allow a more diverse group of observers for the elections, especially local NGOs who were prevented from observing the elections by the Electoral Decree 2014;
- the Commission to take a more proactive role in the build-up to the elections to engender public confidence in the neutrality of the process;
- the excessive penalty for any person who contravened the Electoral Decree, who would be liable upon conviction to a fine not exceeding FJD$10,000 or to a term of imprisonment not exceeding 5 years, or to both; and
- to amend the provisions in the Electoral Decree 2014 that allowed the Supervisor of Elections and his staff indemnity from court actions as a result of decisions they undertake.

The Electoral Decree stated that the ballot paper was to have only numbers, with no names, no photos and no party symbols. SODELPA, with other political parties, made many representations to the

Commission to seek changes to the ballot paper, particularly the need to have party symbols to assist voters. This eventually culminated in the production of a handbook that had the names, photos and numbers of candidates, which could be consulted by voters before placing a tick on the number of the candidate of their choice on the ballot paper. But this made little difference, as the ballot paper only had the number and was clearly to the advantage of FijiFirst, which was promoting just one number.

> It is abundantly clear now that the entire electoral system and electoral decree was cunningly designed to suit the Bainimarama campaign for voters to remember only one number (279) while ignoring all other candidates. (Narsey 2014)

It was quite apparent that the FijiFirst strategy was to ask voters to vote for just the one number representing Bainimarama, and this was heavily advertised through the media and campaign material. The large number of votes for Bainimarama hauled in many of his FijiFirst colleagues with fewer votes than those for SODELPA candidates who did not get into Parliament. Many will question whether this was a 'democratic' representation of voters and the validity of the mantra of 'one man, one vote, one value'.

The electoral system had also imposed a 5 per cent threshold rule that disadvantaged small parties and independents. The total votes lost due to the very high threshold resulted in FijiFirst getting 3 extra seats. This was another gain to the regime's party that was foreseen and written into the relevant decree.

The elections authorities

To ensure control over the process of elections, the Bainimarama regime chose as the Minister of Elections its own Attorney General (Aiyaz Sayed-Khaiyum), who was also the secretary-general of FijiFirst Party. This was a blatant exposition of political control to ensure an election that was in all ways and means to their advantage.

In addition, the Supervisor of Elections, Electoral Commission members, and the MIDA chairman were all seen by the party as pawns in the build-up to elections, as most of them were well known regime sympathisers.

The Electoral Decree also deemed:

> it shall be unlawful for any person, entity or organization that receives any funding or assistance from a foreign government, inter-governmental or non-governmental organization or multilateral agency to engage in, participate in or conduct any campaign (including organizing debates, public forum, meetings, interviews, panel discussions, or publishing any material) that is related to the election or any election issue or matter. (Fiji Government 2014)

This provision barred local NGOs from educational activities related to the elections and effectively restricted the boundaries for free and fair elections. The Electoral Commission was going to conduct all the training and from the party's perspective that was inadequately done.

There was also the decision by the Minister for Elections and secretary of the FijiFirst Party that while international observers of his choice would be allowed to monitor the elections, no local observers would be allowed, although it was clear that local observers would have had a better understanding of local issues and possible discrepancies in the process.

It was abundantly clear that after numerous efforts by SODELPA for a level playing field, the election authorities were doing very little to try to make the elections genuinely 'free and fair', despite the restrictive Electoral Decree and the compromised media environment.

SODELPA at the polls

The SODELPA party executives were well aware that it was going to be a hard-fought battle at the polls. The base voters of the party would have to be the iTaukei, with a total of 297,818 votes comprising nearly 60 per cent of the total votes of 496,364. The party had to win 52 per cent of the total national votes to get the 26 seats required to govern on its own. This meant that if it wanted to target just the iTaukei then it had to win over 80 per cent of their votes. This was a near impossible task.

The strategy was to go after the iTaukei votes with the hope that the other two major political parties, the National Federation Party (NFP) and the Fiji Labour Party (FLP), would win enough seats to form a coalition government. This was first articulated by party leader Ro Teimumu Kepa in his maiden speech as party leader of SODELPA, where he invited other opposition parties to be part of a grand coalition. This was the only feasible strategy in the face of overwhelming odds, given that FijiFirst had been in power for nearly eight years and controlled the media and the rules for elections.

SODELPA won 139,857 votes, which translated into 15 seats in Parliament; and with NFP winning three seats and the FLP winning none the party fell short of the targeted 26 seats.

> FijiFirst also had the advantage over other parties in terms of resources and the fact that they were in power in the form of the post-coup regime and had control over the political and coercive means to restrict the media and freedom of association and was in control of development projects which it marketed effectively to voters.
>
> Eight years of authoritarian rule and unrivalled hegemony entrenched their visibility, familiarity and relevance in the consciousness of voters. (Ratuva 2014)

Although SODELPA could not form government as a coalition as intended, the result was positively considered as a first step towards parliamentary democracy.

Conclusion

The triumph of coup perpetrator Bainimarama and his FijiFirst Party illustrates how a military commander treasonably deposed a lawfully elected government and yet managed to become legitimised as an elected prime minister. All it took was a systematic approach to controlling the election boundaries and the decrees that were, for all intents and purposes, engineered to give him victory at the polls.

Bainimarama has frequently stated that the coup's objective was to bring about a more united Fiji, with a new vision of statehood. But as Jon Fraenkel observes:

> Surveying the international experience of coups aimed at bridging ethnic divisions, it is striking how few cases give credence to that objective. West African military coups after independence were frequently depicted as efforts to counter tribalism or tackle civilian

corruption, but almost invariably proved to be instruments for the triumph of militarised ethnocracy. Coups aimed at countering ethnic polarisation tend to morph quickly into vehicles for the ascendancy of one or the other group. (Fraenkel 2009)

Another chapter could be written on the continuation of military dictatorship under the guise of parliamentary democracy; while the country boasts a democratically elected government, Frank Bainimarama and Aiyaz Sayed-Khaiyum's modus operandi for the past eight years has not changed. Some claimed that the country merely transitioned to a parliamentary dictatorship.

For the SODELPA party, winning 15 seats was a consolation of sorts after eight long years of a military regime. The party fielded 48 candidates, with the strategy of getting as many votes as possible and to cover a wider geographical area. Many observers stated that SODELPA should have done better, but with the cards stacked high against it the party was always realistic that without the support of other parties, it would be extremely difficult to be in government on its own.

References

Fiji Constitution 1997, *Constitution of the Republic of the Fiji Islands Amendment Act 1997,* Fiji Government Printer, Suva, Fiji.

Fiji Government 2013, *Constitution of the Republic of the Fiji Islands 2013,* Fiji Government Printer, Suva, Fiji (September 2013).

Fiji Government 2014, Fiji Electoral Decree, Fiji Government, Suva.

Fraenkel, Jon 2009, 'The Fiji coup and the politics of ethnicity'. Available from insidestory.org.au/the-fiji-coup-and-the-politics-of-ethnicity.

Fraenkel, Jon 2014, 'Observations on Fiji's 2014 election'. Available from pidp.eastwestcenter.org/pireport/2014/September/09-24-an.htm.

Narsey, Wadan 2014, 'Fiji elections: Another victory for treason, lies, money and the culture of silence', Pacific.Scoop. Available from pacific.scoop.co.nz/2014/09/fiji-elections-another-victory-for-treason-lies-and-the-culture-of-silence/.

Ratuva, Steven 2014, 'A symbol of hope—reflections on the Fiji election'. Available from pacific.scoop.co.nz/category/opinions/.

Sayed-Khaiyum, A 2002, 'Cultural autonomy—Its implication on the nation state: The Fijian experience', unpublished Master in Law thesis, University of Hong Kong.

SODELPA 2013a, 'Party Constitution', Social Democratic Liberal Party Secretariat, Suva, Fiji (June 2013).

SODELPA 2013b, 'Party Manifesto', Social Democratic Liberal Party Secretariat, Suva, Fiji (August 2013).

11

'Not with a bang but a whimper': SODELPA and the 2014 elections

Scott MacWilliam

Introduction

At the 2014 elections, the Social Democratic Liberal Party (SODELPA), the party representing Fiji's chiefly aristocracy and indigenous commercial buccaneers (see below), gained more than one quarter of the popular vote and seats. Under a constitution designed by the military regime headed by Prime Minister Voreqe (Frank) Bainimarama, SODELPA was forced to compete in conditions that favoured the regime's own newly founded party, FijiFirst. In such circumstances, the outcome might seem as if SODELPA's achievement was both against the odds and substantial. A closer examination, however, suggests otherwise and raises the question: Has the political and commercial alliance clustered under the party's banner reached a terminal condition in Fiji's political economy? To reframe a line from TS Eliot's poem *The Hollow Men*, is this 'the way the world ends' for the aristocracy and the buccaneers? Is a further extra-parliamentary attempt to capture state power, along the lines of the 1987 coup and the 2000 revolt in the name of indigenous rights, the only means by which they can regain office?

This chapter commences with a consideration of the wider constitutional and electoral terms under which SODELPA fought to secure votes. It then examines the strategy employed by the party, emphasising how playing to the strengths of the party's appeal and candidates was the best alternative possible but also highlighted its weaknesses. The final section develops the conclusion that the party's achievement was probably as successful as could be expected in electoral and parliamentary terms, but that its prospects for improving on this in the future are doubtful.

The electoral arena

In order to consider the 'best case' scenario for SODELPA's future, it is necessary to examine how the 2013 Constitution and changes to Fiji's political economy operated to affect the party's strategy and electoral chances. Some fairly obvious changes had occurred since the May 2006 elections, which was won by SODELPA's precursor, the Laisenia Qarase-led Soqosoqo Duavata ni Lewenivanua (SDL), which had subsequently absorbed an even more nationalistic Conservative Alliance Matanitu Vanua (CAMV). Not only did SDL figures lose their hold on state power in the coup of December 2006, they were also marginalised by the military regime's deliberate strategy of inserting senior officers and reliable allies into the most important administrative departments in the government bureaucracy. The media had been muzzled, with the ownership of one leading paper localised and the other becoming little more than a government mouthpiece. Under Rupert Murdoch's ownership, *The Fiji Times* had been a staunch SDL supporter and military regime critic, but with the change of ownership to a local businessman in 2010, the paper meticulously avoided controversy and punitive regime action. By comparison, the other national English-language newspaper, *Fiji Sun,* became an uncritical supporter of the military regime and consistently backed FijiFirst's election campaign. Although there had been some relaxing of repression prior to the elections, campaigning nonetheless occurred in a highly constrained atmosphere.

Under the 1997 Constitution, the 1999, 2001 and 2006 elections had been conducted on the basis of a single member electorate arrangement under the alternative voting system, with constituencies grossly malapportioned in favour of rural areas (see Ratuva, this volume). In addition, seats were divided between 'open' or non-race based electorates and the more numerous race-based or 'communal' electorates, and were weighted in favour of rural voters. These arrangements therefore favoured parties which had strong rural support, the Soqosoqo Vakavulewa ni Taukei (SVT), precursor to the SDL–CAMV alliance in 2001, and the Fiji Labour Party (FLP), with its strong support among Indo-Fijian cane farmers, rural workers and newly urbanised former farmers. The communal electoral system also underpinned the continuing parliamentary dominance of the chiefly aristocracy and further advances by the Taukei bourgeoisie (MacWilliam 2001; MacWilliam with Daveta 2003; MacWilliam 2014). The 2013 Constitution and associated decrees removed single-member electorates, instituted 'one person, one vote, one value', set a minimum figure for obtaining a seat on a proportional basis, abolished compulsory voting, and lowered the voting age to 18.[1] In short, the changes in constitutional and associated electoral rules negated the main advantages that SODELPA's predecessors had enjoyed under the previous arrangements.

There remained other important barriers to electoral success for SODELPA in 2014 in addition to those embodied in the new Constitution and associated decrees. Despite continuing disputes among candidates for high chiefly office, the Great Council of Chiefs (GCC) had become a political and ideological organising centre for opposition to the military regime. The abolition of the GCC, and therefore its removal from any constitutional role, placed SODELPA, the party home of some of the more important and ultra-nationalist chiefs, at a further disadvantage. So too did the attacks against commercial supporters who had previously backed the SDL party. The most prominent of these, Laisenia Qarase, who had been prevented from running as a candidate due to conviction for corruption, spent a considerable amount of time overseas during the final stages of the campaign. The rules that formally limited candidate expenditure on campaigning

---

1   It has been asserted that by establishing a formula for calculating the minimum number of votes that a party needed to obtain to gain a seat, the 'one vote, one value' principle was not followed, since it acted against minor parties. None of these obtained a seat at the September 2014 elections, although the National Federation Party, which won three seats, could be regarded as a minor party, having won no seats in the previous three elections. In any case, the expression 'one vote, one value' is not usually used to refer to the allocation of seats after the votes are cast but to the relative weight of votes in the voting system.

and fundraising overseas were more honoured in the breach than in the observance, but posed a potential threat to opposition parties and other organisations. FijiFirst raised more money than all the other parties, and this was converted into a clear dominance of advertising in the press, TV and other media.

The regime had also put a targeted effort into bringing some chiefs onside, providing infrastructure and natural disaster relief efforts in their areas. With what seemed to be equivalent to a marginal seats strategy, Prime Minister Bainimarama, Attorney General Aiyaz Sayed-Khaiyum and other ministers travelled constantly around the country touting government activities. They were backed by the military, which was especially prominent in relief efforts whenever a major natural disaster struck rural areas in particular. Even if there were no longer individual electorates to be wooed, because of the change to one national constituency, these activities, together with continuous attention to roads, bridges, schools and health centres, were part of a lengthy campaign to bolster the government's and then FijiFirst's position. Once party propaganda was removed during the two-day embargo on campaigning immediately prior to the elections, the posters featuring the Prime Minister and government efforts in various areas remained on display. SODELPA faced the typical dilemma of an opposition that could only attack government efforts without any achievements of its own to publicise.

In addition to the constitutional and other political barriers faced by SODELPA, most of the major demographic and related changes in the country favoured FijiFirst. While SODELPA made much of its rural and Taukei support, this base was being undermined. The year after the military regime took power in 2006, a national census indicated that the population was roughly split between urban and rural areas. Even if these figures are accurate—and there are substantial grounds for doubting them, including questions about what constitutes rural residence when this is located very close to major urban centres and places of work including large tourist resorts—the trend was moving against rural-based parties. By 2014, unofficial estimates suggest that between 40 per cent and 50 per cent of the country's population lived in the Nausori–Suva–Lami conurbation, with a further 20 per cent in the west of Viti Levu from Nadi through Lautoka to Ba. Some support for these estimates is given by the proportion of votes coming from the Central and Western districts: 43 per cent and 38 per cent respectively.

So, however places of residence are officially identified as being urban or rural, over 80 per cent of the total voting population lives on Viti Levu, the most commercialised island in terms of production and consumption. The voting population in the other two districts, Northern and Eastern, amounts to less than 20 per cent of the total, with the Eastern district having fewer than 5 per cent of the voting population.

The voting age was lowered to 18 by the 2013 Constitution, and probably 25 to 30 per cent of voters at the 2014 elections were less than 30 years old and had not had a ballot previously. FijiFirst, as the effective incumbent government, was well placed to capture the bulk of the urban and some of the rural youth vote. This was also probably the segment of the voting population least likely to enthuse over SODELPA's association with chiefly rule, Taukei land rights and demands for a Christian state. Government pre-election moves to reduce the costs of schooling, to strengthen tertiary education and to 'create' jobs appealed not only to parents of school-age children and young people, but to young voters as well. Changing the distribution of lease monies in 2012 away from chiefs to provide equal distribution to all *mataqali* members not only assisted in providing more money for households which could be spent on purchased goods, church levies and the like, but were also designed to undercut SODELPA's popular base, as well as to bolster the government's, and consequently FijiFirst's, support among Taukei. Once again, being in opposition put SODELPA at a decided disadvantage by comparison to FijiFirst because the government could respond directly to these demographic and other changes with policies and expenditure.

SODELPA's strategic definition

As already noted, in previous elections Fiji voters were largely forced into identity politics that emphasised race/ethnicity.[2] The act of voting was constructed on these lines, with voters required to line up as Taukei, Indo-Fijians or 'general' electors (i.e. other races) and to cast votes for seats, the majority of which were defined as communal. Even as population movement occurred out of rural and into urban areas, with production and consumption for the entire voting population increasingly commercialised, voters remained trapped in these identities in part due to the gross malapportionment favouring rural seats.

The broad features of the various communal electoral arrangements sketched above are well known, but less often noted is the fact that these electoral features were installed by, and secured the political power of, the chiefly aristocracy and indigenous commercial buccaneers. The basis of this aristocracy remained heredity, including attachments to particular areas of land and forms of labour, particularly smallholders of landowning units. That many of the aristocrats are becoming increasingly impoverished serves to emphasise the universality of their existence as rentiers. The process of aristocratic impoverishment in Fiji is similar to that which has occurred in other parts of the world, including in Europe. On that continent there is popular comedy about poor nobles, full of pretensions and clinging on to the last vestiges of their castles and manors, the grand estates of the past, of which the British TV sitcom *To the Manor Born* is a good example. There is no less disdain for the aristocracy in Fiji, epitomised with the popular appellation for the now abolished chiefly institution, namely, the Great Council of Thieves.

---

2   The confusion between identities is not only found in public discussion of Fiji's political economy but is also common in academic accounts. For one instance among many, see Lal 2006, pp. 1–2, where race, ethnicity and communities are all employed to distinguish between populations. Lal invokes the predominant Weberian liberal form of describing and analysing Fiji's political sociology, which nominates races, ethnicities and communities as forms of identity, even occasionally referring to class on a similar basis. This is distinct from and opposed to a Marxist understanding, in which race etc. are forms taken by class, that is class *as if* race, *as if* ethnicity, instead of the liberal pluralist rendering of class *and* race, class *and* ethnicity, class *and* community, class *and* gender, and so on. In this essay, it is not necessary to show the relative salience of class over race and ethnicity for Fiji, which would require shifting epistemological ground to that liberal Weberian position which is being criticised.

If the most important and wealthy chiefs were critical for the first phase of indigenous accumulation, in concert with European and Indo-Fijian businesses, from the 1980s the second phase aggressively broke with this past (Ratuva 2013). While holding political power remained important, plundering state assets and using state power as the basis of accumulation characterised a particular form of accumulation. The Fiji Development Bank and the National Bank of Fiji were utilised by politicians and businessmen and women to fund enterprises that largely took over existing commercial operations, including through the use of state power to force out earlier owners or secure joint ventures. Unlike the coup of 1987, which facilitated the commercial advancement of those whose form of accumulation is here characterised as buccaneering, the 2006 coup was important for the political and commercial marginalisation of many of these earlier indigenous accumulators.

In the case of wealthy Taukei and their Indo-Fijian equivalent, the politics of identity could also be used to disguise the causes and effects of commercialisation on the mass of the voting population. Where households have faced stagnant or declining living standards over recent decades, racial and or ethnic identities have been consistently used for electoral and other political purposes by the holders of state power. Electoral laws that forced voters into Taukei, Indo-Fijian and other blocs were only the most obvious expression of the connection between identity, state and political power. Even when the screen of identity weakened, as in the 1999 elections when voters expressed welfare and other grievances against the two main parties, the SVT and the Indo-Fijian-dominated National Federation Party (NFP), they were forced to vote for other parties that were formed largely around racial or ethnic identity. The People's Coalition, which won the 1999 elections, was primarily an amalgam of voters signalling reaction against the SVT government and a rejection of its coalition partner, the NFP. Most electors could express their opposition only by voting for the FLP and a number of Taukei parties where chiefly figures and their associates held power.

Although the 2014 elections were held under rules that aimed to undermine many of the previous advantages held by parties based on understandings of identity, the main opposition party, SODELPA, nevertheless remained as a reminder of that past. That past included the SDL, 'a party defined by the objective of placating indigenous discontent' (Fraenkel & Firth 2007, p. 75). SODELPA's main leadership comprised two high chiefly figures—Ro Teimumu Kepa, the Roko Tui Dreketi of Rewa in south-eastern Viti Levu, and Ratu Naiqama Lalabalavu, the Tui Cakau from Cakaudrove in Vanua Levu—and also the banned but still active figure of deposed prime minister Laisenia Qarase from Lau, who worked his commercial contacts to help finance the party's campaign. Through these figures, SODELPA kept the mantle of its Taukei predecessors—the SVT, SDL and CAMV. Although both Kepa and Lalabalavu are Roman Catholics in a country where Methodists comprise the predominant Christian denomination, a spirit of ecumenism among the party's leadership made it possible for this difference to be glossed over. Instead, their hereditary status and 'Christian-ness' were emphasised in the party's campaign.

Once the 2013 Constitution was promulgated, and the terms of the elections that reshaped the electoral arena for the 2014 contest were set out, SODELPA retained its roots in the SDL–CAMV heritage but worked to rebrand the past. The most obvious way in which this was done involved incorporating the 'old' parties SDL–CAMV in the new party's name, regardless of the confusing and rather antagonistic political ideologies represented in it. The SDL, the party that saw itself as the bastion of indigeneity, was required to anglicise its name under new regulations and chose 'Social Democratic Liberal Party' in an attempt to retain the close association with the SDL acronym, and to continue its 'mighty mission and a sacred cause' for 'the people of Fiji' (SODELPA 2014a). While there is not space here to document completely how the rebranding occurred, two central concerns of the transformation can be noted: religion and land.

Prior to the launch of the SODELPA manifesto, the party struggled to come to terms with a key feature of the 2013 Constitution. Section 4 effectively defined Fiji as a secular state, understood in terms of complete religious freedom with no one religion being privileged. Sub-section 4(1) reads: 'Religious liberty, as recognised in the Bill of Rights, is a founding principle of the State' (Fiji Government 2013). Opposition to this kind of liberal secularism ran deep within the SODELPA leadership and among Taukei supporters, so that for much of the pre-election period SODELPA's leaders insisted that it would change the Constitution to define Fiji as a Christian state. Acknowledging the difficulty of amending the 2013 Constitution to attain this objective, and recognising that the party could not win the elections while retaining the ethnic and religious identity of its predecessors, SODELPA's platform became a mishmash of compromising statements. 'The Guiding Principles and Values' listed in the manifesto included 'The freedom, equality and dignity of all religious denominations'. However, the manifesto, which sought to 'Reclaim Fiji', also declared in its 'Aims and Objectives' a promise 'To uphold Christian values and principles and to respect the beliefs and values of other religious faiths'. Describing the 2013 Constitution as 'Godless', the manifesto spoke of how the Constitution 'ignored the role of Christianity in the development of Fiji'. Secularism became cast as an attempt 'to encourage worship of an unknown deity'. SODELPA insisted that when it formed government, a new constitution would 'Ensure God's rightful place in our supreme law' and 'uphold Christian values and principles '. While ecumenism made it possible to ignore possible clashes between different Christian denominations' values, there was no doubt that religions other than Christianity would have a subordinate place in the proposed new document. Instead, with Christianity dominant, the Constitution would simply 'Ensure respect for all religious faiths and religious freedom of all citizens' (SODELPA 2014a).

While commercialisation and urbanisation have provided increasingly significant forces to counter earlier regional and rural loyalties, the indigenous vote had previously shown great fragmentation in specific circumstances, as in 1999. Industrialisation and its effects should not be confused with one form of industry—manufacturing. In Fiji, the stagnation and even decline of the garment industry has been conflated with the ongoing process of industrialisation, which reigns in construction, tourism, fishing, some areas of agriculture and financial services. To illustrate, the construction of very tall buildings for offices and residential accommodation in city and town centres occurs through industrial labour processes with complex divisions of labour and equipment applied on site in Fiji and in other countries, wherever the cement, steel, glass and machinery is manufactured. The existence of large tourist resorts, one major component of the tourist industry, represents industrialisation in their construction as well as in their daily operations: food is prepared on an industrial scale in large kitchens, to give just another example of the process at work. As the Asian Development Bank (2015, pp. 249–50) has noted recently, since 2010, '[g]rowth was broad based, with investments in finance, construction, and transport leading the trend …'. The drift of population from eastern and northern Fiji, first to the west and south and then to urban and peri-urban areas, is to a substantial extent an effect of these widespread forms of industrialisation.

Even if SODELPA attracted the great majority of Taukei votes, that would give it victory by only a narrow margin. When the votes of the non-indigenous population (around 40 per cent of the total) are also taken into account, SODELPA's stance on the 'respect for all religious faiths and religious freedom' appeared as little more than an opportunistic move to broaden the party's electoral appeal because the Taukei vote alone would be insufficient to ensure victory. Disarray among the leadership of the Methodist Church, with some sections clearly wedded to the initial SODELPA cause of a 'Christian state' while others attempted to avoid continuing conflict with the government, only helped FijiFirst's campaign to tie SODELPA to its past no matter how the final party manifesto glossed over religious fundamentalism. Not surprisingly, Prime Minister Bainimarama and FijiFirst made much of the SODELPA leadership's past statements and the party's heritage to show the confusion within its ranks over its position on secularism in general and Christianity in particular.

Another signature component of SODELPA's position was its stance regarding land. Once again, this provided the party with both an important strength and a fundamental weakness. SODELPA's leadership constantly attacked the Bainimarama Government and the 2013 Constitution for undermining indigenous rights, claiming that by abrogating the 1997 Constitution, the entrenched protection of native land rights had been removed. One specific objection was that without a Senate, and the representation afforded the GCC through this body, all that was required to change Taukei land ownership in the new unicameral legislature was a simple majority vote in parliament. While debate on the accuracy of this claim raged during the campaign (SODELPA 2014b; FijiFirst 2014), other matters regarding land were probably more important in determining voting behaviour.

While SODELPA's stance was undoubtedly effective in securing the votes of Taukei who still farmed land and others who had left the land but remained attached to rural life in some form, such voters had become a declining proportion of the population. Other Taukei were domiciled in villages but employed in wage and salaried positions at tourist resorts and urban centres. Still, others grew crops for urban markets and purchased industrial commodities for consumption. While commercialisation in all forms transformed the meaning of land rights beyond what may be described as traditional production for immediate non-marketed consumption, often described as subsistence farming, these changes also affected how SODELPA was forced to frame its defence of 'native land rights'. In so doing, the party also had to appear inclusive of Indo-Fijian farmers leasing land and to include poverty reduction, education and state services in its proposed policies. SODELPA was forced to shift its terrain and compete directly with FijiFirst as the incumbent government.

The SODELPA defence of indigenous land rights became primarily about the commercial terms of land occupation and ownership, as well as the needs of both Taukei and Indo-Fijians displaced from land ownership, occupation and cultivation (SODELPA 2014b, pp. 21–22, 43–47). Commencing with the usual obligatory reference to the 1874 Deed of Cession as the basis for Taukei monopoly of land ownership, SODELPA's manifesto proceeded to list all the actions of the Bainimarama Government that had purportedly undermined these. The list included appointing government sympathisers to staff the Native Land Trust Board (NTLB, now iTaukei Land Trust Board) and the opposition to the Qarase government's Qoliqoli Bill dealing with the ownership of coastal areas, including those used for surfing. The manifesto also made clear that its principal objection was to the transfer of control over native lands away from the chiefs, manifested in the GCC, to the minister. As noted above, this move by the Bainimarama Government, carried out via decree, had potentially serious implications for the amount and distributions of land rents that previously went to the chiefly aristocracy. SODELPA's role as the party of rentiers became clearly apparent.

Along with 'restor(ing) the protection of native land to what it has been since 1970', SODELPA also saw a need to attract leaseholders, including the mainly Indo-Fijian cane farmers, and to expand the number of people willing to farm increasing amounts of unutilised or underutilised land. A SODELPA government proposed to deal with this problem in concert with an NLTB in which control was once again vested in chiefs, and which would acquire land and lease it to farmers. In order to prevent farmers from avoiding rent payments, these payments would become 'a first charge on the proceeds of the farm', presumably by the expansion of state supervisory capacities over agricultural production. That this proposal collided with other sections of the manifesto, which objected to government intrusion into other areas of the economy, including those dealing with jobs and economic growth (SODELPA 2014a, pp. 14–17), made the document typical of election propaganda in capitalist economies.

When coupled with the leadership of chiefs and with commercial buccaneers, however, the sections of the SODELPA manifesto dealing with religion and land rights clearly identified the party's central concerns. The particular matters that dominated the manifesto, as well as the conduct of the election campaign along the lines outlined by Dr Tupeni Baba below, left the Prime Minister and FijiFirst in a powerful position to appeal to voters as representative of a superior, inclusive civic nationalism. SODELPA, by comparison, represented a particularistic nationalism associated with chiefly rule, the primacy of rural life and Christian dominance, even monopoly, which extended to an attack on secularism understood in terms of the neutrality of the state in matters of religion.

What does the future hold for SODELPA?

On screen during the election night TV coverage, one of SODELPA's designated urban candidates, Dr Tupeni Baba, discussed some early voting figures with Dr Steven Ratuva, Fiji One's principal commentator. Baba, who had tasted electoral victory in 1987 and 1999 with the Fiji Labour Party and subsequent failure with other parties, enthused about the seeming success of SODELPA's campaign strategy. Early results suggested that behind the two main leaders, FijiFirst's Bainimarama and SODELPA's Ro Teimumu Kepa, other SODELPA candidates were prominent in the count and doing better than candidates from other parties, especially FijiFirst. Baba proudly categorised the initial results as an indication that the strategy of selecting candidates, particularly chiefs and others with strong local followings was trumping FijiFirst's preferred direction of concentrating attention on the party leader, Bainimarama. He clearly believed that local identities and particularisms were being favoured by voters over the national unity slogans of the FijiFirst campaign. Ratuva wisely suggested caution in anticipating possible outcomes at a time when Bainimarama was already garnering many more votes than Kepa and all other candidates.

When the votes were finally tallied, Ratuva's caution proved sounder than Baba's enthusiasm. Bainimarama gained over 202,000 of the total number of valid votes of 496,364. Kepa, in second position, received 49,000 votes, less than a quarter of Bainimarama's total. Attorney General Aiyaz Sayed-Khaiyum, also of FijiFirst, finished in third place with 13,753 votes. With NFP leader Biman Prasad fourth, and another four of the first 12 successful candidates coming from FijiFirst, the SODELPA strategy outlined by Baba did not appear highly successful. Once votes were distributed according to the proportional representation method employed for the first time in this election, the redistribution of surpluses gained by Bainimarama, Sayed-Khaiyum and other leading FijiFirst candidates meant the party had 32 members elected, compared to SODELPA's 15. Baba added to the 'unsuccessful candidate' tally, gaining a mere 1,153 votes and finishing 62nd overall when the final parliament of 50 seats was determined.

At first glance, the outcome might appear to be a fairly predictable triumph for a leader and a party that campaigned on the basis that it was the 'party of every common Fijian'. That FijiFirst was constituted as the means for transforming a military dictatorship into an elected government under a constitution formulated by that dictatorship did not seem as significant as the fact that almost 60 per cent of the voters supported the party. Since FijiFirst had also become the clear favourite of many substantial firms and commercial figures, their funding support enabled the party to outspend its opponents many times over. Such funding is now a standard feature of elections in many capitalist democracies.

SODELPA therefore lost out to a party in power that had been able to draw on significant commercial support as well as on the resources of the state machinery, including the army, over the preceding five to eight years to effectively buy votes. Even the overwhelming vote from among military personnel for FijiFirst, possibly over 80 per cent of the votes cast at military polling stations, could be explained by increased salaries and wages and better working and living conditions.[3] Faced with this centralised concentration of power, the only hope SODELPA had was to run a decentralised campaign, counting upon localised support and putting up candidates who best fitted this strategy. In his pronouncement on TV, Baba was simply expressing a wish, rather than a solidly grounded expectation, that the only alternative open to SODELPA would work.

Any separation between local and national campaigns, however, is too simple for several reasons. FijiFirst, particularly its leadership, also conducted a concentrated 'grassroots' campaign. The party had a slate of candidates, most of whom were Taukei. They were not high chiefs but rather former military officers and white-collar professionals. Party leaders, candidates and supporters visited rural areas constantly, while government programs concentrated on improving roads, bridges and health and education facilities in both urban and rural areas. The government, in the form of FijiFirst, also 'thought local and acted local'. It would therefore be simplistic to portray the elections as a clash between parochialism, especially of a rural 'old' past and a 'new' non-racial or multiethnic nationalism, even if this appeared to be the central thrust of FijiFirst's campaign.

SODELPA, too, was forced to devise an election program, as evidenced in its manifesto, that presented it as a suitable national government in the rapidly changing circumstances of post-2006 Fiji. However, in a Fiji where much has changed over the last decade, and where there is a large increase not just in the number of young people but also in the number of young people who had never voted before, FijiFirst, and to a lesser extent the National Federation Party, were better placed to represent those changes.

---

3   A rough estimate using figures provided by the Fijian Electoral Commission of votes cast at polling stations used by military personnel suggests that FijiFirst gained in excess of 80 per cent of the votes cast. However, there are too many unknowns about these figures for a hard and fast conclusion to be drawn; more research is required into a number of matters, including to what extent voting was secret, whether only military personnel voted at these stations and to what extent prior directions were given by senior officers about how other ranks should vote. During informal discussions with young voters prior to the elections, one consistent theme was the appeal of parties, FijiFirst and the NFP in particular, who had highly educated, university-qualified candidates, including those with doctorates. Making Fiji an 'education hub' for the south-west Pacific is only likely to see this feature of candidates become even more prominent in the future.

Conclusion

By some accounts, and hopes, Fiji's democracy has been 'reconstructed', with parliamentary government once again in place. From an optimistic perspective, Fiji's democracy will now revolve steadily around a regular party competition conducted within a set of constitutional rules, with one or more parties forming government and with a formal opposition similarly composed of one or more parties. In the context of the 2014 result, SODELPA are the losers this time but did well enough against considerable odds. Fifteen seats out of 50 and nearly 30 per cent of the vote is a substantial base upon which to build in anticipation of the next elections.

There are several reasons, however, why some caution should be exercised by those who expect, even hope, that electoral and parliamentary democracy will be the principal trajectory of Fiji's political future. This was also how the 1999 elections result was greeted. Instead, as pointed out soon after the 1999 elections (MacWilliam 2001),[4] and again recently (MacWilliam 2014), Fiji remains a militarised democracy with its Constitution, parliament and elections underpinned by a compressed connection between members of the military apparatus and other occupants of government positions who hold the apex of both political and state power. While the leadership of the military has passed from the chiefly families who tied political power to state power in the first decades of independence, military authority is still critical to how the ruling class in Fiji rules. Even as the current Prime Minister and important elected members of his government, as well as senior bureaucrats, have 'retired' from the military positions they held previously, the importance of their successors in the RFMF for the government's power remains. In this sense, the connection between the military and the other apparatuses of state power remains compressed. Fiji continues to be distinct from some other electoral democracies where military power is less overt, even though critical for the exercise of political and state power.

---

4   The near-universal enthusiasm for the 1997 Constitution and the holding of the 1999 elections is undoubted and does not need documentation. Instead MacWilliam's analysis (2001) developed within months of the elections was regarded at the time as 'controversial' and 'sceptical' by Stewart Firth (2001, p. 7). Readers can judge if after the 1999 elections, and now again after the 2014 elections, Fiji's democracy was and is 'thin' and 'militarised'. Also see Lal (2007) who also used the term 'militarized democracy' to refer to Fiji's post-2006 coup political governance.

Optimism about SODELPA's future, as either an opposition party that retains coherence and significance across more than one election, or as a future governing party, needs to be tempered by the factors outlined above. SODELPA remains the organising centre for a chiefly aristocracy that is in the process of being permanently disempowered by industrialisation and commercialisation. Rentiers are under attack everywhere, not only in Fiji, by advocates of land reform, who view rentiers as an undesirable form of the wider class of accumulators. The substantial areas of 'vacant' land across the country suggest that a major shift is taking place in the role of agriculture—whether this sector can be revitalised and further industrialised remains to be seen. However, should such reforms take place, land rents are likely to become a lesser component of farm production costs, further undercutting chiefly incomes and authority. Even if other *mataqali* members receive a greater proportion of rents as a result of the government reforms noted above, a generalised attack on rents will further cut into the amounts received by chiefs and others. The response of *mataqali* members to any reduction in the total they receive, even if is a greater proportion of a smaller total, is unlikely to strengthen chiefly authority either. In this context, it is also worth noting that even if some workers are pushed back into the countryside as farm labourers or smallholders, their existence will not be one of so-called subsistence, but of labour further subject to capital, entirely dependent upon profitability. Chiefly attempts to impose authority will be in competition with commercial criteria.

The political future of the chiefly aristocracy is no brighter as long as the close ties between the elected government and the military leadership remain. As the events of 2000 and 2006 suggest, these ties are critical. With senior military officers less and less drawn from the highest chiefly stratum, it is unlikely that the RFMF can be mobilised to support the aristocracy's demands for a return to greater authority. Further, any revolt in the countryside led by chiefs in the areas where SODELPA's support remains strongest is not likely to succeed, as the military's close attention to rural concerns prior to the recent election suggest.

Given the extremely challenging procedures for constitutional change entrenched in the 2013 Constitution, it is unlikely that future elections in Fiji will be conducted under terms more favourable for SODELPA. The 2014 election result appears likely to be the high-water mark for the party dominated by high chiefs, particular rural concerns and the Taukei buccaneers who were once prominent. How the attachment between political and state power represented by FijiFirst, the military and leading commercial firms will be played out is of course uncertain. But the greater possibility is that the old guard represented by SODELPA in the 2014 election cannot reinvent itself as representative of the rapidly urbanising and commercialised population that inhabits Fiji now.

References

Asian Development Bank 2015, *Asian development outlook 2015: Financing Asia's future growth*, Manila.

FijiFirst 2014, 'Land-The Truth and Nothing But the Trust: Response to SODELPA', *Fiji Sun*, 14 September, p. 17.

Fiji Government 2013, *Constitution of the Republic of Fiji*, Suva.

Firth, Stewart 2001, 'Prologue: The 1999 Fiji election and the legacy of history', *The Journal of Pacific Studies*, vol. 25, no. 1, May, pp. 1–8.

Fraenkel, Jon and Firth, Stewart 2007, 'The cycles of party politics' in J Frankel and S Firth (eds), *From election to coup in Fiji: The 2006 campaign and its aftermath*, ANU E Press and Asia Pacific Press, Canberra, pp. 64–77.

Lal, Brij V 2007, *Islands of turmoil: Elections and politics in Fiji*, ANU E Press and Asia Pacific Press, Canberra.

Lal, B 2006, '"Anxiety, uncertainty and fear in our land": Fiji's road to military coup'. In Jon Fraenkel, Stewart Firth and Brij V. Lal (eds), *The 2006 military takeover in Fiji: a coup to end all coups?* ANU E Press, Canberra.

MacWilliam, Scott 2001, 'Shallow coups, thin democracy? Constitutionalism in Fiji, 1987–1999', *The Journal of Pacific Studies*, vol. 25, no. 1, May, pp. 9–44.

MacWilliam, Scott 2014, 'Militarised democracy and Fiji's 2014 election', Presented to a seminar in the State, Society and Governance in Melanesia Program, October 28, The Australian National University, Canberra.

MacWilliam, Scott with Daveta, Vilitate 2003, 'Electoral democracy, coups and indigenous commerce: The case of tourism in Fiji, 1987–1999', in Tiina Kontinen and Maaria Seppanen (eds), *Development-concepts, policies and practices: Essays in memory of Michael Cowen*, Finnish Society for Development Studies, Helsinki, pp. 45–70.

Ratuva, Steven 2013, *Politics of preferential development: Trans-global study of affirmative action and ethnic conflict in Fiji, Malaysia and South Africa*, ANU E Press, Canberra.

Social Democratic Liberal Party (SODELPA) 2014a, *Reclaiming Fiji: Summary of the Manifesto of SODELPA Social Democratic Liberal Party*, Suva.

Social Democratic Liberal Party (SODELPA) 2014b, 'Land-The Truth And Nothing But The Truth: A statement and a challenge by the Social Democratic Liberal Party (SODELPA)' *Fiji Times*, 11 September, p. 29.

12

Fiji's evolving foreign policy and Pacific multilateral order: Pre- and post-election

Alex Stewart

Introduction

This chapter explores the impact that Fiji's foreign policy since 2006 has had on multilateral relations in the Pacific Islands. While Fiji has launched policy initiatives on the wider global stage, their impact on the Pacific Islands has been indirect and harder to quantify. Therefore this chapter focuses on regionally based organisations, rather than on bodies with a wider global reach, such as the Commonwealth or the G77. In particular, it focuses on the Pacific Islands Forum (PIF), the Pacific Islands Development Forum (PIDF) and the Melanesian Spearhead Group (MSG). These three organisations have formed the focus for the multilateral dimension of Fiji's foreign policy, either as organisations supported by Fiji or standing in opposition in the case of the PIF.

Given the small size of many Pacific Island states, both in terms of population and economy, multilateralism has long been considered an essential part of the region's framework. Small states have problems mustering the human resources, finances and expertise to deliver services and perform sovereign functions adequately when acting alone. Multilateral regional cooperation is seen by most development partners as the key strategy in mitigating this issue by pooling the resources of several states. As such, the state of multilateral cooperation in the region is of crucial interest. Prior to 2006, multilateral action in the Pacific Islands flowed primarily through the PIF and its associated bodies, flanked by a relatively quiescent MSG focused mostly on developing trade within Melanesia.

In recent years, there have been challenges to that order, driven primarily but not exclusively by Fiji. Since the 2006 military takeover, the Fiji Government has launched a series of confident and often controversial foreign policy initiatives. It has repeatedly challenged the established status quo of regional relations, particularly since its suspension from the PIF in 2009. The unprecedented suspension of Fiji from the peak body of Pacific Island multilateral relations was a major turning point in the region. Rather than isolating Fiji and exerting pressure on the Bainimarama Government to step aside, it fuelled Fiji's efforts to create new avenues for its foreign policy and to sideline Australia, New Zealand and the PIF in the process.

As a key part of this new policy drive, the Fiji Government has placed a greater emphasis on its relations with the other Melanesian states and sought to bypass the central nexus of relations represented by the PIF. This new drive has been channelled through bilateral relations, but also through attempts to shift the equilibrium of multilateral organisations. The primary existing platform for this is the Melanesian Spearhead Group. Beyond this Melanesian initiative, Fiji also sought to engage with the broader region through a series of initiatives that culminated in the establishment of the PIDF. In explicitly challenging Australia and New Zealand, Fiji has set itself up as a champion of Pacific Island interests against domination by the two largest regional forces—Australia and New Zealand. According to Fiji, these two countries represent outside powers rather than being part of the Pacific Islands region (Dobell 2014), and have been interfering with the ability of the Pacific Island states to look for solutions to the region's problems in ways that are appropriate to the unique nature of the Pacific Islands (Bainimarama 2013). This has justified a push towards a new regional architecture that excludes Australia and New Zealand. This new architecture means that the PIF, as presently constituted, is incompatible with Fiji's vision of what Pacific Island multilateralism should look like. This has led the Bainimarama Government to ignore the lifting of its suspension from the PIF, at least to date. Bainimarama's position is that Fiji will not rejoin until its own terms are met, including the reclassification of Australia and New Zealand as development partners rather than full members (Bolatiki 2014a).

This chapter assesses how successful Fiji has been in its aims. I argue that while Fiji has had some success at influencing multilateral relations, it has not occurred to the extent that was desired, nor has the intended outcome been achieved. More specifically, although Fiji's foreign policy since 2006 has caused a shift in the institutional landscape of Pacific Island foreign relations and altered the centrality of the PIF to regional cooperation, it has not succeeded in undermining the relevance and importance of the PIF as it is presently constituted. Rather, the organisation retains a vital and powerful role in the region. A shift in the balance of forces has not occurred in the form of a zero sum gain by new organisations at the cost of the PIF. Instead, Fiji's policy initiatives have seen a further diversification of multilateral structures in the Pacific Islands and an overall strengthening of the potential for multilateral cooperation in the region.

These initiatives have received a boost in strength by the Bainimarama Government's substantially increased legitimacy after its significant victory in the 2014 elections. Given that the undemocratic nature of the regime prior to the elections was the central focus of attacks by critics, and formed the justification for Fiji's suspension from the PIF, Fiji's position regionally has undoubtedly been strengthened by its return to democratic rule. Given the bullishness of the rhetoric used by the Bainimarama Government and its stated intent to make 'Fiji Great, the pre-eminent Pacific Island nation and one respected the world over' (Bainimarama, quoted in Morris 2014) it seems clear that Fiji will continue efforts to enhance its status and push its own agenda in the region.

The Pacific Islands Forum

The PIF is both the oldest and the largest multilateral organisation in the Pacific Islands region. Its members include all independent Pacific Island states, as well as Australia and New Zealand. As all of the non-independent states of the region attend summits, at least as observers, the PIF is the only multilateral body in the region to unite all regional states and bodies at the highest level. Together with the stable funding provided by the backing of Australia and New Zealand this means that the PIF is both well entrenched and well resourced for its operations in the region. Added to this is the fact that the PIF Secretariat (PIFS) coordinates the actions of the Council of Regional Organisations in the Pacific (CROP), which comprise the majority of the task-specific multilateral bodies in the region. Other organisations, such as the Secretariat of the Pacific Community (SPC), focus on specific technical and advisory functions, leaving the PIF to serve as the peak political decision-making body. These factors mean that prior to 2009 the PIF was the central hub of virtually all regional multilateral action.

Given the PIF's central role, control of the organisation grants a great deal of influence over the shape of multilateral relations in the region. The common consensus is that the primary influences on the PIF are Australia and New Zealand, thus creating a dominance in regional relations exceeding the soft power already exerted by the bilateral aid provided by these two states. Australia and New Zealand, however, are not the only non-Pacific Island powers exerting influence over the PIF. With large states such as France and the United States having observer status at the PIF, as well as major extra-regional bodies such as the Asia Development Bank, there is a significant top-heavy presence of other actors in the forum. Even if they are only formally observers, the delegations of larger powers at Forum summits can detract attention away from the issues on the agenda. As Maclellan (2012) points out, this can make it hard for the specific concerns of Pacific Island states to be heard, such as in the ongoing issue of West Papua (PACNEWS 2012).

This top-heavy presence and the distraction from Pacific Island issues that it causes is only one of several criticisms made of the PIF. Another important source of dissatisfaction is the fact that it only engages directly with the national governments of its member states. Private sector enterprises and civil society as a whole have inadequate access. This 'democracy deficit' (Pohnpei 2010) is particularly problematic given that many of the Pacific Island states have fairly weak formalised governance over their own territories (Bohane 2010), and rely heavily on civil society groups such as the churches for service delivery and social cohesion. Though these issues were acknowledged in the Pacific Plan reform agenda for the PIF (Huffer 2006), there has been little action on it to this point. A large part of this lack of action has been the accusation against both the PIF and its Pacific Plan reforms that they are mired in too much bureaucracy to be efficient (Komai 2013). So far the reframing of the Pacific Plan as the Framework for Pacific Regionalism (PIFS 2014) has not brought about a significant change in this deficit. As such, there has been an acknowledged need for reform of the PIF, with some commentators speculating that without reform the Forum could find itself losing relevance (Bohane 2010).

Following Fiji's suspension in 2009, the Bainimarama regime fuelled these criticisms, attacking the PIF repeatedly. This has been flanked by attempts to create competition with other multilateral initiatives such as the PIDF, discussed below. These initiatives have been set up to compete with the PIF not only politically, but also physically through cases of overlapping summit dates (Hayward-Jones 2010). Through all of this, Fiji has pushed the notion that, due to its focus on Western over Pacific Island interests and approaches, the PIF has lost touch with its constituents. According to the Bainimarama Government, Australia's and New Zealand's roles as both members and major donors means that the PIF is too unequal to be functional (Bolatiki 2013). As it stands, it is also irrelevant (Pratibha 2013). These criticisms are not undisputed, but have gained enough momentum that even supporters of the PIF have stated the need for the Forum to 'reaffirm' its relevance (O'Keefe 2012). This is particularly important given the Bainimarama Government's refusal to rejoin the organisation even after the lifting of its suspension (Bolatiki 2014a).

Rhetoric aside, the question that must be addressed is: Has the PIF become as irrelevant as the Bainimarama Government suggests? I argue that this is not the case. While the PIF has lost some of its influence, it is still the peak body of Pacific Island regionalism. It is the best resourced organisation of the regional multilateral bodies. What is more, having Australia and New Zealand as members provides it with substantial security that this will continue to be the case in the future. Apart from Fiji, it remains the only one of the generalist multilateral bodies in the Pacific Islands that unites all of the region's states. Currently, the PIF lacks the legitimacy provided by having all Pacific Island states as members. But unlike the MSG, whose membership is restricted by design, and the PIDF, which several states chose not to join despite receiving invitations, Fiji's absence from the PIF was at least initially not by choice. And despite the anti-PIF rhetoric, the Bainimarama Government nominated Kaliopate Tavola for the 2014 election of a new PIF Secretary-General (Newton-Cain 2014), which does indicate a desire for participation on Fiji's part. While other fora are often attended by lower-ranking government representatives, all PIF leaders' summits achieve full attendance by the heads of the Pacific Island governments. Ironically, this is helped by the strong attendance of extra regional observers, despite the fact that this can distract from Pacific issues. Even if they are a distraction from Pacific Island issues, outside observers such as the United States and China represent crucial development partners for the region, and Pacific Island governments have good reason to be eager for close ties. As such, it is difficult to endorse claims of PIF irrelevance. The Forum's credibility has been damaged by its own need for reform and the exclusion of Fiji, but it is far from removed.

The Pacific Islands Development Forum

The PIDF is the end result of the Engaging with the Pacific Leaders (EWTP) summits, a series of conferences held by the Fijian Government since 2010. These summits emerged in response to the suspension of Fiji from the PIF, as well as the cancellation of the 2010 MSG summit (Tarte 2013). The series of EWTP summits led to the formation of the PIDF as a permanent international body with meetings in 2013 and 2014 and plans for future annual summits. The initial PIDF summit drew significant attention from both regional states as well as extra regional players such as Timor Leste and the UAE (Bolatiki 2014c). Despite inviting many extra-regional observers, Bainimarama nonetheless sees the PIDF as a forum for Pacific Islanders based on Pacific Islander values (briefing to USP staffers cited in Tarte 2013).

The stated purposes of the PIDF are to serve as a platform for Pacific Island action on sustainable development and to aggregate the actions of Pacific Island states in the UN Asia-Pacific group (Tarte 2013). However, most scholarly and journalistic commentary on the PIDF has focused on the challenge it potentially poses to the PIF. Although the Fijian Government has denied that the PIDF is intended to compete with the PIF (Kubuabola 2013), this is at odds with Fiji's criticisms of the latter organisation and Bainimarama's thinly veiled barbs aimed at the PIF during the PIDF summits. Fiji's pattern of seeking new partners and new avenues for international cooperation has been too systematic for it to be otherwise, and the PIDF is very clearly designed to be a vehicle for this policy.

The membership provisions for Pacific Island states means that neither Australia nor New Zealand are eligible for membership, though representatives of embassies in Fiji attended as observers (Kubuabola 2013). Thus Fiji's two largest critics and the dominant powers of the PIF were excluded from being able to significantly influence the new forum. While numerous regional multilateral organisations sent observers to the inaugural PIDF meeting, the PIF was notably absent. Significantly, the summit was scheduled to coincide with key meetings of officials at the PIF. As such there has been little doubt that the PIDF was intended by the Fijian Government as at the very least a symbol of protest against the PIF.

The PIDF is the most readily dismissed of Fiji's multilateral initiatives. Even before the launch of the PIDF, experts were voicing scepticism (Pacific Beat 2013). In interviews, experts willing to credit the impact of Fiji's foreign policy on the regional order of the Pacific Islands have been inclined to take a wait and see approach to this particular initiative. There is some evidence to back this position. So far there have been no major substantive outcomes from the new forum beyond statements of general intent and outcome documents released with a delay after the summits. A secretariat has been established in Suva, but beyond this the PIDF has been thin on the ground with results. Recently, the PIDF has been invited to participate in regional fora such as the SPC summit (*Islands Business* 2014), but again this has yet to produce tangible results.

Beyond the lack of substantive results, the funding needed for the ongoing operation of the PIDF is uncertain. To this point, the funding of the PIDF has relied on the Fijian Government, supplemented by one-off donations from development partners such as China (Tarte 2013). The Fijian Government has provided a secretariat and the ongoing funding for the operations of the PIDF in 2014, but its future beyond that point is uncertain. Unlike the PIF, the PIDF does not have fully committed developed states to rely on for funding, nor does it have the trade outcomes and established clout of the MSG to give its members a vested interest in supporting its continued existence. Given the tight budgetary constraints of even a relatively large Pacific

Island state such as Fiji and the shifting priorities of donor states, it is entirely possible that the PIDF may be financially unsustainable. The PIDF may therefore turn out to be a temporary protest action against Fiji's suspension from the PIF. Several prominent regional experts interviewed on the matter expressed the expectation that the PIDF will not be a lasting phenomenon and would be abandoned as soon as Fiji's PIF suspension was revoked. So far, this has not occurred despite the lifting of the suspension.

I suggest this view is overly pessimistic. Apart from the fact that the revocation of Fiji's suspension has not led to the end of the PIDF, the organisation has some strengths. The PIDF is the initiative of a small developing country, and yet managed to garner the attention of not only regional but also extra regional states. Fiji succeeded in launching the PIDF not only with minimal financial support from larger states, but did so despite active attempts by Australia and New Zealand to isolate the Bainimarama regime on the international stage. As such, the PIDF must be viewed as a genuine Pacific Island movement. Though several Polynesian states such as Samoa boycotted the inaugural session (Pacific Beat 2013), there has been an ongoing commitment by key states. And in this context the invitation to participate in other organisations, such as an invitation to join the SPC, should be viewed as a further sign of support.

While the lack of results to date is indeed an issue, it misses part of the point of the PIDF. Pacific Island culture puts great emphasis on inclusiveness and dialogue as methods of decision-making and conflict resolution. In that respect, holding a well-attended conference can be seen as a milestone in and of itself. During the 2013 PIDF summit, the rhetoric of a significant number of the speakers was focused on finding alternative, Pacific Island solutions to the issues facing the region (Tarte 2014). This inclusiveness and the focus on regional culture on the part of the PIDF is particularly important in the context of the Pacific Plan/Framework for Pacific Regionalism critique of the PIF. If the major weakness of the PIF is its lack of inclusiveness of civil society and Western domination, then the potential impact of the PIDF as an alternative platform for discussion should not be undervalued. Jenny Hayward-Jones (2013) of the Lowy Institute has suggested that one possible future for the PIDF could be as an ancillary discussion group to the PIF, or even as a reform template for the PIF. Part of her expectation for negotiations surrounding Fiji's return to the PIF hinges on ensuring that the approach taken by the PIDF is preserved. I suggest that although the PIDF will remain a wholly independent platform, and that its existence will not be part of the negotiations for the conditions under which Fiji would agree to return to the PIF, the notion that the PIDF can complement the PIF is entirely plausible.

It is important, however, not to overstate the PIDF's success. Despite the attention it has garnered, and the rhetoric surrounding its essential mission, it has so far failed in its underlying political goal of undermining the PIF. Attendance at PIF summits has not decreased since the inception of the PIDF, whether from regional states or outside observer bodies. The PIDF was also marred by the absence of some of the Pacific Island states, with Samoa's absence being particularly significant, tied as it was to explicit criticisms of the Bainimarama regime. The PIDF therefore cannot claim the same level of legitimacy in terms of representing Pacific Island states as the PIF. Together with the greater financial stability of the PIF, that has persisted even despite recent Australian aid cuts, this makes it unlikely that the PIDF will detract from, let alone replace, its more established counterpart in the foreseeable future. As noted above, all interview respondents were confident of the long-term survival of the PIF while acknowledging the need for reform. I therefore suggest that although the PIDF will make a lasting and worthwhile contribution to Pacific Island regionalism, it will be as a separate and hopefully complementary platform of cooperation rather than as a challenger to the PIF.

The Melanesian Spearhead Group

The MSG differs from the other two organisations discussed in this chapter in that it does not aim to be a platform for the entire Pacific Islands. However, much like the PIF and PIDF, it provides a broad spectrum political platform rather than an organisation dedicated to a specific topic area such as the CROP organisations that specialise on particular policy areas. As the Melanesian states make up the majority of the region's population and economic power, the influence of the MSG cannot be underestimated. I suggest that the creation of other subregional organisations such as the Polynesian Leaders Group (PLG) (Tavita 2011) are a direct response to the success the Melanesian states have had in creating a common bloc through the MSG. What is more, the strength of this bloc has arguably been increased due to the greater energy and emphasis placed on it by Fiji's foreign policy since 2006.

The Melanesian states have been Fiji's strongest supporters since the takeover in 2006. Not only have MSG states largely refrained from criticising Fiji, there has also been a backlash from prominent Melanesian political figures such as former Solomon Islands Prime Minister Manasseh Sogavare against criticisms from other Pacific Island states (ABC 2009). Even beyond that, MSG states have supported virtually every initiative of the Fijian government, including sending high-level representatives up to and including heads of government to events such as the PIDF summits (Manning 2010). Some commentators suggest that the MSG has presented a common front, one that has 'mobilised around Fiji' (Walsh 2010).

This view, however, is not uncontested and there have been questions raised about the cohesiveness of the MSG and the question of how deep MSG support for the post-2006 shift in Fijian policy really runs. Critics of the Bainimarama regime questioned whether or not the support of the MSG was more than simply political rhetoric for appearance sake (Lal 2012). Following this line of reasoning, the lack of criticism of the 2006 coup and the subsequent abrogation of the Fijian Constitution may be attributed more to diplomatic inhibitions against open criticism of fellow Melanesians. The main argument in this context is the cancellation of the 2010 MSG summit in Fiji by then chair Vanuatu, which was scheduled to hand over the chair of the MSG to Fiji at that summit. Prime Minister Natapei of Vanuatu cancelled the meeting, citing concerns about the suitability of Fiji as an undemocratic state to chair the MSG. Given the general hesitancy of Pacific Island states towards open public displays of conflict, this certainly represented a major breach of the norms of regional politics among Pacific Island states.

More generally, critics of the MSG have questioned how cohesive and effective the MSG is as a multilateral body. There have been other signs that the MSG does not present an entirely unified front. Most recently, the relationship of the MSG has been strained by the question of admitting West Papuan independence movements as members in a similar fashion to the Front de Libération Nationale Kanak et Socialiste (FLNKS, or Kanak and Socialist National Liberation

Front) of New Caledonia. Vanuatu's support for independence for Melanesians under Indonesian rule has clashed with Fiji and Papua New Guinea's desire for closer relations with Indonesia (Australia Network News 2014). Currently, Indonesia has observer status at the MSG while the liberation movements for West Papua have so far been unable to achieve any sort of recognised status. The cohesiveness of the MSG could also be strained by tensions between its two largest member states, Fiji and Papua New Guinea. Issues such as PNG's Manus Island refugee deal with Australia and the Bainimarama Government's refusal to accept PNG High Commissioner Eafeare as the dean of Suva's diplomatic corps caused diplomatic tensions in late 2013. These tensions prompted observers to suggest that there was a real possibility that Melanesia might be facing a fight for leadership between Fiji and PNG (Hayward-Jones 2013).

While there are certainly differences of opinion and goals among Melanesian states, the MSG is a more cohesive body than its critics give it credit for. Though there are some dissenting opinions (Hayward-Jones 2010), the cancellation of the 2010 MSG summit by Vanuatu has been widely regarded in Fiji as due to outside interference on the part of Australia and New Zealand (Kubuabola 2013). Though there is no direct evidence to support the claim, it is consistent with Australia and New Zealand's policy of isolating Fiji. Regardless of the reason for the cancellation, it is notable that the rift between the MSG members was repaired quickly, and apparently to Fiji's satisfaction. In December of the same year, a reconciliation ceremony was held by Sato Kilman, Edward Natapei's successor as Prime Minister of Vanuatu, at a special meeting of the MSG (Tarte 2011). Given that the next MSG summit was held in Suva (Melanesian Spearhead Group 2011), Vanuatu's boycott is best viewed as a momentary ripple, rather than signalling deeper disunity. Similarly, while there have certainly been tensions between Fiji and PNG that point to the two states having agendas that are not completely aligned, the O'Neill government has strongly denied that these are signs of a deeper rift between the two states. It would appear that the relationship between Fiji and its Melanesian neighbours is a robust one that can withstand a certain level of tension without affecting the overall closeness of ties or willingness of the MSG member states to cooperate. Despite the occasional ripple, the MSG is an important avenue of support for the Bainimarama Government's challenge to the previous regional status quo.

The question though is how far that sympathy goes. It is important to note that the suspension of Fiji from the PIF was unanimous. Thus the Melanesian states obviously agreed to it at the time, although they may have had some private misgivings. While the apparent consensus on Fiji's suspension stands at odds with subsequent MSG support for Fiji, the fact remains notable. While the other MSG members have always pushed for Fiji's suspension from the PIF to be lifted, this has always been with the caveat that Fiji returns to democratic rule. This proviso was only removed in the build-up to the 2014 elections, when most observers started to consider Fiji's return to at least nominal civilian rule inevitable (Dorney 2013). Also, Melanesian leaders have not stopped attending PIF summits, nor withdrawn support for PIF initiatives. It appears, then, that the growing strength of the MSG and its support for Fijian initiatives does not necessarily signal lack of support for the PIF.

The way forward: The post-2014 elections

Fiji's foreign policy since 2006 has evinced a confident search for new allies in an attempt to reduce the importance of its relationship with Australia. While the Bainimarama regime's ambitions have not been fully realised, his government's strategies have nevertheless yielded some results. Ironically, despite the fact that the core dynamic of Fiji's policy has been to try to circumvent and marginalise the central body of regional multilateralism, there has been no fragmentation or weakening of the region's existing multilateral architecture. The new channels Fiji has opened up, however, are viable avenues for further cooperation both within the Pacific Islands community and beyond. However, the other states of the region have not adopted these new pathways sufficiently for them to replace the PIF as the main nexus of the region's multilateral architecture.

Given that Fiji is one of the larger and more developed Pacific Island states, it should perhaps come as no great surprise that Fiji has had a significant impact on the region. It is located centrally in the region, and controls a significant amount of the infrastructure that is key to the functioning of its neighbours. From the perspective of a developed nation, Fiji's capacities may seem very limited. But relative to the other states of the region, with the exception of PNG, Fiji is not only large, but also much more sophisticated. Ironically, though Fiji has always held a leadership role in the region, the fact that organisations such as the PIF have been headquartered in Fiji has helped further nurture the growth of a political class with the education and drive to step beyond the national level and onto the international stage.

The main issue for the immediate future of multilateral cooperation in the Pacific Islands is the relationship between Fiji and the PIF. Fiji's suspension highlighted problems surrounding certain elements of PIF practice. Fiji's suspension also undermined the legitimacy of the PIF's status as representing all Pacific Island states as well as standing at odds with the consensus-based 'Pacific Way' (Dobell 2008). The tension caused by this contradiction was exacerbated by the Bainimarama Government's attacks on the Forum over the next several years (Williams 2013). Originally, the suspension was intended and expected to put the government of Fiji under pressure to hold elections sooner rather than later (TVNZ 2009). But this was to prove ineffective and the Bainimarama regime did not become more conciliatory towards its critics. On the contrary, it appeared to gain a certain amount of kudos as a plucky underdog resisting international pressures (Fraenkel 2013). Full reconciliation now appears to be less simple than Australia would have hoped. As Fraenkel (2013) rightly points out, successfully resisting external pressure has brought political benefits to Fiji. Given Bainimarama's rhetoric as a champion of smaller states against metropolitan influences, restoring relations is more than just a matter of 'just kissing cheeks and pretending that nothing ever happened' (Lieutenant-Colonel Sitiveni Qiliho, quoted in Bolatiki 2014a). Accordingly, the Fijian Government has spurned 'olive branches' that amounted to less than full restoration of relations, such as allowing Fiji to participate in the PACER Plus negotiation at lower levels of engagement (Maclellan 2012, p. 364). It was not until Australia and New Zealand unilaterally moved to lift sanctions that Fijian rhetoric against them began to ease. Yet even with bilateral relations between Fiji and the two metropolitan states nominally restored to normal, Fiji is still proceeding at its own pace and on its own terms on issues such as defence cooperation (Bolatiki 2014a).

Rather than making Fiji seem belligerent or uncooperative, the Bainimarama Government has succeeded in continuing to raise questions about the PIF. While this has not been entirely successful, as discussed above, Fiji is not alone in asking difficult questions.

This is shown by the fact that PACER Plus negotiations were moved to a new secretariat, independent of the PIF. Rather than isolating Fiji, the suspension handed down from the PIF has dented the Forum's credibility. This successful, hard-line approach by Fiji strengthens its position as it negotiates its readmission to the Forum leaders meeting. Given Fiji's rhetoric, there is some doubt as to what Fiji will require to agree to attend the Forum again (Pratibha 2013).

Despite Bainimarama's caginess about rejoining the Forum, it is a goal the PIF should pursue. Even leaving aside the potential for there to be a future impact on the credibility of the PIF if Fiji continues to attack its credibility, Fiji has too important a role to play for the region to be excluded from the PIF. The goal of the Forum is regional coordination, an aim that would be severely hampered by the absence of one of the region's most developed states. Add to that the geographical fact that the Forum's secretariat is located in Suva, and there is a significant incentive for the Forum to bring Fiji back to the table. Credibility and logistics are two of the biggest strengths of the PIF, and both selling points are enhanced by cooperation with Fiji.

There is also a strong incentive for the Bainimarama Government to resume its membership of the PIF. Fiji's standoffishness towards the PIF misses certain realities of the Fijian situation. Even as a relatively developed Pacific Island state, Fiji is still a developing country dependent on significant amounts of foreign aid. Furthermore, as a state spread across a large number of islands, Fiji must cope with at least some of the service delivery issues that other Pacific Island states face. The need for cooperation on as wide a basis as possible is still very much in Fiji's interests, as the energetic pursuit of multilateral initiatives demonstrates. Beyond that, Fiji also has an interest in closer ties to development partners, many of whom pay a great deal of attention to the meetings and actions of the PIF. This means that Fiji has much to gain by renewing participation in the PIF. Given the attempt to have a Fijian Secretary-General elected, it is hard to believe that this is a state of affairs that Fiji will wish to sustain much longer. Despite the rhetoric of the Bainimarama Government, the Fijian government will have to face up to the continued significance of the PIF and that attempts to sideline the Forum are going to be unsuccessful. As Brij Lal has pointed out, culturally, geographically and financially, Fiji has more to gain from its traditional allies and development partners than from entirely new affiliations (Lal 2012).

According to Lal, Fiji's return to the PIF is inevitable, not only from the perspective of the Forum, but also on Fiji's part. The analysis put forward in this chapter supports this viewpoint.

The central question facing the PIF is under what conditions will Fiji agree to resume attendance? Bainimarama's demand that Australia and New Zealand cannot be both donors and members will not be met. Not only would the loss of the financial stability Australia and New Zealand provide be disastrous for the PIF, it would also be difficult politically. As much as Australia and New Zealand are more developed and Westernised than the smaller member states, they are still part of the region. New Zealand in particular has a strong claim to being an Islander state through its Maori heritage. If the PIF wants to serve as a platform for all of the Pacific Islands then Australia and New Zealand have a role to play as members. This is not to say that there is no room for a solution. The call for more voice for the nonmetropolitan members has been a strong one, and Bainimarama is in a position to further invigorate that part of the reform agenda for the PIF. Australia and New Zealand should not be excluded, but a shift in the institutional balance of the PIF for the other states is both possible and necessary to strengthen the Forum. In the Pacific Way tradition of compromise and negotiation, I predict an equitable solution in the mid-term, one that will result in a PIF further strengthened by reform.

What this settlement is not likely to involve is an end to the PIDF or a lesser interest in the MSG. Jenny Hayward-Jones's idea of the PIDF becoming a supplementary body of the PIF is an interesting one, but on balance it seems unlikely. Fiji and the other Melanesian states have benefited from establishing alternatives to the PIF. The Bainimarama Government's intention to sideline the PIF may not have succeeded, but there is still sufficient groundwork laid for these organisations to contribute productively to regional cooperation. Moreover, both organisations are sufficiently different from the PIF to have the potential to be complementary rather than conflicting elements of Pacific Island regionalism. The MSG is a specifically subregional grouping and is therefore able to operate in a more focused manner and with fewer stakeholders. However, it lacks the scope to make truly regional decisions. The inclusion of civil society by the PIDF gives it the ability to be more inclusive and find solutions to development issues beyond top-down government policy. On the other hand, including non-governmental bodies means that it is unsuitable for the formation of treaties or other actions that require sovereign power to take their full effect. These differences mean that the MSG and PIDF will operate more effectively as facets of a diversified regional architecture rather than as competitors to an organisation whose role they are unsuited to fully assume.

This more diversified regional architecture is the logical progression once a settlement is reached and Fiji re-engages with the PIF. There is still a potential for duplication of effort, but if both organisations play to their strengths then this will leave Pacific Island regionalism on a stronger footing than it was before 2006. Though the Bainimarama Government did not manage to undercut the PIF, its multilateral policies since 2006 should still be viewed as a success. If the hurdle of re-engagement can be taken properly then it will leave the regional architecture of the Pacific Islands on a stronger footing than it was in 2006.

References

ABC 2009, 'Melanesian's criticise Samoan PM's comments on Fiji', Australian Broadcasting Corporation, Canberra.

Australia Network News 2014, 'Vanuatu defends boycott of Melanesian Spearhead Group delegation to Indonesia's Papua Province', [Online]. Viewed 10 April 2014 at www.abc.net.au/news/2014-01-16/Vanuatu-defends-boycott-of-Melanesian-Spearhead-Group-delegation-to-Indonesia's-Papua-Province.

Bainimarama, V 2013, Address at the inaugural Pacific Islands Development Forum (PIDF) Meeting—PM Bainimarama, [Online]. Viewed 14 April 2014 at www.fiji.gov.fj/Media-Center/Speeches/ADDRESS-AT-THE-INAUGURAL-PACIFIC-ISLANDS-DEVELOPME.aspx.

Bohane, B 2010, 'Islands dreaming: A fresh look at Pacific Regionalism', *Pacific Institute for Public Policy Discussion Papers*, vol. 15, pp. 1–4.

Bolatiki, M 2013, 'Fiji again stresses PIF call over Australia, NZ', *Fiji Sun*, 15 September.

Bolatiki, M 2014a, 'Fiji PM sets conditions for return to Pacific islands Forum', *Fiji Sun*, 25 October.

Bolatiki, M 2014b, 'Fiji, Australia in defence talks', [Online]. Viewed 8 January 2015 at fijisun.com.fj/2014/12/09/fiji-australia-in-defence-talks/.

Bolatiki, M 2014c, 'PACIFIC AFFAIRS – High level Middle East delegate for PIDF meet'. *Fiji Sun*, 3 June.

Dobell, G 2008, 'The Pacific Way wanes', *The Interpreter*, 26 August.

Dobell, G 2014, 'Status quo Australia versus revisionist Fiji', *ASPI Strategist*, 25 February.

Dorney, S 2013, 'Pacific Island leaders welcome the release of Fiji's new constitution', [Online]. Viewed 10 April 2014 at www.radioaustralia.net.au/international/radio/program/pacific-beat/pacific-island-leaders-welcome-the-release-of-fijis-new-constitution/1186459.

Fiji Sun 2010, 'MSG leaders will sort out rift: Haomae', *Fiji Sun*, 15 July.

Fraenkel, J 2013, 'How to respond to the impasse in Fiji?', [Online]. Viewed 17 April 2014 at devpolicy.org/how-to-respond-to-the-impasse-in-fiji-20130815/.

Hayward-Jones, J 2010, 'Undermining the Pacific Islands Forum', [Online]. Viewed 22 November 2014 at www.lowyinterpreter.org/post/2010/07/30/Undermining-the-Pacific-Islands-Forum.aspx.

Hayward-Jones, J 2013, Personal interview, [Interview] (10 March 2013).

Huffer, E 2006, 'Regionalism and cultural identity: Putting the Pacific back into the plan', in *Globalisation and governance in the Pacific Islands*, ANU E Press, Canberra, pp. 43–55.

Islands Business 2014, 'PIDF invited to key regional meetings', *Islands Business*, 4 November.

Komai, M 2013, 'Pacific Plan to become a regional framework on regional integration', *Islands Business*, 2 September.

Kubuabola, I 2013, 'Fiji says Forum a success despite anti-Fiji campaigning', [Interview] (6 August 2013).

Lal, B 2012, Personal interview, [Interview] (13 December 2012).

Maclellan, N 2012, 'The region in review, issues and events 2011', *The Contemporary Pacific*, vol. 24, no. 2, pp. 359–74.

Manning, S 2010, 'Fiji moves to embrace a new Pacific brotherhood leaving Australia and New Zealand estranged', *Pacific Scoop*, 23 July.

Melanesian Spearhead Group 2011, '18th Melanesian Spearhead Group (MSG) Leaders' Summit Communique', Melanesian Spearhead Group, Suva.

Morris, R 2014, 'Bainimarama claims victory', *Republika Magazine*, 14 September.

Newton-Cain, T 2014, 'PIF: New Secretary-General will have a full agenda', [Online]. Viewed 22 November 2014 at www.lowyinterpreter.org/post/2014/06/20/Changing-of-the-Guard-New-Secretary-General-to-be-appointed-by-the-Pacific-Islands-Forum-Secretariat.aspx?COLLCC=114165702&.

O'Keefe, M 2012, 'Pacific Islands Forum needs to reaffirm its relevance', *The Australian*, 27 August.

Pacific Beat 2013, 'PIDF will never replace Forum: Tuilaepa Sailele', [Online]. Viewed 18 January 2015 at www.abc.net.au/news/2013-08-06/pidf-will-never-replace-forum-tuilaepa-sailele/4869092.

PACNEWS 2012, '"Don't ignore West Papua" appeal from human rights advocate', [Online]. Viewed 20 January 2015 at pacific.scoop.co.nz/2012/08/dont-ignore-west-papua-appeal-from-human-rights-advocate/.

PIFS 2014, *The framework for Pacific regionalism*, Pacific Islands Forum Secretariat, Suva.

Pohnpei, P 2010, 'Discussion paper questions relevance of Pacific Islands Forum', [Online]. Viewed 13 April 2014 at www.fsmpio.fm/RELEASES/2010/october/10_41_10.html.

Pratibha, J 2013, 'Who needs Commonwealth, Pacific Islands Forum?', *Fiji Sun*, 20 November.

Qiolevu, J 2013, Research interview, [Interview] (28 July 2013).

Tarte, S 2011, 'Fiji's search for new friends', *East Asia Forum*, 13 January.

Tarte, S 2014, 'A new regional Pacific voice? An observer's on the Pacific Islands Development Forum (PIDF) inaugural summit, Denarau, Fiji Aug 5–7 2013', *Pacific Islands Brief*, vol. 4, pp. 1–6.

Tavita, TT 2011, '"Historical" Polynesian Leaders Group launched', [Online]. Viewed 15 April 2014 at www.savalinews.com/2011/1 1/21/%E2%80%98historical%E2%80%99-polynesian-group-launched/.

TVNZ 2009, 'Deadline looms for Fiji's Pacific suspension', [Online]. Viewed 12 April 2014 at tvnz.co.nz/world-news/deadline-looms-fijis-pacific-suspension-2692046.

Walsh, C 2010, 'Melanesian Spearhead Group Plus … minus, divided and multiplied', *Pacific Scoop*, 22 June.

Williams, M 2013, 'PM Bainimarama takes swipe at Pacific Islands Forum', [Online]. Viewed 15 April 2014 at fijione.tv/prime-minister-expresses-his-gratitude-to-spc/.

A pragmatic approach to a successful election: A personal reflection

Alisi Daurewa

Introduction

Filled with relief, yet a little saddened with the realisation that this moment would not return, I thanked God for gifting Fiji with the grace of a peaceful general election, after eight years under an unelected government led by former military commander Rear Admiral Voreqe Bainimarama, who removed Laisenia Qarase's elected government for alleged corruption and racism in a coup in December 2006.

The night was Wednesday, 17 September 2014, Fiji's general election day.

According to the 2014 Electoral Decree's Part 3, 19 (p. 234), the President, acting in accordance with section 59 of the Constitution must issue a writ to the Electoral Commission in every election. This task was performed by the Chief Justice (Gates) who was acting as president on 4 August, in the absence of His Excellency Ratu Epeli Nailatikau, who was away overseas. On Monday morning, 22 September 2014, upon receipt of the Final National Results Tally from the Supervisor of Elections (SoE) in accordance with section 103 of the Decree, the Fijian Electoral Commission (FEC) allocated the seats of parliament in accordance with 104 and 105 of the Decree and by 11am announced the names of 50 candidates elected to parliament. At noon on that day the writ was returned by FEC to the President of the Republic of Fiji, conveying the decision of the Fijian electorate in accordance with 106 of the Decree. Bainimarama and his FijiFirst Party won 32 seats. They formed the government while the Social Democratic Liberal Party (SODELPA) and National Federation Party won 15 and three seats respectively. They subsequently formed the Opposition. Later that day, we witnessed Bainimarama sworn in as Prime Minister of Fiji by the President, Ratu Epeli Nailatikau.

Appointment of the Electoral Commissioners

The seven members of the FEC were appointed by the President on 9 January 2014 as required under the 2013 Constitution. Chen Bunn Young is the Chairman of the Electoral Commission. He is a lawyer by profession, who has been running his private law firm for the last 30 years. Father David Arms is a priest belonging to the Columban order in the Catholic Church. He is the only member of the Commission to have had some experience with elections, as a member of the former electoral commission. Professor Vijay Naidu is a development scholar in the School of Government, Development and International Affairs at the University of the South Pacific. Jenny Seeto is a senior partner for the international chartered accounting firm PricewaterhouseCoopers. Larry Thomas is a renowned playwright and filmmaker. James Sowane is a successful tour operator in the tourism industry. I am a practitioner and advocate for people-centred development.

At the time of our appointment, the 2014 Electoral Decree was still being drafted, a supervisor of elections had yet to be appointed, and most of the staff at the elections office were on temporary employment. What was reassuring though was the presence of technical consultants funded by Australia, New Zealand and the European Union, who had begun the preparatory work for elections with help from staff at the Fijian Elections Office (FEO) and the Office of the Attorney General.

Initially we realised that we were going to have to take a hands-on approach and began at least with what was doable despite the absence of necessary frameworks and personnel mentioned above. Our first task was the appointment of senior and middle management staff and the members of the FEC participated as chairpersons of several interview panels. This was an ongoing commitment for an additional three months. At times it was onerous because we were still committed to our other work, but we persevered nevertheless because we saw our role as a national calling. I thought the government was wise to appoint seven commissioners because it comfortably accommodated for the quorum of four in cases when some of us were absent.

The Supervisor of Elections

With a similar constitutional process to the appointment of members of the FEC, Mohammed Saneem was appointed by the President of the Republic of Fiji on recommendation by the Constitutional Offices Commission, which prior to the general elections comprised the Prime Minister and the Attorney General, who was also the Minister for Justice and Minister for Elections. Saneem had been an employee of the Ministry of Justice as Acting Permanent Secretary. The Minister for Elections had told some of us that the SoE would be an independent expatriate so it came as a complete surprise when the minister told us of Saneem's appointment. However, being practical people we were prepared to work with Saneem because he was already performing some functions of the SoE and under the circumstances we did not have the luxury of time. For my part, I found Saneem to be readily accessible. Having said this, the issue of who decides on operational policies is unclear. Soon after its appointment, the FEC had begun discussion with some of the technical consultants on developing policies and operational guidelines. However, after the appointment of the SoE this was not given the priority it deserved. On its part, the FEC was limited from pursuing this further in the absence of its own technical consultant, for which it had made an unsuccessful request. The importance of policies with clear operational guidelines cannot be overemphasised. From a governance perspective, this is an area that needs urgent attention and I am hopeful the FEC will be given the institutional support needed to effectively address this issue.

The Electoral Decree and other related decrees

Despite oral and written representation on the draft electoral decree, very little was accepted by the Solicitor General. We were pleased though with the inclusion of two submissions on other decrees: the Immunity Decree and the right to appeal against the police officer making the decision to revoke a meeting permit. This was at the end of March 2014, the same time as Mr Saneem's appointment as SoE. There were concerns raised as some members of the public feared that a new voting system, plus choosing a number as opposed to a name, would be confusing. I believed that the assumption that rural people were ignorant was an insult to their intelligence. When I observed pre-polling in the outer islands of the Lau group, I was impressed to find aged voters voting with ease and without any problems. I soon found out that figures were not foreign to them because of their early exposure as Christians to reading the Bible, where they were required to cite the numbers of chapters and verses daily from the book of Psalms. They also dealt with numerical digits on a daily basis through counting money, remembering and dialling mobile numbers and through other means.

The roadmap to elections

By February 2014, despite our concern with the delay of the Electoral Decree and the appointment of the SoE, we went ahead and created a roadmap for the general elections with emphasis on voter education. We also realised that the success of actualising the roadmap would have to be based on a pragmatic approach, an example of which was utilising the opportunity the government had begun for us in engaging international technical consultants to work at the FEO. Jerome Leyraud, the team leader for the consultants, further developed the roadmap until we were ready to meet with development partners. Leyraud was highly valuable because of his international and legal expertise with elections. Unfortunately, we were not able to retain him to serve the commission after his term expired in April because the Attorney General did not approve our request and instructed us to use the services of the Solicitor General. We did not feel bound to go to the Solicitor General for advice all the time as we wanted to maintain our freedom to obtain legal advice elsewhere to ensure our independence.

Election partners

One of the strategic decisions we made was to ensure that all presentations and dialogue with potential partners and donors were to be conducted at the FEO building, which at that point needed renovation. This was to enable them to experience first-hand the state of our work environment, which at that time needed urgent attention.

Our presentation of the roadmap on 12 March 2014 was met with overwhelming support from the development partners. The roadmap included our strategy for voter education based on three simple questions: 'What is voting?' 'Why Vote?' 'How to vote?' The voter education process was to be staggered in three stages over the six months that were left before the elections. By coincidence and fortunately for us, the Fiji Women's Rights Movement was already engaged in civic education at that time, addressing the 'What' and 'Why' of voting via media outlets. This meant that we only needed to work on the 'How to vote' aspect.

Thus began a series of consultations, which the SoE continued with after his appointment at the end of March 2014. The support of development partners was manifested in the 54 per cent external contribution to the total general elections budget of FJD$39,284,637. According to FEC's 2014 Report (p. 8), the total expenditure for FEO as at 31 December 2014 was FJD$27,763,815.

In addition to development partners, I thought our regular meetings with political parties, media organisations, NGOs (including those concerned with disability issues), the police and representatives of the transport industry were very helpful. This continued well after the appointment of the SoE because we were conscious of the need to be on track with groups we respected as primary partners because of the important role each played. After all, the success of the general elections was also going to be dependent on their collective support.

The task for the FEC was to establish a relationship with the different groups in recognition of the important role each played in the general elections within a very short period of eight working months, for we were appointed in January and the general elections were in September. Our meeting schedule changed according to the need and circumstances and we stepped back while the SoE continued meeting with the different groups. However, the FEC continued to meet with the police for security updates and the transport sector for logistical purposes, to address the rural electorate not regularly serviced by public transport.

Secretariat issues

While each commissioner was tasked with a certain responsibility, overall, the work of the FEC was affected by inadequate secretariat support for the initial five months of our appointment. Part of my task was to ensure that our minutes, correspondence and decisions were registered and regularly updated. Thankfully, the inclusion of two additional staff before the elections helped reduce our burden. Our secretariat staff worked hard, usually under trying conditions, because we were ourselves under a lot of pressure and were thus often demanding. They were always on hand to help us even late at night and they were incredibly patient and tolerant with us. In addition, we did not have a separate budget, which meant that we had to seek financial outlays for the work we did, including our claims for sitting allowance which were being approved by the SoE whose work we had responsibility over. This was an institutional conflict of interest that we tried to deal with as best as we could.

Polling observation

The commissioners participated as observers in both pre-polling and the actual poll day, including the counting of votes. In doing so, we developed our own checklist, which was helpful because lessons learnt from the pre-poll were reported to the SoE for consideration for poll day processes. The commissioners covered all four divisions, travelling the rugged terrain of the Colo (hinterland) in both Viti Levu and Vanua Levu, the coastal areas, and the unpredictable waters of the Lau and Beqa islands.

Lau Province pre-poll

I travelled to Lau in the Eastern Division, where the electorate voted by pre-poll. Lau is one of 14 provinces in Fiji and consists of several small islands. The islands are the farthest from the main island of Viti Levu and some of its islands, such as Ono-i-Lau, are nearer to the nearest Tongan island than to Suva. Amongst the provinces, Lau is considered the most challenged in terms of accessibility because its several small islands are scattered and because of the unpredictability of the weather.

Three groups of officials from the FEO administered the pre-poll in Lau, with each group travelling by ship, the cheaper and more practical option. I accompanied the third and biggest group in the government ship *Iloilovatu,* assigned to Northern Lau, which is made up of the islands of Oneata, Moce, Komo, Vanuavatu, Lakeba, Nayau, Cicia, Vanubalavu and all small surrounding islands—Tuvuca, Ogea, Katafaga, Susui, etc. We left Suva on Wednesday, 3 September 2014 after a delay of one day because of a mechanical problem with the ship. The third group consisted of 22 officials and 14 police officers. They were divided into seven teams. I accompanied the team as far as Cicia Island and returned by plane on Wednesday, 10 September.

While the FEO had already undertaken the task of ensuring protocols were observed and logistical arrangements made in their initial visit to the provinces before the elections, on arrival in the village, the chief and/or elders were presented with *i sevusevu* (ceremonial offering of *yaqona* to the host, made in respect of recognition and acceptance of one another). From then on, the villagers took over the organisation and prepared food and bedding for the visitors. The *Turaga ni Koro* or village headman in each village played an important role in mobilising the villagers to vote. Aside from myself, the only other observers present were polling agents from SODELPA. I did not meet any polling agents from other political parties.

The polling officials worked hard, often under trying conditions. Some who travelled in the *Iloilovatu* suffered from seasickness. For the team leaders, their dilemma was conforming to the voting schedule prepared by the FEO. This was difficult to follow because on sea, the ship's captain dictated which island to berth at first in accordance with the weather pattern. At times, this meant conducting the pre-poll in more than one island in one day, as they did for Nayau and Cicia islands, where Nayau polling was during the day and Cicia polling was in the evening on 8 September 2014. The polling agents did not return to the ship until the early hours of the next morning. On shore, they were met with friendly people but the terrain for some was not friendly. In Nayau, a policeman smashed his expensive mobile phone when he fell down a cliff with the empty ballot box on the team's way to a village on the other side of the island. Miraculously, he recovered in an instant without any damage to himself or the ballot box.

The electorate in most parts of Northern Lau thought voting was easy. The turnout was about 78 per cent. From observation and discussions with the voters, a number of factors were identified as vital in making voting easy and these included the following: a majority of the polling stations were in village community halls, some in schools and one in a private residence; all were within easy walking distance; there was an easy flow of voters into and out of the polling station; the polling officials assisted where necessary, including helping those with disability issues and taking the poll to the sick and the weak at homes and in hospital beds; a boat carting voter instruction booklets arrived in Lau ahead of the polling teams; the booklets were distributed to the people before polling day. By the time the same booklets were given to the voters in the polling stations, most of them were familiar with the process. Some polling officials explained the process whilst handing out the polling paper. Voters who regularly read the Christian bible were not intimidated by numbers and this included the octogenarians, most of whom were women. In some villages there were question and answer sessions with the author after the *sevusevu*, whilst waiting for the polling officials to set up the polling stations.

Table 1: Details of polling in five Lau islands

Date	Island	Station	Voters List	No. Voted	% Voted
4/9/14	Moce	Nasau	286	221	77%
4/9/14	Komo	Komo	112	86	77%
5/9/14	Lakeba	Tubou	490	299	61%
6/9/14	Lakeba	Yadrana	135	107	79%
6/9/14	Lakeba	Waciwaci	154	103	67%
6/9/14	Lakeba	Vakano	52	42	81%
8/9/14	Nayau	Salia	87	68	78%
8/9/14	Cicia	Tarakua	105	89	85%
8/9/14	Cicia	Naceva	53	43	81%
8/9/14	Cicia	Lomati/Tabutoga	119	106	89%
8/9/14	Cicia	Mabula	297	248	84%
Total			1,890	1,412	78%

The table above includes only those polling stations I visited and those I was able to obtain data for from the respective presiding officers. At the Tubou polling station, the low turnout of 61 per cent was partly due to an administrative oversight. Twenty people who produced identification cards were not included in the voters' roll. Secondly, and a common concern shared by all the islanders, the pre-poll was unexpected. Despite radio announcements from the FEO advising the change in the method of voting, it appeared many of the islanders were caught by surprise. A majority still expected to vote on 17 September. Hence those who were elsewhere, like the Methodist Church ministers and their respective island delegations who were in Suva for their annual conference, joined the list of non-voters from Lau.

International interest

The FEC was hosted by the Australian and New Zealand Electoral Commissions in July and August 2014 respectively. These visits provided insight into their electoral systems and increased my appreciation of engaging non-government workers in the administration of elections, which Fiji has now adopted. When the Multinational Observer Group (MOG) arrived later in Fiji, it was good to meet with some of those we had met earlier in Australia and New Zealand.

Conclusion

Overall, for the commissioners, the road to the elections was not an easy walk. There were disagreements between the FEC and SoE, as eventually evidenced in the court proceedings filed in the High Court to determine what the SoE was bound to do upon 'directions' given him by the FEC. But, much like a rough journey, we managed to negotiate our way through sharp pebbles and rocks under the able leadership of our chairman because each one of us was committed and determined to ensuring there was an election to give the Fijian people the opportunity to vote for their government.

In the end, as they say, the rest is history. Fiji went to the polls with 0.7 per cent of invalid votes. Out of a total 591,101 registered voters, 500,078 or 84.6 per cent actually voted.

To be able to pull this off within eight months, it had to be an election with a pragmatic approach plus a lot of faith. I was honoured to have served my country with the other six commissioners, who brought with them their unique professional skills, vast and diverse experiences and deep wisdom. As a team we didn't forget to laugh! The SoE and his team, including over 9,000 poll-day workers and the technical consultants, worked tirelessly. They showed that cooperation and commitment towards a common national purpose could overcome obstacles. I couldn't have asked for more.

Disclaimer

This is the personal opinion of the author and not of the Fijian Electoral Commission of which she is a member.

References

Government of Fiji 2014, *Electoral Decree*, Government Printers, Suva.

Fijian Electoral Commission 2014, *Fijian Electoral Commission Report*, Government Printers, Suva.

Fijian Electoral Commission & Supervisor of Elections 2014, 'Joint Report on General Election by the Fijian Electoral Commission and the Supervisor of Election to H.E. the President of the Republic of Fiji and the Secretary General to Parliament', Suva.

14

Observing the 2014 Fiji general elections

Leonard Chan

Introduction

Having grown up in Fiji, I maintain strong connections with the country through family, friends and work, even though I moved to New Zealand more than a decade ago. As the Fiji Programme Development Manager in the Ministry of Foreign Affairs and Trade (MFAT), I was closely involved in managing New Zealand's assistance for the Fiji elections. Furthermore, I was fortunate to be one of six officials who joined five New Zealand parliamentarians to observe the elections as a member of the Multinational Observer Group (MOG).

In this paper, I describe my experience of participating in the MOG, discuss the role of the MOG, and describe New Zealand's support for Fiji's elections preparations. I hope this is of wide interest and a useful contribution to the body of literature on Fiji's historic 2014 elections. The views and conclusions presented are my own and not the view or position of the New Zealand Government. The MOG's media statements and its subsequent report provide the considered views of the observation team and I draw on those heavily in this chapter.

The paper does not examine or analyse the electoral framework and the pre-election conditions, although they are important determinants of a free and fair election. This task is left to others who are more qualified. The MOG Report findings (2014c, p. 30) concluded that voters, political parties and the media were reasonably free to engage in the electoral process. The elections were well run and there was no evidence of attempts to influence the process or outcome. The elections were credible and reflected the will of the Fijian people.

New Zealand policy settings and assistance for the Fiji elections

Much has been written and said about the merit or otherwise of New Zealand's policy settings toward Commodore Voreqe Bainimarama's Administration (the Administration) after the 2006 military coup. New Zealand did not impose economic sanctions, but restricted travel, official contact with the Administration, and limited aid funds being channelled through central government. New Zealand aid to Fiji continued throughout the period with an average total aid flow of NZ$5.2 million per year. The political and diplomatic sanctions were targeted at the Administration leadership and its associates and not aimed at ordinary Fijians. By the end of March 2014, the New Zealand Cabinet had removed all restrictions on contact and cooperation with Fiji except for defence cooperation. However, these restrictions were also lifted by the end of 2014.

The New Zealand Government had always said it stood ready to assist Fiji's return to an elected government, provided the Administration demonstrated a commitment to holding free and fair elections with a firm date. The initial approach to New Zealand was during the first half of 2012 when the Administration sought assistance from donors for voter registration and the design of a new constitution. This was a significant step forward because New Zealand was able to respond positively to both requests. New Zealand's technical assistance contributed to the successful launch of voter registration in July 2012, using Fiji's newly acquired electronic voter registration (EVR) system. Soon after, New Zealand, along with other donors, funded the Fiji Constitution Commission to undertake nationwide consultations for a new constitution. Although the draft constitution by the Constitution Commission, chaired by Professor Yash Ghai, was rejected by the Administration, the public response was heartening. The Commission's open consultative process provided a platform for the people of Fiji to comment on the future of their country and exercise their political rights for the first time since 2006.

In mid-2013, the Administration invited New Zealand, the European Union (EU) and the Commonwealth to undertake a needs assessment of the Fijian Elections Office (FEO) to gauge its capacity to conduct elections in 2014. Melissa Thorpe of the Zealand Electoral Commission (NZEC) was a member of the assessment team. The New Zealand and EU team members concluded that it was operationally feasible for the FEO to organise a free and fair election by September 2014, provided preparations began immediately or the likelihood of success would diminish rapidly.

It was clear from the outset that timelines would be extremely tight for the FEO to undertake the preparations necessary to hold elections by September 2014. To understand how challenging the timelines were for the FEO, it is worth noting that in the case of New Zealand, the NZEC began planning and preparing for the 2014 elections soon after the 2011 elections. For the FEO, added delays were another issue to contend with as the already compressed timeframe was squeezed further due to holdups in promulgating a new constitution, issuing electoral laws and recruiting staff.

The joint New Zealand and EU assessment helped New Zealand and other donors decide how to assist Fiji's elections preparations. New Zealand's main contribution was the deployment of technical advisers to the FEO to assist with:

- planning;
- developing policy, process and systems; and
- staff recruitment and training.

New Zealand also funded the cardboard voting booths and designed and built a database that helped fast track the processing of over 15,600 applications to recruit 9,000 polling day workers. Assistance was also extended to cover observation visits to New Zealand by the Supervisor of Elections and three members of the Fiji Electoral Commission.

New Zealand's assistance was delivered through the NZEC, which had responsibility for running the New Zealand elections just three days after the Fiji elections. The highly experienced technical advisers deployed in Fiji were drawn from the NZEC's pool of election officers in the field. The New Zealand advisers worked well with the Fiji Supervisor of Elections and his staff and advised the Fiji Electoral Commission when needed. Together with advisers from Australia and those funded by the EU, the New Zealand team made an important contribution to the successful delivery of the Fiji elections.

As Fiji's election day drew nearer, and following an invitation from Fiji, New Zealand also agreed to provide 11 observers to the MOG. The New Zealand team was led by former deputy prime minister the Right Honourable Wyatt Creech, and consisted of four former parliamentarians (Hon. Richard Barker,[1] John Hayes, Dr Paul Hutchison, and Ross Robertson) and six MFAT officials made up the rest of the contingent. All except Creech were short-term observers.

Multinational Observer Group

The Administration invited four countries (Australia, India, Indonesia and Papua New Guinea)[2] to co-lead the MOG. This was a departure from the usual practice of using multilateral or inter-governmental organisation-led missions. The MOG was also very broad with 92 observers representing 15 countries and organisations, which provided greater legitimacy. The Administration also ensured the MOG worked under common terms of reference (agreed between the Administration and the co-leads). This enabled the Administration to keep an overview of the process and ensured the group worked well administratively.

The terms of reference (Multinational Observer Group 2014a, p. 1) stated that the MOG's two objectives were to:

---

1   At the time of MOG mission Hayes, Hutchison, and Robertson were MPs, but have since retired.
2   PNG subsequently declined Fiji's invitation to co-lead the MOG.

assess whether the voter processes of the FEO facilitated and assisted the Fijian voters to exercise their right to freely vote and whether the outcome of the 2014 Fijian General Election broadly represented the will of the Fijian voters; and

provide recommendations going forward on how future elections can be improved in terms of integrity and effectiveness.

This scope allowed the MOG to assess various aspects of the electoral process including the functions of the FEO; voter registration; public education; alternative means of voting; nomination and candidate registration; election day operations; vote counting and results; dispute resolution; and reconciliation of ballot papers.

Countries invited to send observers submitted nominations that were endorsed by the Supervisor of Elections and then formally issued with identification cards. This two-step accreditation process allowed the Administration better management over the process. There were no domestic observers accredited, but this did not stop the Concerned Citizens for Credible Elections, a coalition of Fijian NGOs, from conducting research on the elections and compiling a report of its observations.[3]

Clear and regular communications were an integral part of the MOG Secretariat's business and this was very well managed. Regular briefings to the media and other stakeholders ensured that all were kept informed. The MOG's transparency, professionalism and independence enhanced Fijian confidence in the electoral process. This, according to the MOG Coordinator (27 August 2014, *Fiji Sun*):

goes to the heart of these sorts of observer activities, it's about providing confidence, it's not just about the international [communities'] confidence in what's happening in Fiji it's about providing some level of confidence to the Fijian voting public that in fact this election will be as good as it can be in terms of its integrity and effectiveness.

---

3   The coalition of 10 NGOs included the Fiji Women's Crisis Centre; Pacific Dialogue; Social and Economic Empowerment Programme; Fiji Council of Churches; Ecumenical Centre for Research, Education and Advocacy; Academics from the School of Social Science (Fiji National University); Academics from the School of Government, Development and International Affairs (University of the South Pacific); Citizens' Constitutional Forum; Fiji Women's Rights Movement; and Dialogue Fiji.

The New Zealand team leader, the Rt Hon Wyatt Creech, arrived as one of the long-term observers (LTO) on 22 August. He joined other LTOs and participated in all aspects of MOG Core Group, including pre-election preparation, visiting and talking to villagers throughout Fiji (including the outer islands) to interview voters, parties, election officials, candidates and civil society organisations on election issues generally. More specifically, the observers sought to gauge the public's comprehension of the electoral processes and attitudes towards the elections. Creech took part in pre-polling observation missions as well, and on election day he was in Levuka, Fiji's former capital. During his month-long assignment, Creech reached some of the more remote places in Vanua Levu, Taveuni and the Lau Group, easily making him the most intrepid MOG member. He was tireless and got on with the job, undeterred by long ferry rides, bumpy drives, and having to trek through difficult terrain.

The majority of the MOG, however, were short-term observers (STO) who arrived in time for a comprehensive briefing two days before the elections. This day-long briefing was invaluable in going over the terms of reference, which included a code of conduct. The observers received useful presentations from the Fiji Supervisor of Elections and members of the Fiji Electoral Commission on the technical aspects of the elections. The observers were paired to cover designated areas, met their liaison officers and drivers, and armed with maps, phones and tips on culturally appropriate behaviour they were ready for deployment the next day.

Observing the elections

On Election Day, the MOG members visited a total of 455 out of 1,489 polling stations (approximately 31 per cent of polling stations operating on 17 September) and observed polling and counting across the country. I was paired with a Suva-based South African diplomat and allocated the Lautoka[4] Central area. We visited 11 polling venues that consisted of 40 polling stations.

---

4   Lautoka is the second largest Fijian city, lying in the heart of Fiji's sugar cane growing area in western Viti Levu, 24 kilometres north of Nadi. Lautoka spans an area of 16 square kilometres and had a population of 52,220 (per 2007 census).

Our early arrival in Lautoka on 16 September allowed time to drop into the Elections Office and pick up information on the polling venues we were allocated. All of the venues were schools except for two— one a community centre and the other a building belonging to the Housing Authority of Fiji. The largest polling venue had nine voting stations and the smallest had one. At a couple of venues, I observed the delivery of the sealed ballot boxes containing ballot papers, election materials and documentation. At other venues I witnessed polling-day workers (PDW) setting up in an orderly fashion. Police were present at all polling venues in an unobtrusive manner, away from the polling areas.

On arrival at a polling station, I introduced myself to the presiding officer, who checked my identification card then got me to complete and sign a logbook. The PDWs were meticulous in following process, such as reading aloud from the instruction manual to inform observers about what was being done. This ensured that the political party officials (PPO) and I were following procedures. It was positive to see the high number of women engaged as PDWs, including highly competent women presiding officers.

I also noticed that there were more women than men PPOs observing the elections. The PPO presence at polling stations was generally low and the smaller parties were usually absent. My conversations with a number of PPOs indicated that they were ill-prepared as election scrutineers. This is echoed by the MOG Report (2014c, p. 13), which noted that the:

> Political parties and the FEO gave insufficient weight to the importance of agents (PPOs) in guaranteeing the electoral process. The FEO provided some training, but it was entirely focused on the electoral process, rather than agents' role in the process.

Despite this and a general lack of political party support for PPOs on election day, most officials were stoic and stayed till the votes were counted.

Voting

Early on election day, I made a quick drive by a cluster of venues before calling in at Tilak High School, which had seven polling stations, to observe PDWs set up before polling started at 7.30am. Outside each venue people were queuing up, many arriving over an hour before polling began. It was a public holiday and many people had clearly decided to get the voting over and done with to free up the rest of the day. As it turned out, a smarter choice might have been to vote later in the day when there were fewer queues. Voters appeared genuinely upbeat, good natured and full of anticipation. The atmosphere was generally positive and at times festive. This accords with the MOG's Preliminary Statement that noted:

> The 2014 Fijian Election, the first election since 2006, was enthusiastically embraced by the voters of Fiji who were keen to participate in the democratic process. The election was conducted in an atmosphere of calm, with an absence of electoral misconduct or evident intimidation.

The FEO election material promoted voting as a national responsibility with slogans like 'My election, My Fiji' and 'I'm voting because I'm Fijian'. Fijians were clearly motivated by these messages and the urging of leaders, including the Chair of the Fiji Electoral Commission, with 84 per cent of registered voters casting their votes.

It would appear that the FEO had not anticipated a surge at the start of polling and PDWs were not prepared for this. Better anticipation and planning could have averted some delays and the frustration experienced by some voters. By mid-morning, long, slow-moving queues were frustrating voters who had been standing in the hot sun for two to three hours. At venues with multiple polling stations, PDWs directing voters to the correct queues in the first instance would have prevented people from lining up for the wrong polling station. Proportionally, however, such incidents were few and election officials quickly worked out the issues and managed them. Most able-bodied voters completed their ballots with ease, usually within a few minutes, while those needing assistance took longer. I was pleased to see election officials go out of their way to assist voters who were elderly, pregnant, unwell or had disabilities—they were allowed to vote on arrival without queuing. The slowest aspect of the voting process was verification. Under pressure the PDWs carried out their duties assiduously, with the MOG Report (2014c, p. 3) noting that:

> Despite a new, unfamiliar and complex voting system, the Fijian Elections Office administered the election effectively. Polling officials were well-prepared and voting procedures were generally followed correctly.

The bright orange fluorescent vest, white *bula* shirt[5] with the MOG logo, and large photo IDs worn by MOG observers made them easily identifiable. This also made it easy for observers to interact with voters and election officials. Many voters were curious about my presence, while others welcomed and thanked me for being there. Some voters complained about the delays and the way the elections were run. On a handful of occasions, I helped voters find their designated polling stations by texting the '545' number, a dedicated telephone number set up by the FEO for voters to either text or call to find their polling station. The system was innovative, quick and worked well if one had a mobile phone.

Counting

Polling stations closed at 6pm, but at most venues things had quietened down well before then. I returned to the same polling station at Tilak High School where I had witnessed the start of polling in the morning, this time to observe the conclusion of voting and counting. Again, the presiding officer was meticulous in adhering to procedures, first making a final call before closing the polling station, then reconciling the number of ballot papers used against the roll, followed by the sorting and counting of votes. Counting 500 votes took almost four hours, an indication of the arduous process involved. After the results were double checked, a copy was displayed outside the polling station and the provisional results were reported to a call centre in Suva. Everything was packed into the ballot box, sealed and then sent back to Suva. As with voting, the PDWs were very diligent in adhering to the counting process. I spent Saturday at the

---

5   Fijian name for a Hawaiian-style floral shirt

Vodafone Arena, the vote counting centre in Suva, to observe the counting of postal votes because by then the bulk of the counting had been completed and the results displayed around the hall.

Elections—critical for Fiji's progress

Fiji's 2013 Constitution introduced for the first time an electoral system that was not based on ethnicity. The 2014 elections for a 50-member unicameral legislature was conducted under an open list proportional representation system, which also lowered the voting age from 21 to 18. For many reasons the elections were a much anticipated and closely followed event for Fijians as well as for the broader international community, including the large Fijian diaspora abroad. A credible election would reinstate Fiji as a democratic country and help restore political relations between Fiji and its Pacific neighbours—particularly with Australia and New Zealand. More importantly, the elections answered immediate questions like:

- How well would the new electoral system fare?
- What would voter turnout be?
- What would the elections outcome be?
- Would the results be accepted by Fijians?

According to the MOG, the elections were very well run despite the limited time to prepare and logistical challenges caused by geographical spread and remoteness. While there were some anomalies on election day, these were isolated cases and not unexpected, given that the electoral system was new and untried. In the bigger scheme of things, the administrative issues encountered were minor and did not compromise the integrity of the elections. Voter turnout was high. According to the Fijian Elections Office (2014, p. 2):

> a total of 84.6 per cent of Fiji's 591,101 registered voters voted in the 2014 General Election. Only 0.75 per cent or 3714 of the 500,078 ballots cast were invalid, a record low for an election in Fiji.

A total of 248 candidates from seven political parties and two independent candidates contested the elections. Bainimarama and his FijiFirst Party won close to 60 per cent of the votes to claim 32 of the 50 parliamentary seats. The Opposition (made up of the Social Democratic

Liberal Party and the National Federation Party) secured 15 and three seats respectively. The other political parties and independent candidates did not gain any seats because they did not secure 5 per cent of the total votes cast as required by the 2013 Constitution. Fijians and the international community have largely accepted the result, assured by the MOG's declaration on 18 September 2014 that:

(a) the outcome of the 2014 Fijian Election is on track 'to broadly represent the will of the Fijian voters; and (b) the conditions were in place for Fijians to exercise their right to vote freely'.

Conclusion

Some feel that the Administration's decision to postpone the elections from 2009 helped Frank Bainimarama and FijiFirst get elected. While there may be some truth in this claim, it would be difficult to verify. The additional time certainly allowed the Administration to consolidate power, demonstrate its ability to govern, and implement policies that have had immediate tangible benefits and won support. Examples of such policies include the introduction of free school fees and bus fares, improvements to roads and village infrastructure.

The MOG found (2014c, p. 30) that:

Despite compressed timeframes, a complex voting system and some restrictions in the electoral environment, the conditions were in place for Fijians to exercise their right to vote freely; and

The election broadly represented the will of Fijian voters.

The MOG concluded that the elections were credible and the Fijian people had spoken, with almost 60 per cent of voters choosing FijiFirst. This was a comprehensive show of support for Bainimarama. The elections paved the way for Fiji's return to democracy.

References

Chand, Shalveen, 2014, 'Watch and improve', *Fiji Times*, August 27. www.fijitimes.com/story.aspx?id=278429.

Fijian Elections Office 2014, *2014 General Election – Final Report by Supervisor of Elections*, 22 October, Suva.

Multinational Observer Group 2014a, *Terms of Reference*, Suva.

Multinational Observer Group 2014b, *Preliminary Statement Media Statement*, Suva.

Multinational Observer Group 2014c, *2014 Fijian Elections Final Report of the Multinational Observer Group*, Suva.

15

Concluding note: The election to end all coups?

Steven Ratuva and Stephanie Lawson

Predicting political futures is no easy task, even when there are clear patterns of historical behaviour to act as indicators of likely developments. But in Fiji, the multiplicity of internal and external factors that have shaped the country's social, economic, political and cultural life always has the potential to direct events along an unexpected trajectory. The lessons of the past should keep us alert to the possible widespread resurgence of indigenous nationalism, something that could very well occur in adverse economic circumstances. Another possibility is a split within FijiFirst. If Bainimarama were to vacate the leadership, for one reason or another, is the party likely to retain the coherence it has achieved to date? Bainimarama's departure from the political scene seems unlikely, barring serious illness or worse, but if the stability of a system depends largely on the personality of one individual, as the present system seems to, it does not bode well for the longer term. Then there is the role of the military—one can scarcely rule out the possibility of another coup, although, again, this would be a longer term rather than an immediate prospect. It seems, then, that there can be no certainty about Fiji's political future, especially when it comes to the prospects for the consolidation of democratic constitutionalism. The best we can do is to venture some generalisations based on how we interpret the past and present and how these may be projected into the future.

Between 1987 and 2014 there have been seven elections and four coups. This amounts to a ratio of one coup to every two elections, which has inspired terms such as Fiji's 'coup culture' and 'coup cycle', as well as the epithet 'coup-coup land'. These terms make a point about the ever-present possibility of extra-parliamentary means of regime change in Fiji. This has been evident elsewhere, especially in Latin America, Asia and Africa, although the pattern of coups and military rule has generally withered away as local and international political circumstances have changed; Thailand being a notable exception at the present time. The question for Fiji and its political future is: Have the forces that have fostered coups abated?

The aftermath of the 2014 elections has seen a continuation of indigenous nationalist demands, expressed in different forms. These include an attempt to form a Taukei Christian state in Ra and Nadroga provinces and continuous demands for greater Taukei and land rights by community groups and parliamentary representatives. Then there is the fast-changing arena of industrial, tourism, infrastructural and economic development generally, which, while delivering many benefits, has also widened the socioeconomic gap further, with implications for those who feel left behind in the surge of development. These forces must be handled carefully, not only by the state but by political parties, religious organisations, civil society groups and the community at large, all of which have a role to play in ensuring that stability is maintained in a peaceful and legal manner. The return of parliamentary government can only enhance the ability of all these groups to contribute.

A number of inter-related practical approaches may be useful in addressing the issues outlined above, including expanding the space for continuous dialogue between different political parties and groups, enhancing the ability of the state to respond positively to people's concerns, especially in combating poverty and inequality by ensuring a more equitable distribution of resources and making development more people-centred. If the fostering of neoliberal economic policies comes at the cost of social dislocation and the further marginalisation of poorer communities, this would be recipe for long-term instability in a country that is still going through a transition from semi-subsistence to participation in a globalised capitalist economy. This is especially the case among rural and peri-urban Taukei. A related issue is the growing movement of people between rural and urban areas, which invariably gives rise to new patterns of social interaction, not all of which may be positive. Those at the periphery are at risk of being left out in the South East Asian-style state-driven developmental approach discussed in Chapter One.

There is also the ever-increasing use of the social media through mobile phones and the Internet, alongside traditional media such as radio, newspapers and television, which instantaneously overcome geographical boundaries and enhance active campaigning and mobilisation by political groups and individuals, all making the transmission and sharing of political grievances easier. At the same time, the state's surveillance system has become much more sophisticated, based on lessons learnt internationally as well as the experience since the 2006 coup.

Another issue of concern is that, since coming to power, FijiFirst's strategy of maintaining its hegemony has overshadowed attempts at dialogue or inter-party cooperation. Democratic politics may be adversarial, but consensus and cooperation are still required at various levels, especially in a country traumatised by repeated military intervention. Instead of going through a national reconciliation process to bring the different groups together and mend the fractures, Bainimarama's method of suppression, mainly by deploying legalistic means, is a strategy that is more likely to allow wounds from the coups to continue to fester rather than heal. A subtle but influential strand in Fiji's coup politics is the strong element of victimhood and the way in which the psychology of vengeance and counter-vengeance has motivated coup players. When Chaudhry was prime minister, he saw himself as a victim of the 1987 coup who had managed to survive and turn the table on his former adversaries. He attempted to reintroduce some original Labour Party policies in relation to land development. But this simply intensified indigenous nationalist passion and he was swept from power in 2000 by the Speight coup.

Then there was the attempted mutiny in 2000 by members of the Fijian special forces against Bainimarama, to avenge what they saw as Bainimarama's betrayal of the Speight coup. There can be little

THE PEOPLE HAVE SPOKEN

doubt that the traumatic effect of the attempt on his life during the mutiny became a deeply embedded psychological force, which helps to explain Bainimarama's unrelentingly vengeful attitude towards those involved in the 2000 coup and, beyond that, towards those who oppose him politically. On the other hand, the Social Democratic Liberal Party's attitude towards FijiFirst and Bainimarama has to some extent been shaped by the personal experiences of some party leaders and members who were victims of Bainimarama's repressive policies after the 2006 coup.

The cycle of vengeance and counter-vengeance has the potential to nurture and amplify discord and to threaten national security in the long run. In politics, time does not necessarily heal the pain. Rather, time may provide a reservoir of memories where grievances and the desire for vengeance are stored until circumstances appear ripe for their resurrection. We have seen this in Fiji time and again. This is also the key reason transpolitical dialogue is so important at the present time to provide a democratic space for political players to engage in serious discourse about both the past as well as the future of Fiji's security and stability.

Although there is now a government installed through a democratic process, creating a democratic political culture involves more than just an election. A distinction needs to be made here between formal democracy and people's democracy. The former refers to adherence to legal and constitutional rules, while the latter involves human relationships and interaction in a participatory and mutually consensual way. While formal democracy provides the basis for the rule of law, people's democracy ensures that citizens participate or are engaged both directly and indirectly in a meaningful way in the political process without stifling restrictions imposed by authorities. The future growth of democratic political culture in Fiji will depend on the interplay between the two aspects of democracy. This also highlights the importance of the role of civil society organisations, faith-based organisations, media, youth, women and other citizen groups in providing avenues for meaningful participation for ordinary people. These diverse voices need to be incorporated into an inclusive framework of national engagement. Constant dialogue, transparency, communication, listening, acceptance of diversity, inclusiveness and sensitivity to different views have the potential to put an end to vengeful behaviour.

One of Fiji's great assets is the resilience of its people and their ability to overcome constant disruptions to democratic governance. While it is true that many people left the country following coups, the population by and large has confronted the challenges and adapted to changing circumstances. While scholars have largely focused on issues of ethnic or racial tension and political fragmentation, there is little recognition of the reservoir of goodwill and resilience which has kept the country free of civil war or serious violence, as has occurred in the Solomon Islands and Bougainville and in other regions such as the Balkans or parts of Africa in recent years.

Civil wars generally erupt on the basis of deeply embedded fractures within society that give rise to a desire by competing groups to completely subjugate or even 'cleanse' the country of the other group by violent means. This has not been the case in Fiji, where tension has been limited largely to competing ethnic elites and has not necessarily been replicated between communities on the ground. While there were isolated cases of intimidation and violence during and following the coups, there has been no large-scale, organised or spontaneous inter-group violence. There are several reasons for this. First, there is the absence of military-style organisation within the communities, due at least in part to lack of arms. Virtually all arms in Fiji are in the hands of well-disciplined security forces and this, ironically, has been a key stabilising factor. A second factor is the restraining capacity of the Taukei cultural system itself. While indigenous nationalists have used 'culture' as leverage against other ethnic groups to serve their political interests, this has been balanced by the Taukei sense of social accommodation and peace-building. Arguably, this has acted as a powerful restraining force. Having said that, other groups have also adhered strongly to non-violence, including the Indo-Fijian community, which has been the main target of indigenous nationalist groups but which has always exercised considerable restraint.

An important historical factor underlying restraint in all communities is the post-independence multiracial experiment under Ratu Mara's Alliance Party, which, despite its problems, contributed to an atmosphere in which mutual coexistence was recognised as the only viable way forward for Fiji's society as a whole after independence. This followed a peaceful transition to independence in which all political groups cooperated to ensure that the process was smooth and without rancour. Thus, although Fiji's history shows there are issues that have the potential to inflame passions, there are other factors that have the capacity to minimise and absorb conflict and to encourage peaceable coexistence and interaction. Fiji's future stability depends on nurturing the latter rather than simply suppressing discontent.

It is important to note that the threshold for violent conflict or extra-parliamentary intervention can be dangerously lowered when tension is protracted and unchecked. Judging by the deep-seated tension between political parties and political leaders in the new parliament, it will take a considerable effort to move towards a political culture in which such tensions are ameliorated and democratic constitutionalism can be consolidated. This means, above all, a system under which those who win office through free and fair elections are recognised as the legitimate government, regardless of its ethnic composition.

By the same token, opposition parties also have a legitimate and important role to play in offering criticism and alternative views. Indeed, democratic constitutionalism depends on the legitimacy of both government *and* opposition. But democracy in Fiji will no doubt fare much better when the dividing line between government and opposition is not demarcated largely by ethnicity. As the 2014 elections results indicate, the dichotomous pattern of Taukei vs Indo-Fijian parties of the past is no longer the dominant pattern. Instead, FijiFirst has become the centripetal political force, attracting by far the most cross-ethnic support. Under the new electoral system, ethnically based parties cannot win elections purely on the basis of their traditional support. Having said that, communal identity and loyalty will remain major factors in Fiji's social and political life.

We have noted previously, however, that politics in Fiji has never been 'all about race' and other factors such as socioeconomic disparity, commercial interests, power plays within communities, and so forth, have been and will remain important elements in Fiji's complex political dynamics. Then there is the paradoxical role of the military, the most powerful institution in the country. Bainimarama claimed an impressive victory in September 2014 on a platform that was explicitly anti-communal. Yet the very institution that underpinned his rise to power and subsequent victory, and which has greatly enhanced status under the current Constitution, remains almost 100 per cent Taukei, with no indication that this will change in the foreseeable future.

The greatest challenge facing the future of democracy in Fiji remains the legitimation of the parliamentary system to the extent that it becomes integral to a democratic political culture and accepted as such by all participants in the political process, including the military. Fiji has learnt the hard way that extra-parliamentary means are painful and destructive. For all the criticisms that can be made of Fiji's 2014 general elections, it has at least seen the return of electoral democracy and parliamentary politics, which in turn provides the key forum for the expression of diverse views, interests and agendas. The various authors of this book have themselves put forward diverse views, but there is no doubt that each has sought to seriously explore the conditions under which democratic stability can be achieved and, with it, a coup-free future for Fiji.

Contributors

Jone Baledrokadroka is an advisor on security and development with the United Nations Development Programme in Papua New Guinea. With a PhD from The Australian National University, he specialises on issues of security, military and political transformation.

Leonard Chan works for the Ministry of Foreign Affairs in New Zealand and was a member of the Multinational Observer Group during the 2014 Fiji elections.

Alisi Daurewa, a rural development expert, is a member of the Fiji Election Commission.

Brij Lal is Professor in Pacific History at The Australian National University and founding Director of the Centre for the Contemporary Pacific. Amongst his numerous works is the acclaimed *Broken waves: A history of the Fiji Islands in the 20th century*.

Stephanie Lawson is Professor of Politics and International Relations at Macquarie University, Sydney, and Senior Research Associate, Faculty of Humanities, University of Johannesburg. Among her many publications is the award-winning *The failure of democratic politics in Fiji*.

Scott MacWilliam is a visiting fellow with the State, Society and Governance in Melanesia program at The Australian National University. He has carried out intensive research on Fiji politics over the years.

Lynda Newland is a lecturer in anthropology at the St Andrews University in Scotland. She recently worked at the University of the South Pacific and has carried out extensive ethnographic research in Indonesia and Fiji.

Steven Ratuva is Director of the Macmillan Brown Centre for Pacific Studies and Professor in the Department of Anthropology and Sociology at the University of Canterbury, New Zealand. His latest book is *Politics of preferential development: Trans-global study of affirmative action and ethnic conflict in Fiji, Malaysia and South Africa.*

David Robie is Professor and the founding director of the Pacific Media Centre, and editor of the *Pacific Journalism Review*, *Pacific Scoop* and Pacific Media Centre Online at the Auckland University of Technology. He is author of a number of books on peace and conflict in the Pacific.

Sefanaia Sakai is a teaching assistant in governance at the University of the South Pacific. His area of research is land and politics in Fiji.

Alexander Stewart is a PhD scholar at Swinburne University in Melbourne and specialises in international relations and Pacific regional politics.

Pio Tabaiwalu holds an MA in international relations and has worked for the Pacific Islands Forum. He is a former assistant minister in Fiji and is currently secretary of Social Democratic Liberal Party, the major opposition party in Fiji.

Patrick Vakaoti is a lecturer in social work at the University of Otago. He recently worked at the University of the South Pacific and his major area of research is youth in a changing world.

www.ingramcontent.com/pod-product-compliance
Lightning Source LLC
Chambersburg PA
CBHW040152270326
41928CB00040B/3307